SMALL BUSINESS IN
TRANSITION ECONOMIES

SMALL BUSINESS IN TRANSITION ECONOMIES

Promoting enterprise in Central and Eastern Europe and the former Soviet Union

Edited by JACOB LEVITSKY

INTERMEDIATE TECHNOLOGY PUBLICATIONS 1996

Intermediate Technology Publications Ltd
103–105 Southampton Row, London WC1B 4HH, UK

© IT Publications 1996

A CIP record for this book is available from
the British Library

ISBN 1 85339 343 6

Typeset by Dorwyn Ltd, Rowlands Castle, Hants
Printed in the UK by SRP, Exeter

Contents

Abbreviations

AA	Autonomia Alapitvany (Hungarian Foundation for Self-reliance)
BIC	Business Innovation Centre
CARESBAC-Polska	A Polish venture capital fund
CIDA	Canadian International Development Agency
CIS countries	Commonwealth of Independent States (most of the former Soviet Union)
EBRD	European Bank for Reconstruction and Development
EIB	European Investment Bank
FSU	Former Soviet Union
G-7 countries	Group of major industrial nations
G-24 countries	Wider group of countries, including some middle-income states
GTZ	Gesellschaft für Technische Zusammenarbeit (German aid organization for technical co-operation)
IBD	Integrated Advisory Service for Private Business Promotion
IBRD	International Bank for Reconstruction and Development
IPC	Interdisziplinare ProjektConsult
ITC	International Trade Centre
KfW	Kreditanstalt für Wiederaufbau (German Development Bank)
NADSME	National Agency for the Development of Small and Medium Enterprises (Slovak Republic)
PBEP	Polish-British Enterprise Project
PARD	Polish Agency for Regional Development
PHARE	Poland, Hungary Action for the Reconstruction of Economies (name given in 1989 to the now general programme of EU support activities in Central and Eastern Europe)
RDA	Regional Development Agency (Poland)
RODA	Romanian Development Agency
RPF	Regional Development Fund (Ostrava)

RAIC	Regional Advisory and Information Centre
RSBF	Russia Small Business Fund
SEAF	Small Enterprise Assistance Funds
SME	Small and medium enterprise
TACIS	Technical Assistance for Commonwealth of Independent States (EU programme of aid for former Soviet Union countries)
UNIDO	United Nations Industrial Development Organization
USAID	United States Agency for International Development

Preface

A conference was organized in Budapest from 6 to 8 June 1995 by the Committee of Donor Agencies for Small Enterprise Development. The conference was entitled 'Innovative approaches to financial and technical services for small enterprises' and the intention was to bring together representatives of entrepreneurs, small business associations, SME support agencies, financial institutions and government organizations from all over Central and Eastern Europe and the former Soviet Union (CEE/FSU). Representatives from donor agencies active in the relevant countries and some selected key international experts participated in the discussion of successful programmes to support SMEs in the region. Many of the participants came from key positions in organizations or agencies playing a central support role in SME development. The multilateral UN agencies UNDP, ILO and UNIDO, as well as bilateral aid agencies from Austria, Canada, Germany, Netherlands, Sweden, Switzerland, UK and USA, together with the host Soros Foundation provided the finance to cover the costs of the Budapest meeting. Other sponsors of the conference included the World Bank, PHARE and TACIS, the European Union support programme for CEE and FSU respectively, and the European Bank for Reconstruction and Development (EBRD), the bank set up by the industrial nations to provide finance to the CEE/FSU countries.

The conference themes addressed four major questions considered of central importance to SME development: financial support, technical and management services, policies conducive to SME development and the focus of international donor agencies' assistance in promoting SME in the region. The proceedings were tailored to stimulate the widest possible direct involvement of the participants. Following the welcoming address by the President of Hungary, Arpad Goncz, keynote speakers provided an overview of the conference themes. Allan Gibb, Professor at the Business School of Durham University, UK and B. Muller-Kastner of KfW Germany, spoke of the need to foster an entrepreneurial culture in the countries of the region. This was in Gibb's view an educational challenge extending far beyond the vocational training system. Besides financial help for business 'start-ups', there was also a need to assist existing businesses. Gibb called for a 'mutual learning partnership between the transition economies and those of the West'.

The second keynote speaker, B. Muller-Kastner of the KfW, said that promotional banks should be set up in the countries of the region to ensure that there was a development orientation in loan decisions. The commercial banks, in his view, were not likely to provide the financial services required and respond adequately to SME requests.

Danuta Hübner, Deputy Minister of Industry in Poland, also spoke at the opening session, as did Leila Webster of the World Bank, on behalf of the Donor Committee. The only other plenary session was a panel discussion chaired by Nancy Barry, President of Women's World Banking, which reviewed the main conclusions during the final session. Representatives from Russia, Poland and Hungary stressed the learning value of the presentations and particularly welcomed the opportunity afforded to hear the experiences of support programmes in other countries of the region.

Workshop sessions

The other sessions over two days were organized in the form of workshops focused on specific case studies based mainly on the experience of donor-supported projects in providing financial, technical or management services to help SME development. Six sessions of 90 minutes each focused upon themes relating to the start-up of new small enterprises, their expansion and growth and various aspects of policies and institutional development. Parallel workshop groups at each of these sessions covered the following subjects:

○ *The business environment*, including government policies towards SMEs; taxation and regulations; small-scale privatizations and 'spin-offs'.
○ *Finance for SMEs*, including: micro-credits and start-up loans; grants and seed capital; bank lending for SMEs; loan guarantee schemes; equity and venture capital; and combining financial and technical support.
○ *Institutional support framework*, including: incubators and business innovation centres; regional business services and advice centres; community-based economic development initiatives; and the role of business membership organizations.
○ *Training and more general support projects*, including: management training and development; entrepreneurship identification and training and targeted enterprise development.

The workshop sessions gave opportunities for participants responsible for SME projects and programmes to present papers (two at each session) describing the experience of organizations and individuals working in countries in the region. Presenters were from business membership associations, banks, government agencies, local enterprise agencies, business support institutions, local government, non-government organizations (NGOs), and in some cases consultants or academics who have worked with or studied the SME sector in different countries. Through both the plenary and workshop sessions, simultaneous English and Russian interpretation facilities were available.

A novel event was organized on the second day of the conference—a project market place—to facilitate further exchange of information, experiences and ideas in an informal atmosphere. Around 20 projects, generally different from the cases dealt with in the workshop sessions, were displayed in stalls with posters, literature, photographs and visual aids, manned by persons able to explain the background of the projects or institution involved, and to answer directly the questions of those interested in further information. Participants showed great interest in the projects exhibited, circulated around the stalls at the market place, generating lively discussions and exchanges, and engaged in comparison of different approaches and varying experiences and results. Interpretation services were at hand when needed. GTZ of Germany were responsible for organizing this event.

Overall, over 230 participants attended the conference, including representatives from 19 countries in the region, 10 of these from the countries of the former Soviet Union. There were 48 representatives of donor agencies present, not including all those living in the region. In all 47 papers were presented, 24 of them from participants of the countries of the region. It has unfortunately not been possible to reproduce all the papers in this volume; a selection has therefore been made, and it is hoped that a representative sample has been offered. They give a cross-section of the type of projects initiated by donors, an account of the conditions prevailing in relation to SME in the various countries and the degree of progress and success achieved in the SME sector's development and the support framework created.

Special thanks are due to David Wright of the ODA and Eva Bakonyi of the Soros Foundation of Hungary for their leadership in organizing the conference. Thanks are due to the help given in producing this compilation of the conference proceedings by Steven Johnson, of Graham Bannock and Partners, who played a key role in organizing the meeting, and by Clare Tawney, for her assistance in editing and proofing the papers.

Introduction

The growth of the private sector, and in particular of SMEs in Central and Eastern Europe and the former Soviet Union, has been phenomenal. According to the London-based journal *The Economist*, by the end of 1994, 65 per cent of GDP in the Czech Republic, 60 per cent in Poland and Hungary, 50 per cent in the Russian Federation and 50–55 per cent in the Baltic countries were the contributions of private sector business activities. There is also considerable variation between different countries, however, with the private sector in Romania reaching only 35 per cent of GDP (Gheranescu) and 40 per cent in Bulgaria. It is argued by some that the lower figures in these latter countries are explained by a slower speed of privatization—particularly of the smaller units of the service and distribution sector—rather than a dearth of entrepreneurship. The variety of experience across the region of Central and Eastern Europe and the former Soviet Union is reflected in the papers presented at the conference and published in this book, as well as in the conference workshops.

Small business entrepreneurs have tended to flourish in all the countries of Central and Eastern Europe and the former Soviet Union (CEE/ FSU, referred to here as 'the region'). Even in Russia the number of private enterprises had grown to around two million, as against less than 40 000 five years previously (Ermakov). Hübner speaks of 2.1 million enterprises in Poland of which 92 per cent employ less than five people. A large number of the new entrepreneurs are in the 'grey' or informal economy, mostly in retail trade, offering services or 'buying and selling' merchandise.

The years of communist control, centralized planning and state control of all economic activity have inevitably left a legacy. Laczkó points to the general negative attitude prevailing in Hungary and taken by many of the authorities throughout Eastern European countries to the contribution made by the self-employed and those engaged in the 'subsistence informal economy', despite this providing a more acceptable alternative to unemployment and welfare. Those involved in self-employment usually do so after facing a situation in the market economy that cannot offer them suitable formal employment, he pointed out.

Some economic thinkers and some sections of the population in former communist countries generally also still have a negative view to those living off commercial profits. The emergence of vicious criminal elements, whose activities are not always clearly differentiated from legitimate business in the eyes of many in the population at large, has hardly helped to raise the status of private business. The extent of the criminal element's influence on the private business sector may be exaggerated in the West, but there does exist a pressing problem still to be overcome in countries such as Russia and elsewhere in the region, to separate and protect private business, especially successful and prospering SMEs, from entanglements with organized criminal groups.

The business environment

Most governments in the region have approved programmes and legislation aimed at stimulating SME development. In Russia, in June 1993, a federal law was drafted providing support for SMEs which has, over the subsequent two years, slowly made its way through the various levels of the State Duma and the legislative process (Ermakov). In Spring 1995 the Polish Government finally approved a wide-ranging policy programme for the SME sector (Hübner). The presentation by Komsa and Merkulov describes a state programme of support for developing entrepreneurship approved in Belarus in November 1992. In Slovakia, as Brhel and Foltin report, the government has in various resolutions declared its support for SME development and recognized the need for the government to create the necessary environment for entrepreneurial development. Privatization laws have, according to Gheranescu, provided the framework in Romania—as in other countries of Central and Eastern Europe—for government support for private SMEs.

Despite the enactment of a range of laws and the promulgation of decrees which give support to the creation and development of SMEs, a proper legal system able to defend private property and enterprise and to enforce contracts is still lacking in most countries. Various speakers at the conference, particularly those representing associations of private entrepreneurs, chambers of commerce, and those who spoke for the growing business community, all complained that the legal framework was still inadequate for the needs of a market economy and a growing private sector. Hübner, speaking for the Government of Poland, recognizes 'that a proper emphasis should be put on creating an all-embracing legal environment conducive to the development of the SME sector'. Representatives of business associations in Lithuania and Estonia have also complained of an inadequate legal framework in their countries for SMEs to develop.

Taxation and regulation.
SMEs in all countries complain of high taxation, and the enterprises in this region are no exception. Indeed, the history of the past decades in the

Central and Eastern European countries or 70 years in the FSU—has made everyone unused to paying taxes. Past experience has also tended to make everyone reluctant to pay into the government treasury. On paper the taxes, if paid in full, appear high, but in practice tax avoidance and evasion is prevalent on a wide scale, demonstrated also by the large underground economy and widespread informal sector operations. After a few years of movement to a market economy and the growth of a private sector, legislation has been introduced in several countries, e.g. Russia (see Ermakov's paper), simplifying the taxation system and the introduction of tax concessions, for SMEs and microenterprises. New SMEs working in priority areas (such as agricultural products, consumer goods, medical supplies and construction) in Russia are exempt from income tax for the first two years and subsequently benefit from a reduction of the tax rate for the third and fourth years of business activity. SMEs are exempt from property tax for the first year of operation and from the requirement to pay in advance the assessed tax on profits. Tax procedures in Russia have also been simplified for microenterprises, which are defined as businesses with less than 20 employees in consumer goods manufacture, and 10 employees in trade and services.

As most SMEs in the region are relatively recent start-ups (63 per cent are post-1990 arrivals in Poland, as Hübner points out) and were started with very little capital mostly based on personal family savings, it follows that capital accumulation and retained earnings are most important for growth prospects. Tax concessions in the first years can therefore be significant, bearing in mind that access to bank finance is still limited in these countries.

Serious efforts have been made to reduce regulations and towards simplification of administrative procedures. The registration period for new SMEs has been shortened considerably in most of these countries, making it much easier to license a new enterprise compared to a few years ago, when it was still a bureaucratic nightmare. Demands for statistical reports have been reduced, lightening the administrative burden on entrepreneurs.

Finance for SMEs

As might have been expected, finance has emerged as a most pressing problem for new and expanding SMEs in the region. The banking system left behind by the communist regime was rudimentary and unsuitable for the financing needs of a growing private sector, and especially of SMEs.

During the years 1990–5 the banking system has been transformed, to a greater or lesser degree, in all the countries. There are now thousands of private commercial banks operating throughout the Russian Federation, and also a significant growth of private banks in Central and Eastern Europe. This has occurred both through the gradual privatization of existing banks and also through the growth of new private ones. Many of these banks are severely undercapitalized and managed in a heavily bureaucratic, conservative fashion. According to Wallace, the RSBF is encountering a major barrier in the 'over-bureaucratic procedures' of the banks. She tells of 27 documents—many requiring notarization—being required after loan approval, before disbursement. This complaint was echoed by several other participants.

Banks are still very much in need of training and advice on how to deal with SME borrowers. However, the RSBF and other credit programmes in Poland, Hungary, Romania and in other countries of Central and Eastern Europe have shown that under certain circumstances the financial institutions can be responsive to the needs of SMEs.

Equity finance

Several innovative financial support projects have been developed in the region. One such scheme was the Ostrava Regional Fund (RPF) in the Czech Republic which was created as a venture capital company, and which by early 1995 had received 230 requests for funding (Boot). More than 200 of these applications were rejected, and after further analysis the number actually implemented went down to single figures. This is not out of line with the proportion of projects actually financed by venture capital companies in more developed countries.

Another equity financing organization is the Small Enterprise Assistance Fund (SEAF) which operates with USAID funds (and in some areas with EBRD funds) in Poland, Bulgaria and Russia. The size of investments by the SEAF are from $25 000 to $300 000 in enterprises with 15 to 150 employees and assets of up to $250 000. Gibson's paper makes the interesting point that SEAF avoids investing in completely new start-ups and maintains there are already enough operating businesses in the countries involved to provide suitable partners to SEAF for equity financing as minority shareholders. SEAF has started working with EBRD on the equity financing component of the RSBF in Nizhny Novgorod in Russia. Like most such institutions, the RPF and SEAF provide both equity and loans.

Credit and grant finance

The KfW (Kreditanstalt für Wiederaufbau) of Germany has developed a credit project for SME in Kyrgyztan (a former Asian Soviet republic). Some 200 applications were received for a total credit of DM140 million in the first six months of the project. Lindlein, the consultant working on the projects, explained in his paper that only seven of the loan requests for a total amount of DM7 million were approved. He pointed out that many requests came from the 'old guard' who had run industries before. Most of the applications needed technical assistance to assess market potential and to prepare realistic business plans.

The PHARE (EU) programme has helped develop SME loan financing programmes in Slovakia (Brhel and Foltin) and helped finance the STRUDER regional development scheme in Poland (Structured Development in Selected Regions) which uniquely offers (non-repayable) grants of up to 25 per cent of the costs of a new investment, mainly in fixed assets, provided a minimum part of the project cost is contributed by the entrepreneur (15 per cent if project is above 200 000 ecu, (or $250 000). The maximum grant given is 100 000 ecu ($125 000). The panel set up by PARD (Polish Agency for Regional Development) had by the end of April 1995 approved grants to over 200 projects for a total of 7 million ecu (nearly US$9 million). The STRUDER scheme, described by Kozak in his paper, was launched in April 1995. When questioned why 'grants' were provided rather than loans, the justification was given that through providing grants it was easier for entrepreneurs to obtain the rest of the capital needed, apart from their own contribution, in the form of loans from the banks. Having received the grant, the entrepreneur is able to comply with collateral requirements, and with a reduced debt burden, the risk of lending by the bank is lower.

In Belarus also loans are given at preferential rates 'from a fund for the financial support of entrepreneurs set up by the government for small business start-ups'. TACIS (EU) is now assisting in that country with a large new financial support project (Komsa and Merkulov).

Few data were provided in these papers on the loan repayment levels of the various financial assistance projects. Part of the explanation may be that many of these lending projects are relatively recent, having been started only up to two years ago. There were statements, however, that some lending programmes were facing some repayment problems. A lack of adequate information and reporting systems, it was commented by some, contribute to a lack of up-to-date detailed data on levels of repayment.

Wallace reports that after granting 90 small loans in RSBF the arrears rate was 20 per cent, and there had been one loan loss. Zeitinger does not give a figure of actual arrears or losses in the 'micro-credits' lending of the RSBF, but expects annual loan losses to be 'in the range of 6 per cent'. Significantly, Zeitinger puts more emphasis on striving 'towards a break-even' point in the micro-lending of the RSBF by achieving greater efficiency in the number of credits handled by each loan officer. This he sets at 16 (expected to be reached by the end of 1995), but the achievable number could ultimately be 50 (loan portfolio of US$150 000), at which point the programme will definitely be profitable for the banks.

Loan guarantees

Clearly, bearing in mind past history, most potential SME borrowers cannot provide the collateral which the cautious policy of the conservative and inexperienced banks demand. Accordingly, there has been great interest in setting up risk-sharing loan guarantee schemes to overcome this problem. One of the first external organizations to try to help set up credit guarantee schemes (CGS) was the Burgesforderungsbank of Austria, which has for a number of years operated a CGS for SME in that country, and since 1991 has helped set up a CGS in the Czech Republic, Slovakia, Hungary, Slovenia and Romania.

Most donors have included a proposal for a guarantee scheme in their SME assistance programme: ODA in Eastern Poland (Hardy); PHARE (EU) in Slovakia with the Slovak Guarantee bank (Foltin and Brhel); and Canadian CIDA in Romania. The Romanian Fund for Loan Guarantees (RLGF) has been in operation since early 1994 (Coclitu and Bratescu). It offers guarantees to lending banks of 70 per cent of loans against default. The Romanian Fund is owned by the National Privatization Agency, together with four major commercial banks.

Several proposals for setting up local guarantee funds were presented at the conference, especially in Poland. It is clear, however, at this early stage that the actual operation of a CGS is more problematic than appears when discussing the proposal, not least when ensuring the co-operation and proper use of the schemes by the banks. Some schemes have already been abandoned. Several participants at the conference thought that guarantee funds could respond to a major need, however, and that it was definitely worth continuing to negotiate with banks to work out acceptable arrangements.

Finance available on reasonable terms will remain a central requirement for SME development. Inevitably, access to finance by SMEs is bound up with such macroeconomic factors as the general economic and monetary situation of the country, exchange rates, inflationary pressures, interest rates, and so on. It is generally accepted, however, that excessive subsidization of SMEs would prove counterproductive in the long term.

Institutional support framework

In 1990, there was virtually no institutional nor government support for SMEs. It is remarkable how, five years later, there is such a large proliferation of business advisory centres, foundations for assistance and promoting SMEs, local and regional enterprise agencies and support institutions of different kinds. Associations of small business entrepreneurs, chambers of commerce, economic societies and other private sector membership organizations have also sprung up, both to lobby government for a better environment and policy and legal framework for

SMEs, and to help entrepreneurs to promote and market their products. These organizations also help entrepreneurs make commercial contacts both in the domestic business community and abroad. In several of the Central and Eastern European countries national and regional development agencies with funding from the central government (sometimes with banks as shareholders) have been established (as in Poland, Slovakia, Romania, and the Czech Republic), although the foundation structure is often favoured as more flexible for such organizations, making it easier to obtain external funding.

The councils of the foundations in Hungary and Poland are mixes of public and private sector representatives from government, chambers, NGOs, associations of regional development agencies, banks and business associations.

Support institutions and training courses have been set up in Bulgaria, the Baltic countries, in Siberian regions of Russia and of course throughout the countries of Central and Eastern Europe. An example of a more comprehensive service for SME is the Integrated Advisory Service (IBD), described by Gheranesu, set up in Romania with help from GTZ of Germany. Small Business Development Centres have been established in Romania and in Krasnoyarsk in the Siberian region of the Russian Federation, through help from Washington State University financed by USAID, as described by Tolar, and Business Centres in the Moscow region were set up with help from Canadian experts funded by CIDA.

Many centres and institutions have only relatively recently started operating (in 1994–5) and were struggling to find appropriate qualified and experienced staff as well as funding to increase their operations. The papers in a number of such cases presented a picture of ambitious plans rather than concrete results or achievements. Some of the centres reflected healthy local and grass-roots initiatives but were started sometimes without adequate information on the problems to be dealt with and the needs of potential clients, and with insufficient resources to accomplish the role they had allotted themselves.

Donor approaches

Donor agencies have been very active in setting up centres and SME support institutions. EU's PHARE programme has helped set up agencies and centres in Slovakia, UNIDO has been involved in Romania (see Allen on the UN ROM Centre), EU through TACIS have helped in Belarus (see Komsa and Merkulov), several different bilateral donors have helped the Foundation for Enterprise Development in Hungary, and the British Council and UK Know-How Fund have provided assistance in setting up support centres in Eastern Poland, in the Lublin and Bialystok areas (Hardy). As in Hungary, Poland has sought to co-ordinate the various centres and agencies (32 Business and Information Centres helped by the PHARE programme) through the Poland Foundation for the Promotion and Development of SME which has now been set up, as described in Gurbiel's paper.

The support centres and agencies set up with donor help often reflect the approach of the adviser sent by the aid agency and sometimes the experience of the donor home country. USAID support for SME, for example, has in some cases taken the form of contracting a US university, with experience in operating a Small Business Development Centre (SBDC) in the US, which then attempts to replicate the US experience of the SBDC in Eastern Europe and the former Soviet Union. UK assistance, both through ODA and the Know-How fund, have tried in some cases to press the idea of creating enterprise agencies as in the UK; the GTZ of Germany has used the CEFE (entrepreneurial development) approach and also, in a few cases (for example, Hungary), the creation of a *Handwerkskammer* type (craft chamber) training organization. In Hungary, donors are trying their different approaches where a variety of bilateral agencies from different countries are working within the Hungarian Foundation for Enterprise Promotion (HFEP). This is not to say that these efforts are inappropriate on all occasions, so long as the local agencies and groups are given a suitable opportunity to decide on the applicability of the approach in their own situations.

In some cases, however, local counterparts want donors to recognize more the special conditions prevailing in their countries and to listen closely to local counterparts. Hübner of Poland comments that 'foreign assistance is most successful in those cases where it is really based on a partnership concept (equal partners not donor and recipient). . . . A local partner should be a real partner in defining the needs and ways of meeting them, not just the recipient of widsom. . . .' In opening the conference, Arped Goncz, the President of Hungary, echoed some of this sentiment when he asked those who came from Western industrialized countries to have patience when programmes seemed slow and to take account of the history, culture and social backgrounds of the people they were helping.

Donors have in fact, in many cases, gradually adapted their programmes as they became more acquainted with the countries in which they were working. The high technical and educational levels in many of the countries have made local professional staff quick learners, and in more than a few cases they have soon taken the lead and adapted projects to the special conditions prevailing.

Donors have generally encouraged local support institutions to consider charging for services and to plan for 'future sustainability' after donor funding has eventually been phased out. This may also have encouraged some centres and agencies to spread out into too wide a range of services as they look for those which could raise more income, but for which the staff is inadequately prepared or which may be less related to the main *raison d'être* of the institution. More patience and a longer time perspective may be in order to press the institutions towards sustainability. Circumstances may not make this feasible for some years, even though the goal should be maintained. Furthermore, while the decentralization of support services is desirable and certainly more effective in reaching out to SMEs, an over-abundance or proliferation of local institutions, as appears to be happening in countries such as Poland, Hungary and others, could put strain on available funds and qualified staff, both of which may be in short supply. An assessment of potential demand may be called for in order to balance the efficacy of operation to available resources, both staff and financial.

The trend towards 'innovation centres' may reflect the higher technical level of entrepreneurs, who justifiably aspire to set up SMEs using modern, 'state of the art' technology to compete on world markets. Ermakov reports that, according to statistics, 37 per cent of employees of SMEs in the Russian Federation, including the entrepreneurs, are university graduates (a World Bank study of SMEs in St Petersburg found 60 per cent of SME owners were graduates), and there are similar numbers from other countries in the region.

Training

Training was usually one of the first forms of assistance provided by donors. Hübner refers to 112 institutions throughout Poland and the number expanding rapidly in the east of the country, all providing business training for SMEs. She makes particular mention of the Polish-American institutions supported by USAID. Ermakov describes recent TACIS (EU) training activities implemented by French, Italian and British companies. In Slovakia, the Business Innovation Centres (BICs) and the Regional Advisory or Information Centres (RAICs) supported by PHARE (EU) have provided training for entrepreneurs on 'how to start a business' and specifically on the 'development of business plans' and on 'legislation, tax and accounting'.

Significantly, most training activities have been combined with consultancy and direct advice to enterprises. Several speakers at the conference stressed the need to develop more training material and courses directly related to the situation prevailing in these countries. A paper from Uzbekistan described how the GTZ entrepreneurship development and training programme (CEFE) was adapted to the special conditions of the country. Local training in Uzbekistan was first given to 'trainers', who then adapted the programme for delivering in the local language, in this case, to women entrepreneurs.

There is a need to focus more training on marketing. An interesting paper on marketing SME training activities in Slovenia was presented by Godina of the Economic Institute in Maribor, which highlighted some of the difficulties experienced in selling the institute's training to SMEs, after the first programmes had been carried out. 'Marketing' and 'modern financial accounting for a competitive market economy' were the biggest gaps in small business management left as a legacy of the past.

Target groups

The target group of SMEs that needs help differs in size from country to country, depending on historical, social, economic and technological development. As has been mentioned, the societies and governments of the countries of the region aim at an industrial economy, including SMEs, based on high technological standards to suit the technically educated entrepreneurs and the pressing need to compete in world markets. These countries under the former centralized control had large complex industries which in many cases exported their products quite widely. It is not surprising therefore that target groups of SMEs in the region are generally larger in size and more in keeping with SMEs in industrialized countries than in the Third World. In Romania, Gheranescu refers to 'small companies with fewer than 400 employees'. Even in distant Kyrgyztan, Lindlein explains that the KfW defines SMEs as firms with 'up to 500 employees' as potential beneficiaries of the credit project they are financing. Hardy refers to the 'programmes [being] open to private enterprises employing between 1 and 100 full-time equivalents'.

Bearing in mind the type of economies that existed previously in these countries, with an emphasis on heavy industry and the relatively high level of technical education, it is not surprising that the definition of SMEs to be supported should be rather larger, and the technologies proposed somewhat more sophisticated, than might be the case in parts of the Third World, and donors have to take this into account in their projects. However, partly under the influence of some donors, and to some extent as a result of rising unemployment, these countries are also faced with a challenge to provide programmes for a growing microenterprise sector, although, as referred to earlier, there are some differences as to the support that governments are prepared to give in helping this burgeoning 'informal sector'.

The 'target group' issue is exemplified in the papers on the experience of the (RSBF) Russian Small Business Fund (Wallace and Zeitinger). The RSBF has two principal products: small loans and micro-credits. Small loans of up to $75 000 are for firms with up to 50 employees, and micro-credits for those with fewer than 20 employees. The average loan size in the small loans programme is $50 000. Micro-credits can go up to $20 000, which is high by comparison with the size of such credit in other parts of the world. Zeitinger also points out that 'most micro-credits (average $2500) finance trade, although there is a minority of borrowers for production ventures' which are usually linked to trading and services.

Projects with specific focus

Most donors have provided assistance along more conventional lines for support to SMEs in the region, namely through projects that combine in a package helping set up business advisory and promotional centres together with financial assistance through credits, equity capital, grants, and so on. The conference also included accounts of innovative projects based on more targeted or focused approaches.

Business incubators have been set up in these countries aimed at providing operating premises and support services in an organized form in one place. Hübner mentions '20 incubators in operation' in Poland which provide 'training and advice and offer space to entrepreneurs to run small businesses'. Khaled Malik, the UNDP resident representative presented an account of a 'pilot incubator programme' in Uzbekistan, being planned by UNDP. There was a general interest in the business incubator as a possible instrument for SME promotion, especially in less-developed regions or localities, but there was too little information given to enable any evaluation to be made of the efficacy of this approach and its widespread applicability to countries in the region.

Programmes have also been set up targeting particular regions or ethnic groups. One of these was aimed at developing small private business in co-operation with the regional employment service (with Canada CIDA's help) in a district outside Moscow where there was an urgent need to diversify away from the military industries which had been heavily concentrated in the locality. Progress has been slow but the paper by Ponomarev and Gribankova of the Employment Service document the setting up of business support centres throughout the district and the types of advice and financial support offered to those starting up their own businesses.

Assistance has also been targeted at a historically disadvantaged ethnic minority: the Roma ('gypsy') community in Hungary (Biro and Csongor). The Hungarian Foundation for Self Reliance is helping this ethnic minority by training them in how to become self-employed and start businesses and offering small amounts of financial help to get these small projects off the ground. The experience of this work has helped refute the conventional view that members of this minority lack initiative and are unsuitable for entrepreneurship.

Finally, one paper which potentially could be of great value, not only throughout all countries of the region, but even beyond, was that of Lyapunov (assisted by Allan Gibb of the UK) in ways of 'creating small businesses out of large'. The past regimes of these countries believed strongly in large industries and often built up giant monopolistic enterprises which manufactured most components and operated all services needed within their own walls. Now as the countries move towards a market economy, this approach is unsuitable. Lyapunov and Gibb describe the experience of the Prompribor Association in Chuvash, Russia, transforming large enterprise into '25 smaller linked companies of which 22 are located inside the plant' in 1994. The paper makes a significant contribution to how small business development can be achieved through the down-sizing and disaggregation of large state-owned companies.

Conclusions

The Budapest Conference was probably the first major effort to collate donor experience in helping promote private SME development in the countries of Eastern and Central Europe and the former Soviet Union. There has been significant progress in the introduction of favourable policies to create the appropriate enabling environment and in the development of an institutional support framework, but a great amount still remains to be done. Many support projects are still in an early phase having been in operation for only one to two years or even less: too short a time to draw final conclusions on the experience.

Some more general perhaps preliminary conclusions may be drawn from the presentations and discussion at the conference. Among these are:

○ Although the whole vast region of Central and Eastern Europe and the former Soviet Union has many common features in the economic and social problems they face, based on their similar recent history, there are differences between the situations in each country. There are distinct historical, social, cultural, economic and political factors that must be taken into account.

○ The legal systems still remain inadequate to stimulate and protect the small-scale private sector and to facilitate its growth and development. More needs to be done in this respect quickly to ensure the strengthening and continuity of SME.

○ Access to finance remains a major issue. Part of the problem lies in the financial instability of many of these countries (high inflation and high interest rates), but more resources are needed and more pressure on the commercial banks to respond to the needs of the SME sector. Programmes involving loans, grants, equity finance schemes, and leasing arrangements should all be expanded further to broaden the outreach of financial assistance. The introduction of more loan guarantee schemes should also be explored.

○ Entrepreneurs in all the countries need advice and help in marketing their products to overcome the deficiencies of the distribution system and the insufficient development of business linkages and public procurement from SMEs.

○ The institutional support framework needs to be assessed to ensure that local and regional support institutions are to be encouraged where there is sufficient demand for the services. Care should be taken that limited financial and staff resources are not overstretched and are used effectively.

○ Training for SMEs is important, especially in marketing, financial accounting and entrepreneurship development, but more must be done to develop and use local materials and cases and to link training with advice, consultancies and financial support.

The above are but some of the conclusions that came out of an assessment of the conference proceedings.

As regards donor agencies, the conference showed that a substantial contribution has already been made through the donors' contributions and projects. As for the next years, the feeling of most participants from the region was that there was now a need to hand over more of the management and direction of support services and training programmes to local personnel, and that there were now sufficient qualified and informed professionals in most of the countries to take over.

PART I

Background to the Small and Medium Enterprise Sector

Improving the support for small business development in Central and Eastern Europe and the former Soviet Union

ALLAN GIBB

THE SMALL BUSINESS BASE in Central and Eastern Europe and the former Soviet Union is growing rapidly, and is equally rapidly acquiring all the characteristics that make it difficult to deal with from the viewpoint of government, and the institutional and assistance support environment. In particular there is the problem of its diversity, and consequently the very different needs which arise within it. Equally important is its contempt for government, bureaucracy and indeed any sort of intervention other than that which 'leaves it alone'. Surveys of small businesses in Central and Eastern Europe already indicate that they have much in common with Western counterparts, in terms of complaints against the politicians, the banks and the regulatory bureaucracy, and that they seek refuge in the 'informal' economy as a result. In respect of public policy relating effectively to this diverse community, it may be worth reflecting on two key issues. Firstly on the most effective ways of monitoring the health and needs of the small business community over time, both generally and sectorially in a manner that is useful for policymakers rather than academics. Secondly, on how to create an effective dialogue with this sector, given the distinctive problems that Western governments have in this respect.

The culture of small business

Most people who run small or medium businesses do so as a 'way of life' which has a particular culture (values, attitudes and beliefs) shaped by a particular set of characteristics which are endemic in, and important to, that way of life. It is important firstly to recognize the nature of the environment with which the entrepreneur seeks to cope on a day-to-day basis. Essentially the task of the entrepreneur can be characterized as that of managing a series of largely personalized interdependencies, under conditions of uncertainty, with limited resources. The world of small business people is that of their relationships with customers, marketing channels, suppliers, employees, family, regulatory authorities, banks, accountants,

Allan Gibb is Professor at Durham University Business School, UK.

3

competitors, and indeed all those with whom they must necessarily transact. In managing these transactions the major concern is to reduce uncertainty and transaction costs, mainly via the strength of personal networks.

This view reminds us that our own efforts to support small enterprise will be judged by the degree to which they make this task easier. It is also a reminder that if we are to achieve a level playing field it is not only the entrepreneur that needs to learn, but perhaps even more importantly all those with whom he transacts, particularly government. Coping with uncertainty is the stimulus to entrepreneurial behaviour. All too frequently governments can be seen to be enhancing such behaviour (albeit unproductively) by creating ever-increasing levels of uncertainty and complexity in the entrepreneurial environment, rather than reducing it. Thus, they divert entrepreneurial behaviour and initiative away from its major goal of meeting the needs of customers. The world of the entrepreneur is one where personal contact, trust and judgement is more important than business plans and formal information: it is a world where credibility is based upon 'know how' and 'know who', and it is a world where business improvement comes via contextual knowledge gained by the experience of handling business and organization development processes under pressure, rather than by formal learning, objective knowledge and systems.

Perhaps therefore when we look at examples of good practice in the other chapters in this book it might be useful to reflect on the degree to which they embody in their approaches what I call the four keys to effective small business support, namely: empathy with the *cultural context* of the small business person; understanding of the necessary *know how* rather than know what; real understanding of the importance of *knowing who*; and being aware more precisely of the business development processes through which the '*need to know*' arises. If there is any overall criticism that might be made of support services for small businesses across the world it is that they: too often design their institutions and offerings in the mode of the corporate bureaucratic organization (the cultural metaphors are wrong); they too often focus upon 'know what' instead of 'know how' and offer support at an inappropriate decontextualized level of abstract knowledge; they do not work closely with or become part of the transactional network of the owner (they have no credibility with the 'know whos' of the business world); and their offerings take little account of the learning environment of the small business manager, based as it is around the experience of problems and opportunities. This leaves the busy owner managers with the impossible task of transferring and translating abstract knowledge into their own context, or coping with 'professional' and weighty systems and techniques that they do not need at the current (or indeed immediate future) stage of development.

4

In summary, key questions that might be asked about the support activities for small business in Eastern Europe and the former Soviet Union are:

o To what degree are they based on a monitoring of the health and the real needs of the small business community?
o To what degree are they the result of effective communications with the small business sector itself?
o To what degree do they target carefully (and possibly segment) the small business population?
o To what degree do they embody in their design a real understanding of entrepreneurial culture?
o To what degree do they deliver and facilitate the accumulation of know how?
o To what degree do they assist the entrepreneur in developing the necessary 'know who' to deal effectively with the network of relationships?
o To what degree do they provide support on a 'need to know' and 'problem solving' basis?

These, in my view are not academic questions, but ones of great importance for the practitioner and donor.

Developing the entrepreneurial culture

Business development begins, in my view, with the educational system and not just at the advanced level. In almost all of the transition economies there is currently a major focus on educational reform at all levels from primary, through secondary and vocational, to higher education. Within this reform there is a growing awareness of the scope for influencing societal culture, attitudes to work, to business and to entrepreneurship.

The culture which supports small enterprise development has broadly been described above as sets of values, beliefs, attitudes and norms of behaviour which underpin a role model of success in society via individual or collective entrepreneurial endeavour. That such a culture is to be shared and embedded in all levels of society is undoubtedly important if small business is to have a respectable place in the community. Arguably, however, it is of particular importance in the education system. In all of the transition economies basic changes are being made or considered in educational curricula and pedagogy. In particular there is a marked desire to change the vocational educational training (VET) system in view of the break-up of the relationships between school and business embodied in the old structures. The new context is that of preparing people for a flexible labour market with recognition that young people will no longer be guaranteed a job in the industry sector or in the company in which they learn their trade. One distinct challenge in the vocational education system is that of developing in young people an awareness and capability of how they may use their skills in self employment. This is in recognition of the fact that in a market economy as many as one in five or six of them may ultimately end up with their own business.

The educational challenge, however, extends far beyond the vocational educational system. There are, in the wider curriculum, numerous gateways available to develop an understanding of small and medium business, including ethics, economics, sociology and psychology, as well as in the content of traditional mainstream subjects such as history, geography and mathematics. This challenge also extends to that of the design or re-design of pedagogies to allow greater scope for the development of personal skills and the acquisition of knowledge in an entrepreneurial manner. Many of these changes are in hand. There are already numerous models of 'add-ons' in the curriculum, often based on Western programmes such as 'junior achievement' or 'mini-enterprise' in schools. The real issue, however, is one of embedding entrepreneurial education within the standard curriculum, backed up by appropriate teacher retraining. Of equal importance also is the need to establish different models of school-industry linkages to replace those of the old regimes. In all of these respects considerable progress is being made in the Central European countries and there is growing interest in the former Soviet Union. The main problem, as ever, is that of finance for new materials and for teacher training, and the motivation of teachers suffering from low salaries, but faced with severe changes in their environment.

At all levels small business entrepreneurial education should not be confused with business education or indeed management education and training in the traditional sense. Teaching business management in a conventional manner can be the antithesis of developing understanding of small business management. At management school level, conventional management courses based on Western MBA or other standard subject content frameworks are, by and large, scarcely relevant to the small business: precisely the opposite. As argued earlier, teaching small business demands from the teacher the creation of an appropriate cultural context for learning, a concentration on know how and know who and an understanding of the business processes which generate the 'need to know'. This is a highly important challenge requiring specialist materials and special teacher competencies.

Assisting the start-up process

The case for specialist support for the start-up process lies in the fact that this is where there is the greatest gap between existing knowledge and resource and the knowledge and resource necessary for survival and growth. It is in this process of start-up and in the early survival years that

6

most learning probably takes place in any business. It is an enormous market for all kinds of interventions. It is possible to argue the case for and against public or subsidized interventions: but this seems almost to be irrelevant as there are a myriad of such interventions in the transition economies. It is less clear, however, whether this 'market' has been targeted carefully enough. Very different needs arise within different market segments, for example in: spin-offs from large companies; youth; ethnic groups; the unemployed; transfers out of the armed forces; transfers from defence industries; franchise models; and the agricultural sector. There are nevertheless problems which are more or less common to all small businesses, such as those of inadequate infrastructure, registration tax, the regulatory environment and, of course, security.

A particular challenge which seems to be greater the further east one travels, is that of creating manufacturing and industrial service (as opposed to trading) businesses, and in particular helping entrepreneurs to find ways around the obvious resource gaps in terms of security of property and finance. In the latter respect we should remember that (as often in the West) bank finance is not the critical source of early funding of most small businesses, and the role of the banks can be exaggerated.

Support interventions are, however, difficult when large numbers of would-be entrepreneurs wish to operate in the informal economy: and many legitimate businesses are reluctant to make widely known their business intentions (or their results for that matter). This seems to be a particular deterrent to using the banks in parts of the former Soviet Union. The biggest barrier to 'legitimacy' appears, however, to be high tax and social insurance liabilities.

It is clear that in Central and Eastern Europe in particular the 'market' for start-up support is undergoing a radical re-appraisal in which it is no longer simply enough to have a 'Western model'. The focus of interest of the small business seems to be on regulatory and resource issues: but there is substantial scope for building out from these interests to help companies deal with their early problems of survival.

Assisting the development of existing businesses

This is an area into which many agencies are now moving in their financing, counselling and training efforts, and there is a growing number of supply offers. There is as yet, however, little sign of careful segmentation of this highly differentiated market. Much of the supply in training is of standard functional courses on marketing, finance, production, and so on. There is some specialization on the business plan, reflecting the problems in acquiring resources and the role the plan plays in this respect. There is also a long list of short courses focused on the difficulties that small businesses have with the regulatory environment and on languages. One way of exploring

7

the adequacy of the existing training and counselling services is to divide them into: programmes delivering information on changes in the regulatory and broader environment; programmes providing basic business techniques and systems (for example, managing cash flow, debtor–creditor relations, producing adequate costing systems, and so on); personal development programmes focused on enhancing the entrepreneur's negotiating, selling, persuading and other soft skills; and finally business development programmes dealing with problems and opportunities arising from survival and growth. When examined against this typology, the supply side still seems woefully inadequate in terms of a distinctive focus on the 'need to know' of the entrepreneur.

On the hardware (financial) side it seems unlikely that conventional Western approaches to soft bank lending, perhaps including loan guarantees, will result in spectacular returns (they do not in the West). The problem here, as with the start-up situation already described, is the absence in the West of well tried and verified models that work on any real scale and can be sustained and disseminated more widely in the future. In the absence of foreign funds for disseminating and marketing these models, if indeed they exist, a key may be to seek greater entrepreneurial involvement in their development and management. We should bear in mind that entrepreneurs probably learn better and most frequently from each other, by co-operation with each other and from the recommendations of other entrepreneurs, and that bottom-up financial initiatives such as credit unions and co-operative (sector) banks are likely to provide in many cases a more appropriate response to needs than loosening the norms of conventional banking.

Overall we can question whether support is geared closely enough to the overall small business development processes taking place, although this is a generic problem in the West and not particularly one of the transition economies alone. Moreover there are very distinctive transition economy conditions which may cast doubt on the relevance of some of the Western approaches. I read somewhere recently that the extremely turbulent conditions in Central and particularly Eastern Europe reinforce substantially the need for business plans. One could in my view argue exactly the opposite: that in conditions of great turbulence, complexity and uncertainty the concept of planning as opposed to the art of judgement and know who, is very much less relevant in business dealing.

One market for small business development which seems to have been somewhat neglected is that which arises from the restructuring of large companies. Notwithstanding the debate on the 'scale' problem in transition economies, it is clear that under the former system, large numbers of small businesses were internalized within large firms. It is clear also that the restructuring of these large organizations to achieve the necessary flexibility in the new market economy is involving, and will continue to involve, the externalization (putting out) of many small companies. Research demonstrates this has already happened informally in a variety of ways: but there is an almost universal need for this to happen more quickly, so that management and organization restructuring occur alongside business privatization.

Network development: Institutions

Much of donor support and assistance over the past five years or so has been concerned with developing the institutional capacity to provide financial and other services to small business. In the West there are still a number of unresolved issues as to best practice, including: the degree to which institutions should be standardized as opposed to regionally and locally differentiated; whether their ownership should be private, public or mixed; the degree of specialization (who does what among the different kinds of institutions); the issue of linkage, integration with, and servicing of, each other (for example, co-operation between banks and counselling, information and training services); their financing in terms of the mix of 'for profit' or 'not-for-profit' activity; the role of membership and particularly small company membership and representation; and the creation of real long-run sustainability where necessary. Relevant to many of these issues at the regional or local level is that of the need for, nature of, and means of providing, any central support.

The chapters in this book concentrate, probably rightly, more upon activities than institutions, although the two are not easily separated. In particular the strategic vision as to who will 'own' the supply of small business support services at the local and regional level when Western assistance has disappeared seems to be somewhat missing. The choice is generally between chambers of commerce, local authorities and local and regional governments and other business associations. It is a debate that still rages in many Western countries. No less relevant to the future of small business institutional support in transition economies is the degree to which local initiatives have been developed as real 'bottom-up' endogenous ventures as opposed to being externally (centrally) determined in activity and scope by formal standard business plans and 'accountable' top-down approaches.

In respect of the future of business advice centres, local enterprise agencies and the like, the real dilemma seems to be not only that of who will ultimately own them, but whether they can continue to afford to try to meet broader social and economic development needs or whether they should focus upon commercial 'for profit' activities. The latter makes them in the long run mere clones of commercial consulting services; but if they bravely choose the former option then they will need strategically to build long-term support networks. In some cases they also need to sort out

9

clearly their mission between small business development agency and a local and regional development portfolio, which is much broader. The issue of networking and creating networks at the local and regional level is not one that is resolved by appointing representative Boards of Directors for agencies. Nor, in my view, is it solved by the designation of 'one-stop shops' for small business advice and assistance. It is more a function of developing a regional strategy focused upon meeting the needs of each of the future key players in the region, while creating additionality. Here there seems to be substantial scope for learning by experience exchange between transition economies.

Not to be neglected in the debate about institutional development is the issue of the creation of regulatory and other service delivery institutions that are really user-friendly to the small and medium enterprise community. This raises the issue of the basic design and competency of such institutions at the local level, and in particular that they should have real empathy with the culture of small business. This seems to be an area of neglect (as it is in the West) but of critical importance if many of the problems of the small business attitudes to the 'formal' environment are to be solved. Sadly, the convention seems to be that it is the small business that needs to be developed to cope with the institutional environment, and not the other way round.

Finally there is the highly important issue, now becoming critical, of the nature of any future central support for regional and local differentiated SME services. Here there is something of a problem in that the major role of many central agencies has been that of the conduit for donor funds with a corresponding emphasis upon developing plans, allocating budgets, controlling finance and accountability, and counting the numbers. This of course is an exaggeration, but it seems to have led to the neglect in developing essential long-term central services for local development bodies. It has also created tensions, as the 'centre' is seen by local agencies as a controller, not a facilitator. The potential range of central support services is considerable and includes: central support for the development of promotional materials; updating agencies on legislation; updating data banks; provision for experience exchange; providing region-to-region business links; providing a conduit for foreign funds; support for special credit schemes; lobbying and pressure group activities; central purchasing; research and development into needs and new programme opportunities; development, testing and dissemination of new programme models; building from a bench marking of best practice; the transfer, adaptation and dissemination of programme models from abroad; comparative evaluation; monitoring of the health of the small and medium enterprise community, and its needs; the provision of on-going training facilities for trainers, consultants and agency staff; the development of programmes for staff of the regulatory and service environment; small business advocacy in the development of legislation; and, perhaps most importantly, the on-going education of bureaucrats, policymakers and politicians.

Assistance

The ultimate shape of the institutional environment within which small and medium businesses will operate at the local and regional level is as yet unclear. In most transition economies there is therefore a premium upon ensuring that models of assistance for SMEs (be they ultimately commercially viable or dependent upon subsidy) are highly credible and capable of being delivered by a variety of competent personnel, no matter what their ultimate institutional delivery context. The key isues therefore seem to be those of:

o the application of the 'culture context', with the 'know how', 'know who', and 'need to know' message incorporated in the design of all support models;

o the development of well-targeted, customer-segmented, training, counselling and financial models, capable of being widely disseminated;

o the ongoing exchange of best practice and bench marking in this respect;

o the development of (locally serviced) systems of ensuring that those who deal with the small business are competent, via programmes for training trainers (local capacity) and training counsellors and consultants;

o developing the capability to use successful business persons for small firm support (particularly given the acute problems of retaining good core advice centre and even financial services staff at relatively low salaries);

o ensuring that all those who work with small business are themselves deeply embedded in the local transactional environment with which the business deals, so they have street-wise credibility;

o the development of programmes to raise the competence of all those in the regulatory and professional service environment;

o ensuring that information services for small businesses are not characterized by the technical and impersonal sophistication and linkage of data banks, but are personalized as much as possible to the small business on a need-to-know and possibly therefore cluster basis; and

o ensuring that there are close links between essential services to small business and a mutual understanding between those who offer their services, in particular that maximum use is made of local and regional networks and joint ventures in the development of programmes and their marketing.

Against these criteria there still seems to be much scope for action. The key questions I often ask when visiting small business development institutions at the national or regional level are: 'Who are the outstanding people in the provision of services to small businesses, and which are the outstanding programme models? Where are the entrepreneurs involved and where are the good examples of network co-operation and joint venturing?' Probably too often those asked these questions still find difficulty in answering, indicating that a major challenge still lies ahead.

Improving support programmes and the transfer process

It seems to me that small business support for Eastern Europe and the former Soviet Union is really about the transfer of learning *both ways*. Effective transfer occurs when ones existing way of looking at things or way of doing things is replaced by another way of looking at things or another way of doing things on a sustainable and continuous basis. The most common way of entrepreneurial learning is to learn by doing, by solving problems and grasping opportunities and by giving broader meaning to that process of learning (so that next time the problem can be averted or dealt with more easily). These principles are simple, fundamental and easily ignored. It can be argued that the rapid dissemination of Western practice into different cultures and countries with different problems of development can create discontinuities in education systems, financial systems, regulatory systems and transition systems which make it difficult for the small firm to grow incrementally or indeed for agencies to cope. It can also distort the learning effect as the focus may become one of how better to make the 'imported' system work than pragmatically to solve local problems. I was reminded recently by a colleague in the UK that in respect of the transfer of Local Enterprise Agency experience from the UK to Central Europe we had collated ten years of experience into one start-up package. Another classic case is, of course, that of the business school teaching the translated cases, concepts and Western economy models to managers whose contextual knowledge and skill needs are those related to restructuring. For small business managers time spent on knowledge acquisition out of the context of their problems is likely to be time wasted.

This experience calls for the concept of mutual learning partnerships between transition economies and those from the West. There needs to be a greater allowance for experimentation and making mistakes on both sides, for differentiation and flexibility, greater vision in terms of what embedding means in terms of change, recognition that the vision and image of what might be in the future comes from within the society and not from Western transplants, and openly and honestly recognizing that many of the models used in the West are not wholly validated. There is much to learn from what does not work (perhaps more than from what does), in the banking system particularly. Overshadowing all of this is the issue of sustainability and continuous learning, in terms of building upon successful institutional behaviour and programme models as well as taking a strategic policy view of the ultimate vision of support for, and finance of, small business development. If institutions are grafted onto transition economies in the shape of small business centres or various kinds of local and regional development agencies, it must be recognized that these are not without their problems in the West and indeed have their own ultimate sustainability continuously open to question. Agencies have no god-given right to exist, and neither do their programme models. They exist only by courtesy of the needs and demands of the entrepreneur (and the ideologies and whims of governments). Giving meaning to the needs of entrepreneurs and converting needs into demands is the most difficult and demanding task of all, particularly as the entrepreneur does not speak with one voice. Yet failure to listen leads to the dictat of providing 'what is good for them' via the professional and bureaucratic culture of the business school, accounting company, bank, or government department. What strikes me is the remarkable absence of evidence at present of programmes designed by entrepreneurs and small business people to help us understand them; programmes designed by those in the transition economies to help Western consultants and advisers to understand better the cultural context, and the 'know how', 'know who', and 'need-to-know' basis upon which their approaches should be modelled; and programmes to help politicians (whatever their ideology) better understand the nature of the stable environment they need to create for entrepreneurs.

Institutional support for small business in Poland

DANUTA HÜBNER

SUSTAINING THE GROWTH of small and medium enterprises in economies in transition is important for a number of reasons:

○ the private sector and, in particular, SMEs form the backbone of a market economy and in future will provide most of the employment;
○ small enterprises help in the de-monopolization and restructuring of large state-owned companies;
○ SMEs play the pivotal role in changing export patterns, thus contributing to the international competitiveness of the economy;
○ the shift from a few large state-owned enterprises to many privately owned SMEs will increase the number of people with a direct stake, as owners, in the economy and therefore with a vested interest in social stability;
○ an increase of the number of SMEs will also bring flexibility to the economy and facilitate technological research and development;
○ new business development, including SMEs, is a key factor for the success of regional reconversion, where traditional and heavy industries will have to be restructured.

The contribution of SMEs to the market economy is therefore now widely recognized.

The small and medium enterprise sector in Poland

The Main Statistical Office (GUS) data lists over 2.1 million enterprises in Poland, of which about 92 per cent employ up to five people; about six per cent employ between 5 and 50; and about two per cent have more than 50 employees. It is estimated that there are more businesses than this active on the market in Poland, which are not shown in official statistics. This 'grey area' of the economy could possibly account for up to 40 per cent of private economy activity. The private sector dominates the retail trade and the construction sector (providing respectively 89 and 86 per cent of the output), is strong in transport (43 per cent) and gaining strength in industrial production—SME industrial output accounted for 38 per cent of national figures in 1994.

Danuta Hübner is the Deputy Minister of Industry and Trade in Poland.

The majority of Polish businesses are very new; only two per cent have been running more than 25 years; 35 per cent were established between 1970 and 1990; and 63 per cent, being new, are post-1990 arrivals. The SMEs currently employ about 60 per cent of the workforce and in the period 1990–94 as a sector increased employment by 1.5 million employees. National statistics also show that SMEs account for more than half of Poland's GDP and their growth rates are significantly superior to the public sector.

While in the first years of transformation Poland witnessed an unprecedented increase in the number and longevity of SMEs, in the mid-nineties the pace of firm growth is slowing, yet the sophistication and breadth of the sector is expanding. The sector may be approaching the maturity phase. For each phase of SME development both structural characteristics and key success factors change. For the start-up period the freedom of economic activity was the basic stimulus. On the side of the government, refraining from any action was a conducive factor. The rapid growth phase then required first of all macroeconomic stabilization but the maturity phase means that companies now need a stable institutional environment.

SME support institutions in Poland

Around 1989–90, no institutional infrastructure serving the needs of the SME sector existed. Since then, a lot of activities in the development of such institutions have been undertaken, resulting in a great number of both non-profit and commercial organizations which provide services to Polish businessmen.

Two main categories of those institutions can be distinguished:

o Financial institutions: state banks, private and co-operative banks, brokerage houses, and insurance institutions.
o Other institutions and organizations, including: regional development agencies and foundations, centres of innovation and entrepreneurship, advisory, information and training institutions, economic chambers and associations, promotion and commercial institutions.

Financial institutions can be best described by their high dynamics. That applies in particular to banks. The large urban areas lead this process. However, banks are not interested in rendering services to SMEs, they do not grant preferential credits, and, in general, tend to be rather reluctant to deal with SMEs. High interest rate and high collateral requirements make credit quite an inaccessible source of finance for private firms and especially those newly set-up companies which do not possess sufficient collateral and operate in conditions of high risk. In order to facilitate access to credit for Polish entrepreneurs, the government co-funded the credit guarantee fund designated for the SME sector, to be operated by one of the state banks.

15

These guarantees can be obtained by enterprises (independently of their legal status and property form) with no more than 250 employees, annual turnover below 20 million ecu and total assets below 10 million ecu. Credits provided by Polish banks can be guaranteed, if they are used for investment or purchase of raw materials, in the following areas: start-up or increase of export production, the implementation of high-tech innovations, the purchase of privatized enterprises' inventory, environmental protection and the creation of new work-places (including new enterprises).

Non-financial organizations developed rapidly as well. At the end of 1993 a total of over 600 institutions were supporting small businesses, including:

o 123 regional development agencies and foundations;
o 52 innovation and entrepreneurship centres;
o 314 chambers of commerce and business associations;
o 112 advisory, information and training institutions;
o 72 promotion and trade institutions.

Regional development agencies (RDAs) are established in the legal form of joint stock companies, with the Treasury, *voivods* (regional governments) and banks acting as shareholders, or alternatively as foundations with the same categories of founders, playing a significant role in several regions. In particular, RDAs have been established in regions facing structural unemployment. The principal goals of RDAs include: preparing restructuring programmes and SME development programmes; entrepreneurship promotion, including information, advice and training; establishing investment funds in the form of equity, loans and guarantees; promoting Polish businesses on foreign markets; and organizing auctions and business fairs.

The agencies promote and support all efforts geared to regional development, as well as establishing and developing contacts with local institutions and organizations. They also promote social and economic initiatives in support of SMEs. Agencies of local initiatives, also belonging to this group, have been operating since 1990 as the regional network of FISE (Foundation for Social and Economic Initiatives). Their purpose is to support local small businesses, in particular start-ups. They also provide assistance to local governments.

Innovation and entrepreneurship centres. This group is represented by 52 centres, and further expansion is planned. In different regions of the country business incubators are being established. Currently there are over 20 incubators. They provide training and advice and offer space for entrepreneurs to run small businesses. The users of the incubator can obtain secretarial, administrative, legal and financial services, i.e. full office service for start-ups.

Chambers and business associations. Chambers of Commerce (119 in number) are self-governing organizations at the regional level. Their members represent all business sectors and all types of economic activity. The activities of the chambers include: lobbying the state authorities on the interests of members at the regional level and in the local administration; the organization of fairs and exhibitions; promotion and marketing of local products; rendering fiscal, legal and financial advisory services; the organization of training courses; and assistance in establishing business contacts, both locally and abroad.

The National Chamber of Commerce (KIG) is an organization representing regional chambers. The Chamber deals with the promotion of Polish entrepreneurs locally and abroad; has a data bank including information on more than 40 000 Polish and foreign firms; organizes trade missions and promotes fairs, exhibitions and auctions, and also conducts publishing activities.

The Craft Chamber is a self-governing structure of craftsmen, operating on a regional level. The Association of Polish Crafts consists of 26 chambers. The activity of Craft Chambers is focused on advocating the interests of members to the government, self-governing administrations and other institutions. They also provide assistance in legal, organizational, fiscal, economic and financial issues, and organize training courses on vocational competence. They also help with international business contacts and organize exhibitions of craft products.

Economic societies and associations, of which there are 132, are in most cases established by local communities and they play a significant role in the integration and activation of local private entrepreneurs. These associations have been established in order to represent and protect the interests of particular groups of entrepreneurs or to promote entrepreneurship at the regional level in order to undertake joint actions in support of the development of the local business community.

Advisory, information and training institutions. In addition to the above, there is a large group of institutions which, according to their statutes, exclusively provide information, advisory and training services. This group is quite numerous (112), and currently is expanding more rapidly in the eastern part of the country (where the number of this kind of institutions is not large). Among these institutions are:

○ the Economic Solidarity Foundation with 12 local branches;
○ Polish–American Entrepreneurship Clubs;
○ Polish–American Advisory Foundations for Small Enterprises;
○ consulting institutions;
○ promotion centres.

Promotion and trade institutions. The group of promotion and trade institutions includes the Offices for Economic Promotion and Foreign

Co-operation, which have been established since 1990 in the economics departments of regional offices. These institutions promote regions and businesses, both locally and abroad, with a special focus on the private sector. They are also involved in publishing catalogues and promotional brochures, preparing offers of sale of state enterprises, maintaining data banks concerning underutilized assets, providing consulting and information services, and organizing fairs and auctions.

A significant role in business promotion is played by institutions organizing fairs, exhibitions and auctions. Recently, a considerable increase in the number of these institutions has been seen in some cities in Poland.

Generally, the small business environment is characterized by a broad regional diversification of institutions both in number and in financial resources. Much of the advisory and financial infrastructure is concentrated in large urban areas like Warsaw, Lódź, Poznań, Gdańsk, Szczecin and Cracow. The SME environment is better developed in the western part of the country, while its underdevelopment is clearly visible in eastern regions.

Towards government policy for the SME sector

Bearing in mind the importance of the SME sector for the development of the Polish economy, the Government of Poland approved a policy programme for this sector in the Spring 1995. The policy document was elaborated and presented for the approval by the Ministry of Industry and Trade. It forms an integral part of the industrial policy, and at the same time has an independent legal status.

The formulation of the SME policy programme has been, in the case of Poland, a corollary of many factors:

○ pressure on the SME community based on their actual needs in terms of growth barriers (financing, information);
○ difficulties of SMEs stemming from the instability of economic activity and economic policy;
○ pressure on SMEs due to their inherited risk aversion;
○ problems of SMEs stemming from the historical position (private sector development under the centrally planned system faced many barriers, but the environment was a constant);
○ a discrepancy between an extremely rapid expansion of certain small businesses during the first years of transformation, generating requirements towards certain areas of business environment, and a much slower development of others.

In general, government had to fill the institutional vacuum in the short-term by a programme planning the future development of institutions and processes to meet the expectations of the SMEs. This required an objective look at the role of the SME sector in the development of Poland and proper attention by the government to support SMEs and encourage employment, investment, exports, structural change, the private sector, the middle class and budget revenues.

In other words, Poland has been going through a process of building an awareness of the role of SMEs in its economic and social development, and this process has been both a bottom-up and top-down one. On the one hand, small businesses have built their own identity by experiencing ups and downs in their activities, and have found the way to approach politicians and governments. On the other hand, the Government of Poland has become more aware of the role SMEs play in the process of transformation. Such a process takes time, it requires information, interest and commitment, and finally it requires institutions to become independent and sustainable.

This process has not taken place in a political, social and economic vacuum. It has also required a great deal of personal commitment of many people involved, among those being the G–24 Task Force for Small Business whose initiative culminated in the 1993 document, *Investing in the Future*.

The institutionalization of the SMEs' development has its roots also in the involvement of academic communities. From vocational skills training programmes in construction trades to the Warsaw Institute of Banking, from MBA curricula at the Warsaw School of Economics to high-level scientific research and commercialization of new technologies, and seminars and workshops on the role or definition of SMEs (which turned out to be a serious problem in the formulation of the policy programme), the importance of education and research cannot be overemphasized.

The main direction of the proposed government SME policy programme is to create and maintain a positive environment for the sector's development, including, in particular, legal regulations, and the adaptation of fiscal and financial banking systems.

The second important direction of the policy programme is to create conditions to increase SMEs' access to finance. This requires new legal regulations to help develop local guarantee and credit funds.

The third important element is the creation of a convenient environment for entrepreneurs (and potential entrepreneurs) in order to improve their access to management, marketing, quality control, strategy and production, and new technologies training. This will be done by support to institutions providing training, editing and consulting activities for SMEs.

The fourth important direction of SME policy is to create proper conditions for increasing the production capacity and competitiveness of SME products on domestic and foreign markets. This will be achieved through ensuring better access to business information, promoting the implementation of new technologies, and facilitating standards and quality assurance

19

procedures. The Ministry of Industry and Trade, responsible for SME development and policy, has established the Polish Foundation for the Promotion and Development of Small and Medium-sized Enterprises, which will be responsible for the practical implementation and co-ordination of activities and programmes in this area.

Conclusions

The development of the SME sector in Poland points to some general tendencies:

o Initially, SME development and expansion was a spontaneous process, based on hidden reserves, a spontaneous response of potential entrepreneurs to the freedom of economic activity, and on existing legal gaps. The stage, however, has been reached when well-prepared and focused measures are needed to continue the momentum of sector expansion. Further development will be hardly possible without stabilization of the institutional environment.

o In the initial stage, basic services were developed, which were very useful for starting businesses. Now there is a need to develop more specialized and in-depth services to cater to the needs of those who have already reached some experience and require more comprehensive assistance.

o At first, different types of institutions and services were developed without much co-ordination and co-operation. This was not necessarily bad (and was perhaps unavoidable) at the beginning. However, experience shows that in order to fully utilize potential assistance, complete service packages should be provided to SMEs, including both financial and non-financial services (otherwise SMEs cannot properly use the finance available, and do not have the motivation to reach out for non-financial services).

o The question of the sustainability of institutions created basically with financial input from foreign sources becomes more and more important as foreign assistance decreases and national and local sources are not ready to provide substantial funding. The SME service providers have therefore to operate more on market terms, but since the SME clients cannot yet pay full prices, future sources of subsidizing these kind of activities have to be identified.

o Foreign assistance is most successful in those cases when it is really based on a partnership concept (equal partners, not 'donor' and 'recipient', with both parties recognizing mutual benefits to be gained from the relationship). Local partners should be real partners in defining their needs, and not just a recipient of 'wisdom'. The possibility of co-financing local costs of project is still very important, otherwise, taking into account the lack of local resources, it may prove difficult to obtain any meaningful results.

o Small and medium enterprises are present in all industries. Government policies oriented towards the development of SMEs have to be carefully designed and well co-ordinated. They have to be well poised, coherent, aware of the role played by regional and local partners, well integrated with other programmes of structural policies and based on sound and realistic estimates of financial possibilities.

o The question arises whether the institutionalization of government activities aimed at supporting SME development is required in the form of a formalized policy programme. In my opinion this depends on the following factors: the tradition and history of SME development in a given country; the strength of the sector in terms of capital, competitiveness, and the differentiation of vested interests and lobbying; and the cohesion and maturity of the business environment.

Transformation is a process of institutional change. Its success in the long run will not be possible unless necessary institutions are created and developed. Some of those institutions develop in response to demands created by the very functioning of SMEs, some have to be carefully designed and established by governments. When we discuss the issue of institutional environment or SME development it does not seem adequate to adopt the narrow understanding of 'institutions' as organizations. In its broader sense 'institution' also means rules and principles, or systems. In case of Central and East European countries, it is the latter that really matter. Organizations are built up, and some of them disappear after some time, others emerge. What really matters is the legal system, which takes time to be established. That is why from the very beginning a proper emphasis should be put on creating an all-embracing legal environment conducive to the development of the SME sector.

Government policy for small and medium enterprises in the Russian Federation

VICTOR ERMAKOV

AT THE START of the nineties, at the same time as the breakup of the centralized socialist economy, the rapid growth of the private sector of the economy began in Russia. By 1995 the number of independent enterprises in the country amounted to about 2 million, compared to about 40000 at the end of the eighties. The number employed in the small and medium enterprise (SME) sector has reached about 10 million. In trade, domestic services, building and commercial activities, SMEs account for approximately one half of the total number of enterprises and half of those employed in them. It is estimated that the number of SMEs will increase in the coming years by at least 30 per cent annually, although a temporary reduction in the growth rates is possible.

SME employees have a high level of qualifications: 37 per cent of workers have tertiary education, and 39.4 per cent secondary. Judging by surveys of businessmen, 40 per cent of them have savings at the bank (on average 10.2 per cent of the total value of the firm), 74 per cent used personal savings as start-up capital, and the average profit came to 16.2 per cent of the volume of turnover. The average income of 61 per cent increased in 1994. The statistics testify, particularly against the background of the general fall in output and the crisis of many large enterprises, that small business has a significant domestic potential, and is a high-paying, efficient and profitable sector of the economy.

The total proportion of SMEs in the Russian GDP, does not exceed 15 per cent, and the share of the total working population is about 13 per cent (without counting those holding more than one job). On the whole, SMEs in Russia do not yet play the role in the national economy which they do in economically developed countries. The process of development of small business in Russia is, doubtless, closely connected with the development of the general politico-economic and social situation in the country, and comes under the influence of a series of unfavourable factors, which will be discussed later.

Legal provision for SMEs at the federal level

There is now no doubt that the efficient development of SMEs, and an increase in their contribution to the national economy, is only possible with

Victor Ermakov is the President of the Russian Small Business Support Agency.

state support. This is particularly true in Russian conditions, where market relations are only just being formed, where state monopoly is still strong and the deep restructuring of the economy has hardly begun.

In 1993–4 a series of steps was taken in Russia, aimed at state support for small business. Under the Government of the Russian Federation's programme 'Development of reform and stabilization of the Russian economy' for 1993–5, native enterprise was identified as the chief driving force for market reforms and the guarantee of their stability and irreversibility. The special significance of small business as the most dynamic sector of the economy was underlined.

By its own Resolution of April 1993, the Government approved the federal programme of state support for SMEs for 1994–95. In June of the same year the Government approved the draft federal law on this subject. By the middle of April of this year it passed the second and third readings in the State Duma and again was submitted for consideration to the Council of the Federation. Small business has high expectations of this draft law. The next programme of support for SMEs in 1996–97 is now in the stage of being worked out.

The resolution of the government on the network of regional agencies for the support of small business, taken in December 1994, deserves separate mention and appraisal. The draft federal law on the simplification of the system of taxation and accounting for small business, prepared in April 1995 for consideration in the State Duma, is highly important. The law is aimed at altering the bias of Russian tax legislation, which has not until now encouraged the development of SMEs in industry. The draft law aims to simplify tax procedure for 'microenterprises' (20 people in consumer goods industries and up to 10 people in trade and services). SMEs will only need to make two payments: for a licence, and for income tax for the whole quarter. Payments to off-budget funds have, it is true, been preserved. However, the combined payments to federal, regional and local budgets, if this law is passed, will not exceed 30 per cent of profits. The implementation of this will probably begin in 1996.

At the moment Russian tax legislation has only the following privileges for SMEs: tax exemption for newly founded SMEs working in priority areas (such as agricultural products, consumer goods, medical supplies and construction) for the first two years, and a reduction of the tax rate in the third and fourth year of activity, the exemption of 'new' SMEs from property tax in the first year of activity, and exemption from the payment of advance contributions for the tax on profit.

Tax incentives in the form of privileged rates of tax on profit have also been applied to credit and insurance organizations working principally with SMEs. A fund for the support of enterprise and the development of competition has been created and is operating, as well as a fund for the promotion of SMEs in science and technology.

Work on the deregulation of enterprise and the simplification of administrative procedures is going on: the process has been sorted out, the registration period for new SMEs has been shortened, the volume of statistical reporting has been reduced four times, and the procedure for licensing SMEs has been made easier in a number of districts. Legislation aimed at supporting SMEs makes a fairly long list, the length of which will grow.

On the whole, measures for the direct stimulation of small business and indirect regulation, creating a favourable climate for enterprise, are combined in the activity of the Russian Government. However, an overall system of state support for SMEs has not yet been created. An adequate legislative and normative basis has not yet been worked out, there is no mechanism for carrying out decisions and supervising their implementation, and there is no unified system of state support for small business on the federal, regional and local level. Finally, state provisions that have been made for this are insufficient.

Federal agencies that support SMEs

The variety of agencies supporting SMEs in foreign countries makes it difficult for Russia to borrow directly from any one foreign model. The Russian structure of support for SMEs is currently as follows. In the Federal Assembly (i.e. in the Parliament of the Russian Federation) SMEs are dealt with by several committees under one or another aspect: the committee on property and on economic reform and property relations (these committees belong to the Council of the Federation, or Senate); on economic policy and on property; and privatization and economic activity (part of the State Duma). In the last committee there is a separate subcommittee for SMEs.

In the Russian federal executive agencies, small business issues fall under the authority of the Economics Ministry, the Antimonopoly Committee, the Ministry of Finance, the State Property Committee, the Committee for industrial policy and the Federal Employment Agency. These ministries and committees are represented on the supervisory council of the fund for the support of enterprise and the development of competition. This allows conflict of interests in implementing measures for the financial support of small business to be avoided. Inside these ministries, specially created subdivisions are concerned with SME issues, and issues of SME support are also considered in other ministries.

The setting up of a system of state support for SMEs is, it must be acknowledged, difficult. The defence of departmental interests, and weak communications and co-ordination, are as yet characteristic of this arrangement. This leads to a parallelism and duplication of a series of functions in co-ordination with regions and associations of SMEs, and in the preparation of international contacts and programmes. The problem is to determine the authority of the separate agencies and distribute functions between them. Specialists in the field of SME support have already been found and they have some resources, but they are uncoordinated, and this hinders the state from arranging effective programmes for SMEs.

Financial support for SMEs at the federal level

The main agency for the financial support of small business on the part of the state is the fund for the support of enterprise and the development of competition already mentioned. It was created in accordance with the resolution of the Government of Russia of 1 April 1993. Initially it was attached to the Antimonopoly committee, but in that year it became an independent organization. It began its practical work at the end of 1993.

During this time the Supervisory Council of the Fund prepared procedures for the use of the resources of the fund, and the financing of entrepreneurial projects and regional programmes was begun. The function of state customer of the federal programme of state support for SMEs in the Russian Federation 1994–5 was given to the Fund. The creation of the fund was a stimulus to the development of similar funds in the regions of Russia, and led to an increase in the resources from regional budgets aimed at the support of SMEs. By 1995 regional funds had been founded in 70 subjects of the Federation, and the volume of corresponding resources exceeded 50 billion roubles (currently 7100 roubles is equivalent to £1).

There are serious weaknesses in the work of the fund, connected with the newness of its task, its lack of experience and subjective circumstances. These include the limited range of firms and financing techniques, leading to a dispersion of resources and a reduction in the number of SME beneficiaries; the complicated procedure of selection, examination and financing of the SME projects through commercial banks; the passivity of the management of the fund in attracting financial resources from private banks and investors, including foreign ones; and the lack of a clear procedure for the supervision of the activity of the executive on the part of the Supervisory Council.

In total in 1994, for example, only 0.001 per cent of the expenditure of the federal budget was given for state support of SMEs, and the fund only spent about 5 per cent of the resources it had for the implementation of the federal programme for the support of SMEs. In the current year a series of measures are being considered, which are aimed at increasing the role of the fund as the main instrument for the implementation of state policy in support of SMEs in Russia.

State support for SMEs at the regional level

The increasing economic independence of the regions belonging to the Russian Federation is one of the most important traits influencing the establishment of market relations in our country. Economists consider the general development of small business as the fundamental factor for building up regional economies. Executive agencies in the Russian regions now have sufficient powers and resources to help in the establishment and development of enterprises.

The actual development of SMEs in the different regions is, however, very uneven. The absolute leader in this field is Moscow. By the beginning of 1994, 220000 SMEs had been registered there. As yet scientific enterprises (16 per cent) and commercial SMEs providing consumer goods (18 per cent) predominate. Only 15 per cent are engaged in trade and public catering, and significantly less in production. It is a different picture in St Petersburg. There the number of industrial SMEs amounts to 24 per cent, construction SMEs 20.5 per cent, but the total number of them is not great: about 25000 in total.

In some regions, although they are sufficiently developed, the number of SMEs does not exceed two thousand. SMEs in Russia are as a rule concentrated in the big cities. This can be explained as a characteristic of the branching structure of the regional economy and of the policies of the regional authorities, who are by no means everywhere committed to the development of small business. In several regions they have not yet realized the importance of the development of SMEs for the solution of urgent socio-economic problems.

The resolution of the Government of the Russian Federation 'On the network of regional agencies of support for small business' in 1994 is of key significance for the development of small business in the regions. The Government approved measures, with the participation of the EU, for the founding and development in 21 regions of networks of non-state regional agencies for the support of small business. The aims were: training and consultancy services for entrepreneurs, the supervision of business programmes and projects, the provision of information for SMEs, and assistance to SME employees in the preparation and registration of their founding documents.

The creation of a network of regional agencies was included in the 1994–5 federal programme of state support for SMEs. There will be an allocation of 1.4 billion roubles for these purposes out of the federal budget in 1995, and equal participation of the regions is envisaged in the financing of the creation of a network of regional agencies. It is proposed that the executive bodies help create these agencies, including by the initial provision of working premises. The Russian Federal Employment Service is being enlisted in this work, which ought to help involve the unemployed in the SME sphere, and to organize the professional reorientation of laid-off workers (see Ponomarev's and Gribankova's chapter on this subject).

Support for enterprise at the regional level

In Russia there is no unified system for the support of small business by executive bodies. The guidelines for the demarcation of powers in this field are stipulated in the draft federal law 'On state support for small-scale enterprise', but it has not yet been passed. Now in the regions of Russia where the State Committee for antimonopoly policy has its own regional administration—the majority of regions—a policy of support for SMEs co-ordinated with the local authority is being carried out (see Komsa's and Merkulov's chapter dealing with such regional support in Belarus). On the whole a tendency for the further decentralization and broadening of the rights of local government in this field can be observed.

Many regions have instituted their own regional programmes for the support of SMEs. They have a list of concrete business projects, for the realization of which state and above all financial support is demanded. The number of such projects under regional programmes varies from five to several dozen. They include business parks, science and technology parks, business incubators, business centres and SME support agencies. About 20 similar projects were registered with the federal programme of state support for SMEs and are entitled to part financing by the fund for the support of enterprise and the development of competition. In 1993–4 regional programmes were instituted in 12 of the members of the Russian Federation and by 1994–5 there were already 24.

The predominant form of small business support in Russia at the regional level is the funds for SME support. The first such fund was already established in 1990–1 and now they are found in 70 out of 89 of the members of the Russian Federation. The main sources of financing for the funds are: regional budgets, resources from the privatization of state enterprises, the property of the founders, income from the activity of the fund, the repayment of credit, and contributions by legal bodies. The organizational and legal forms of the regional funds are varied: state institutions or enterprises, non-commercial organizations, voluntary organizations, closed (or open) partnerships (or joint-stock companies). The following figures give some idea of the resources of these funds: in 1993 they financed business projects to the sum of 29.2 billion roubles, and in 1995 this sum will amount to about 240 billion roubles, on preliminary data. If the Russian economy improves, then the volume of resources allocated by the regions for the support of regional SME funds will grow at a much greater rate.

Co-operation with foreign companies and organizations

Between 1993 and the beginning of 1994 the experimental stage of founding small and medium business support agencies was carried out in a number of Russian regions, with the assistance of the British KnowHow fund. Taking their experience into account in some respects, the TACIS programme for the support of the creation of a network of regional small business agencies began in 1994. The consortium CORE, which included a

French, Italian and three English companies under the leadership of Focus Consultancy, started a two-year programme of technical aid for the creation of this network on behalf of the Commission of the European Union. The experts of the countries mentioned took part in the preparation for the opening or development of agencies in 21 Russian regions, and made suggestions of possible new 'points' for the creation of such agencies. In Moscow in early 1995, in co-operation with the Russian agency, they successfully held the first two seminars for instructors and directors of the regional agencies, with the aim of working out business courses for new Russian entrepreneurs, taking European experience into account. Supplies of technical and office equipment for the network of regional agencies are being planned, as well as regular seminars and internships for the staff of the regional agencies in European business centres. In the framework of the TACIS programme, technical assistance is being provided to the Moscow agency for the development of enterprise by providing information and consultancy services, including connections with services abroad.

In April 1995, under another TACIS project in Russia aimed at applying European experience in the development of small business, a special seminar was held in Moscow with the participation of representatives of a number of European research centres, Russian Government and other bodies in charge of small business issues. The implementation of the project will be continued through visits familiarizing our specialists with the development of small enterprise in a number of European countries.

In the Moscow district a programme of assistance to private enterprise at the regional level is being realized with the assistance of the Consultative Society of the Board of Guardians. It is aimed at the creation of infrastructure and the training and advising of local government employees. There has been, on the whole, a good start to co-operation between Russian small business and European experts in this field. The Russian counterparts are ready for the development and deepening of this co-operation.

A number of projects have also been worked out and implemented with non-European countries who have experience with small business. In Vladivostok, a Far East international policy centre was created with the active support of the Primorski Krai administration and of the Japanese Ministry of International Trade and Industry, which includes several technology and training centres for SMEs using Japanese technology. Chinese, South Korean and American organizations are taking part in separate projects at the Far East centre.

Factors hindering the establishment of small business

Small business in Russia functions in conditions where it is adversely affected by such large-scale factors as general political and economic instability, the crisis situation of industry, under-developed infrastructure, the payments crisis, the lack (for politico-economic reasons) of internal incentives for long-term investment and the introduction of new technology.

The continuation of the monopoly position of industrial suppliers, pressure from large (including foreign) competitors, inequality in the market for credit and investment, the lack of managerial skills of new SME owners and managers and finally the ongoing criminalization of the economy are hindering SME development.

In addition to this, a number of specific obstacles stand out. These include:

○ an incomplete legislative basis for SME activity;
○ the ill-considered, unthought-out nature of the present system for taxing business people;
○ the difficulty and high cost of registering business services;
○ the incomplete system for licensing businesses and for certifying goods and services;
○ the abundance of supervisory bodies and the parallelism and duplication of their functions; and
○ the actions of local executive bodies, at times hindering the development of business.

Conclusion

Hardly anyone will take it upon themselves to predict the direction of the general politico-economic development of Russia in the coming years. As for small businesses, their specific difficulties have a temporary character and it is possible to overcome them. In our opinion, the outlined long-term tendency for an increase in SME potential and dynamism will be of decisive significance. As the situation gradually normalizes and those forces which support the revival of small enterprise in Russia become stronger, new promising futures should be opening up for these sectors in the final years of this century.

Helping businesses in the 'subsistence economy' in Hungary

ZSUZSA LACZKÓ

EVERY TRANSITION has its own social costs—every change has losers and winners. This simple truth has many consequences which need to tie the economy to a broader frame globally and locally. According to Peter Drucker, economic theory is behind the times, in that it assumes perfect competition, overlooks the qualitative aspects which are essential in the present argument and, puts forward alternatives which are highly contrasting, such as between consumption and investment, protectionism and free trade, and so on. The economy cannot be regarded simply as the world economy, however; there is a lower level: the local market and the subsistence economy. This term covers 'more or less stable activities which ensure that basic needs have been satisfied, but do not provide for any form of accumulation or growth for the majority of the population.

The subsistence economy in Hungary falls into the following categories. The household or family economy involves production especially for own consumption and acts as compensation for household members in low-prestige, low-salary employment. It also includes informal market activities, whose underground nature reflects their lack of viability with legislation in the present state, and one-person microenterprises and small businesses which provide a 'survival' income; retailers, craftspeople, other small businesses. These activities are clearly not profit-making under normal conditions regarding wages and living standards, but they nevertheless provide an entry into self-employment and into business for people who are able to be absorbed into the labour market.

The authorities of Eastern European countries usually tend to overlook the contribution that these activities can make to economic development. On a modest estimate, there are about 1 million small businesses and microentrepreneurs in the subsistence economy. The subsistence economy is primarily a place for learning. On the assumption that the subsistence economy provides for the basic needs of very many people, the above mentioned types of subsistence market activity, and especially the informal economy, should move into the sphere of the 'normal' market. If this does not happen it means that the legislative and economic environment is unsuitable and needs to be changed so as to allow these activities to

Zsuzsa Laczkó is from the SEED (Small Enterprise for Economic Development) Foundation, Hungary.

30

become socially recognized. When some people work very hard for theireconomic survival in microenterprises, we might ask whether it is the best use of public resources to make them turn instead to reliance on welfare by making the market more competitive? The position of such businesses is weakened by not accepting a degree of distortion in the rules of competition. Eastern European governments are very rigorous on creating economic stability, but perhaps at a high social cost.

Over the past four years the numbers of the young unemployed have become much larger than their share in the population, and among them the ratio of the long-term unemployed has been increasing continuously. This tendency is dangerous, because it is a general experience that the chances of finding another job deteriorate in proportion to the length of the time spent unemployed. Hungary has a middle position concerning the ratio of long-term unemployment, in comparison to both the Central and Western European countries. Unfortunately, it is a particular feature of these economies that economic development does not greatly affect the unemployment rate of first job seekers. This means, that we cannot anticipate any substantial improvement in the existing conditions, even implementing a successful economic development and employment policy.

Perhaps in response to this, the data reflecting the first part of the 1990s already indicate that a higher percentage of the young are attempting to involve themselves in the private sector than older generations. Who are these young people? First of all, there are those who have finished their education as a mature or graduate student and are facing an uncertain future. There are also those who—even though in the Hungarian society the level of awareness about self-employment was very low, especially in the early 1990s—have recognized that they must solve their own problems, and cannot wait for an effective outside solution. However, the lack of seed and working capital, which is generally characteristic of the SME sector is especially true in the case of young people.

The Életpálya Foundation began its activity in July 1993. The two founders, Shell Hungary Ltd and the Millennium Foundation, realized that amidst growing unemployment, the possibility of finding a job is becoming increasingly difficult for those who have just finished their education, and that this could result in serious social unrest. By creating the Életpálya Foundation the founders wish to promote the option of self-employment and make it available for more and more young people.

In its activity and methods, and in the image it has chosen, the Foundation follows the experience and methods of the organization named Livewire, which has been operating successfully since 1982 in the United Kingdom. In the first stage of its activity the target is to adapt the programmes and materials of Livewire to take into account the specific circumstances which arise in Hungary.

Focusing on enterprise opportunities for young people aged 18–30 Élet-pálya has four objectives:

o to promote awareness of the importance of enterprise among young people;
o to help young people interested in setting up a new business to make the key preliminary decisions;
o to render professional help to enable young people to establish and run their own small businesses; and
o to give opportunities to share experiences.

The Foundation tries to establish broad co-operation with local organizations and others operating in the country providing support to young people, the unemployed and to those who run their own business. It is necessary to rely on people with experience (entrepreneurs and businessmen) who volunteer to act as advisers and tutors to those who are interested in setting up their own business. It is not the Foundation's goal to duplicate services that already exist, but to promote their better utilization and to add elements that are still missing.

Between November 1993 and June 1994, 300 clients were registered. The second week of January proved to be the most successful, when 27 young entrepreneurs approached the Foundation, since then an average of 10 youngsters have turned to Életpálya weekly. However, the actual number of the clients is less important than the percentage of the clients who get effective support from Életpálya, since this support has enabled many of them to be referred to advisers and to prepare their business plans. Many entrepreneurs approached the Foundation when they heard about the entrepreneurship competition which it used to publicize its activities.

Half of the clients live in the country, where the coverage of the Élet-pálya service is limited. Nevertheless several young entrepreneurs entered the competition, preparing the business plan on their own by using the guidelines provided. Most of those who registered and who lived in the countryside did not respond to our first letter, however. Those applicants to whom we could provide advice, proved to be more active: only 32 per cent of them dropped out.

The majority of those registered, living in Budapest or in the surrounding area were interviewed in the Életpálya office in Budapest. The purpose of these interviews was to inform the client about the service provided by Életpálya, and for the co-ordinator to get to know the client's ideas and to find the best adviser for him or her. The co-ordinators do not link the clients up with an adviser immediately: the young people are first asked to work out a marketing plan following the business plan guidelines, carry out a simple market study and identify the questions which will be addressed by the adviser.

A total of 54 young people approached the co-ordinators, and 36 of them have been linked up with advisers. It is difficult to evaluate the clients: they vary, depending on their character and social background. However, the main motivation for approaching Életpálya was definitely the entrepreneurship competition. Many young entrepreneurs have a good business idea but they cannot get credit to carry it out, and they turned to the Foundation because a sum of around HUF 100 000 (£580), which is the second prize of the competition, would help solve their finance problems.

The first batch of the most promising young entrepreneurs have already started their businesses, or have worked together with someone and they are now taking over. This group has businesses with the most financial and market potential. These entrepreneurs were primarily interested in the competition prize, but when they were linked up with an adviser they came to appreciate the help they received. Such promising young entrepreneurs generally accept the support provided by Életpálya positively. Through their own or their parents' experience, they appreciate the importance of the advice, networking and publicity gained through the competition.

A significant number of the applicants came to Életpálya with ambiguous ideas. These applicants do not have business experience; they only have an idea, whose feasibility they have not worked out. Through the interviews it becomes apparent that they are not really clear about the business they are entering and that they are lacking in experience. Other young people want very specific help, such as where to find premises, sponsors, market data, cheap supply sources and credit, and they are disappointed when they learn that they have to look for the answers themselves. Életpálya's activity presupposes certain levels of independence, which disappoints some clients.

Although the tradition of self-employment does not have such a long history in Hungary as in England, Hungarian young entrepreneurs are not lacking in ideas. Many ideas similar to those tried out in England can be found: self-employment in the craft and hobby industries, and local community service is quite typical. During the exploration and the realization of the idea it is evident, however, that there are fewer young people in Hungary who can rely on the business experience of their parents or friends.

Recognizing the critical influence of family background for these young people, highlights the importance of supporting the development of family businesses. Hungarian Womens' World Banking Association is running a programme for women entrepreneurs running small enterprises and family businesses, called Enterprise Learning and Networks Initiative. In addition, SEED (Small Enterprise Economic Development) Foundation identifies young people, women and family businesses as its target groups, but frequently handles these groups as a unit, designing its programmes to deal with them all.

Creating small businesses out of large enterprises

STANISLAV LYAPUNOV AND ALLAN A. GIBB

THE DEVELOPMENT of the small business sector has undoubtedly been the most visible manifestation of the move to the market economy in Central and Eastern Europe (CEE). Most of the former communist economies can now boast several hundreds of thousands (if not millions) of small, private-sector businesses (Charap, 1992). Small business has also, so far, been the success story of the privatization process. Auctions and sales of small, usually service sector, businesses have proceeded relatively successfully and the process of restitution of property in Central European countries has led both to the restarting of family businesses and, via the sale of property of such businesses, to an improvement in the capital availability for small business start-ups (Kayser, 1991). Within the state sector many small businesses have been started as off-shoots of state companies (although this is now illegal in some countries) or have sprung up informally within the company enabling the use of otherwise under-utilized resources (Webster, 1992 and de Melo and Ofer, 1994).

The weaknesses of the existing small and medium business base in economies in transition

The 'success' of the development of the sector is, however, in reality substantially less than would superficially appear. Many of the small business registrations represent second or third jobs of those desperate to supplement low state salaries eroded substantially by inflation. Such registrations are also made to facilitate one-off deals of the 'middleman' kind for the purposes of avoiding taxation (Kupserberg, 1992). Many small businesses are still forced to behave illegitimately to circumvent unfair and cumbersome legal procedures in the regulatory environment and/or to avoid the attentions (in Russia in particular) of the Mafia or of corrupt officialdom. Premises are not easily available on secure terms of tenure, the taxation system is confused and the banking system is even more inadequately equipped than in the West to respond to small business needs. All of these factors encourage the development of the informal small business sector.

Allan A. Gibb is a Professor at Durham University Business School, UK and Stanislav Lyapunov is the Chairman and Chief Executive at the Prompribor Industrial Association, Chuvash, Russia.

These difficulties, when added to the absence of capital for growth and development, ensure that the small business sector, as it is now constituted, is predominantly that of the microenterprise working on a quick turn-round of services and transactions. There is a considerable weakness in that part of the small business sector which might be job generating (such as the microenterprise business and the under-twenty-employee small business sector in Europe) (European Network, 1994). And there is a very substantial absence of the medium-sized manufacturing and service business with national and international markets. There is thus still a 'hole' in the middle of the industry/service-sized distribution of firms. On the one hand are the large, mainly state, companies and medium-sized service-sector businesses (which, when privatized, tend to rapidly reduce numbers) and, on the other, numerous microenterprises and self-employed businesses, many in the informal sector.

It has been argued elsewhere that without the emergence of a well-rounded small and medium business sector, the vital role that small business plays in the distribution of ownership in the economy, providing flexibility of response and the growth of a culture of management of business under conditions of market uncertainty, will not be underpinned. Most cornerstones of the market economy will also not be fully established, including: the concept of widespread individual ownership and the right of the individual to transfer property and land; the key role played by consumer demand in the allocation of resources (as opposed to being dictated to by monopoly power and bargaining); the organization of a production sector under conditions of uncertainty and in advance (most often) of demand, with the associated risks involved; competition with large numbers of buyers and sellers; freedom of entry to compete; a scale of business dictated not by political and commercial power but by technology and real economics; and with price as a major arbitrator in the allocation of resources. Privatizing the existing state-owned structure will arguably not by itself lead naturally to the market economy criteria described above: individual ownership will remain divorced from management by institutional investors; property will be dominated by large power blocks; the consumer will remain dictated to as before (by a different group, or by the same group in disguise); competition will be limited; uncertainties will be removed by agreement between power groups; and scale will be dictated by power, as will resource exchange. This is particularly evident in Russia at present.

It is almost self-evident from the above that the future strength of the small business economy in Central and Eastern Europe is still very much a function of decisions to be made by large company managers as well as by politicians and bureaucrats who establish the rules of the game in power and exchange relationships in the economy, as well as being a function of changing the mentality of the majority of the population. Against this backcloth this chapter looks more closely at the relationship of the restructuring of large companies to small enterprise development, with particular respect to Russia, although the principles are arguably the same in most restructuring processes. It firstly takes a brief, but critical look at the impact of the privatization and restructuring process. It then reviews the basic argument for regarding large state businesses as a potential source of small enterprise development. After reviewing the broad range of issues associated with the restructuring process in practice it considers the case of the restructuring of a large state company in Cheboksary in the Autonomous Russian Republic of Chuvash. It draws some principles from this review which might be applied to other cases. Finally it considers the implications of this for forms of external support.

The impact of free markets and privatization on small businesses

The philosophy of Western support for the market economy in Central and Eastern Europe has been underpinned by the belief that releasing market forces via the deregulation of markets, the abolition of state control mechanisms over resources and behaviour, the associated removal of centralized decision-making and the influx of foreign competition, and (hopefully) capital, together with privatization of state companies and the establishment of broad financial mechanisms of market regulation as per Western models, will be enough to release market forces. Once such conditions are established, under this model everything else is deemed to fall into place (with the addition of some banker training, retraining of the unemployed and a dash of management training, Western business school-style). The immediate 'success' stories of Western capital involvement in Eastern Europe where conditions are more difficult are likely to be in areas where there are very substantial returns, resulting from the ability to charge high hard-currency prices with low local currency costs (for example, hotels), and via the acquisition of property and trading ventures with quick returns and high margins. Western purchases or buy-ins of state companies are confined to the best parts of the economy and frequently involve a subsequent sizing-down of a company from several thousand employees to its 'core' of several hundred jobs and therefore Western-style commercial viability.

The position has been further complicated, particularly in the Commonwealth of Independent States (CIS), by the struggle of those forces with power, via their previous influence in the party, to retain it via control of property and business dealings and distribution of the major part of resources, especially of those which are in short supply. Thus, for example, in Russia some local authorities hang on to premises and property and impede the process of its privatization. Some state supply ministries have been replaced by industry associations composed largely of the same people. The chief executives of state monopolies, partly or wholly in the process of being privatized, make, in some fields, considerable fortunes in the absence of competition while the new (old) industry associations still operate, and with considerable control, as do Mafia and racketeering gangs. There is, for example, in Russia, evidence that in certain key industries a not inconsiderable proportion of transactions activity goes through the same channels (disguised) as of old (Boeva and Shironin, 1992), rather than via new market exchanges, and that a great deal of service-sector activity is Mafia controlled.

The net immediate result of these Western 'macro framework' approaches in the East has therefore been to reduce output dramatically, create unemployment, create massive redistribution of incomes, sponsor inflation via the exercise of monopoly power in situations of chronic shortage, and create circumstances where Mafia regulation of the playing field is possibly needed to protect new small businesses from all of those who wish to exploit it via bribes and 'negotiated' services. There is some evidence that it has also created a growing disenchantment with the concept of entrepreneurship and private competitive enterprise among the majority who cannot benefit substantially from it but are obliged to seek a range of supplementary additions to their normal income in order to survive. In these circumstances the process of privatization is seen to be associated with unemployment and its particularly heavy social consequences in circumstances where there is no underpinning by a well-developed social security system. Auction activity and/or voucher presentation schemes are in danger of becoming discredited by the insolvency of many of the former state companies.

Against this backcloth there has been some growth of small business activity within the large company sector. Until recently in Russia, for example, state monopolies have frequently sought to establish small businesses either as a vehicle for their managers to create their own companies or as a means of settling the problem of raising the efficiency of a large monopoly company or a way of creating jobs. Some of these companies constitute ways of getting around restrictions, exploiting new opportunities and utilizing spare resources in the state firm. By this process individuals are themselves encouraged to carry parts of the former state company into independent activity.

Large businesses as an opportunity for small business development

The latter-mentioned examples are a reminder that within every large business there are many potential small businesses. The large company can indeed be seen as a conglomerate of small businesses representing a wide range of services; some directly, and others indirectly, production oriented; and a great many processes and often products that could be operated independently should the costs and benefits merit it. The typical large Western manufacturing company, for example, probably has more service-sector than strictly manufacturing jobs within it (many of which could be externalized as independent businesses). A process of disaggregation where many of these 'businesses' have been 'spun off' has been observed in many large firms in the West over the past decade (Harrison and Maryellen, 1993).

When the large firm is viewed as an agglomeration of the small business, the potential for disaggregation can be seen to be considerable. In Table 1 some examples are given of areas within the large company that can operate as independent businesses. They are broadly divided into: internal business services; internal personnel services; and internal stand-alone production processes. They constitute potentially: tasks that could be carried out on a 'self-employment' basis; processes that could stand alone (which are not technically on-line linked with other processes); products and processes that have market potential elsewhere (customers outside of the business); areas of chronic under-utilization of capacity (machine or labour); 'top-up' services and processes subject to internal cyclical demand (for example, changing the rolls in a steel-rolling mill); internal products and services with distinct independent customer segments; parts of the business that could easily be locally supplied (and do not therefore need the large company sourcing capability); technologies that have use elsewhere (perhaps with radically different customer sets); parts of the

Table 1. Creating small businesses out of a large company

'Internal' business services		
Sales	Maintenance	Warehousing
Marketing	Materials handling	Computer
P.R.	Distribution transport	Wages/tax
Printing	Personnel transport	Recruitment
Design	Gatekeepers	Travel
R & D	Guards	Accounts
Environment protection	Stock management	Procurement
Health and safety	Training	Stores
Inspection	Education	
'Internal' personnel services		
Pensions	Canteen	
Redeployment	Bars	
Gardens	Accommodation	
Sports	Cleaning	
'Internal' stand alone products/processes		
Products		
Components		
Processes		

business that outsiders could buy into without damage to the company; and (linked with several of the above) parts of the business that could meet locally unmet or partly met needs if allowed to expand.

The strategic issues involved in 'large into small'

It is one point to argue that in every large organization there are numerous potential small businesses, and that the potential is even greater in the former command economy large organizations. It is another point altogether as to what criteria might be used in making the decision to retain or 'externalize' a product, process or service. This is a strategic management issue of equal importance in West and East. It is an issue fundamental to the size and shape of any market economy structure. At its root is the economists' transactions cost theory of the firm which argues that decisions in favour of 'internalization' of a product or service will occur when the 'market transactions costs' (dealing with the product or process as an external agent) exceed the cost of managing the product/process internally (Williamson, 1985). In reality this somewhat simplistic concept, even when modified, cannot truly be said to 'explain' decisions of this nature in the business world. In practice the decision to 'externalize' or 'internalize' is likely to be a result of a combination of strategic production and management decisions.

Strategic issues will be those related to: the position of the company in the environment; and decisions concerning what should be the 'core' business of the company. The strategic environment arguments for 'internalizing' a particular product or service revolve around the need (or otherwise) to reduce uncertainty in the supply and/or demand side by 'controlling' suppliers and outlets. Such actions may therefore be taken in order to: secure supply; secure market outlets; deprive competitors of supply sources or markets; and deny key technologies to competitors. Products or processes may also be internalized when there is insecure supply or indeed no supplier (as arguably was the case in many command-economy state businesses—see below). The 'core business' strategic arguments for internalization are likely to revolve around: the company mission statement (what business it is or should be in); what the company is best at; where it has an existing or future unique selling proposition or market lead; and what are likely to be the key technologies of the future it ought to retain and develop.

Decisions to 'externalize' parts of the company represent the residue of the resolution of many of the issues identified above. 'Environment' arguments are likely to revolve around whether it is in the company's interest to stimulate a competitive supply situation and to take advantage of new market opportunities which cannot easily be grasped by internal departments. It may also be possible to release areas of company technology with potential elsewhere and to take advantage of new technologies and processes, and overall to devote more energy to the key customers and markets. Internal strategic consideration will probably focus upon issues such as: releasing entrepreneurial energies, consumed internally, into the market; perhaps weakening union control of labour in key areas where more flexibility is needed; and simplifying the organization and reducing overheads in the process.

Production and management issues in the external/internal debate

The immediate pressures relating to the external/internal debate stem from issues relating to the control of production and production costs. The arguments for the internalization of services and processes are essentially of a control nature. Controlling production standards and reject costs, ensuring 'just-in-time' and reducing inspection costs are the main arguments, along with the contention that up-to-dateness in technical development can be better ensured by internal organization. The production case for externalization relates mainly to the need to reduce the chronic and cyclical under-utilization of resources, consequently to reduce overheads and reduce the costs of control of internal production processes and services.

The broader management control argument for internalization focuses upon the reduced management energy arguably to be devoted to searching the environment for supplies and the associated resources involved in managing the purchasing process. There is also an argument that having 'a broader' organization will make it easier to attract a talented workforce. In contrast the 'externalization' argument makes a case for reducing internal communication costs and focusing management control issues on what really matters to the organization.

The opportunities in the CEE/FSU

The potential for such a disaggregation process as described above, almost as a necessary part of restructuring of large firms, *is very great* in Eastern Europe in particular. Many large companies have been built up over time without market or process logic. They may, for example, embrace many different products which are unrelated to each other (or are only marginally related), all operating within the same physical and managerial infrastructure and having a great many auxiliary services. Most self-employment or micro-businesses services were internalized because, for political reasons, they were not allowed to be available externally. And the same is true for many sub-contracting processes and component supply services.

As a result of the 'tradition' within which large companies have developed there are many internal supply-side products and processes which are not fully utilized in the overall balance of production. They are chronically under-utilized or used fully only on a cyclical basis. They therefore represent major sources of inefficiency. As a result also of the tradition: there are many internalized products and services with market potential outside of the company; there are many parts of existing business which could easily be locally supplied and therefore run independently; there are parts of the business where the technology has many uses elsewhere; and there are parts of many companies which might meet locally unmet or poorly met needs if allowed to expand.

Thus, overall, if businesses are to operate at higher levels of utilization, and if entrepreneurial resources within them are to be fully released, then a radical review of the restructuring and down-sizing potential and therefore of the possibilities for retaining small businesses arguably needs to take place before, or alongside, privatization. The case for prior restructuring is strong. Companies need to be prepared, as in the West, for the privatization process. In Russia there are further complications that arise from the 'social aspects' of the business. It seems to be frequently assumed that large companies in Russia are merely inefficient versions of Western large companies. This is not the case. The purpose of the large firm in Russia was different. It was a social institution providing a wide range of services to its workers, including: housing accommodation; clinics and medical facilities; the provision of food (by its own farms); leisure benefits; holiday and vacation benefits; and a range of other social services. It also, in effect, internalized unemployment and therefore the social costs. These services, many desirable in themselves, need to be continued and handled in a different way or by different authorities.

Problems in restructuring large businesses into small—the Russian case

There are major problems in re-constructing and downsizing large companies in Russia. Perhaps the most important is that there is an absence of resources available for this process and in particular for the management of independent businesses. Many small businesses created cannot (unless they are almost wholly local in their supply and customer chain) easily obtain necessary resources because a substantial proportion are still without the influence of the large 'power blocks'. Therefore some relationship needs to be retained between downsized small businesses and their previous owners. There is also a drastic shortage of capital and little prospect of access to it via the banking system. The 'spun-off' small company therefore is likely to be dependent upon its former large firm for sources of capital and will continue to be so in the foreseeable future. Managers of large companies face considerable personal risks in disintegrating their firms and therefore their power base. By this process they see that they may lose influence and control over the market. There are also major problems of ensuring that incentives are given to the managers of 'new' small companies in respect of the current shareholding and ownership regulations being pursued. These arrangements do not normally provide substantial potential for managers to take over and own the business or indeed buy out the company.

There are, in addition, major issues as to how the management of the company adapts to a different culture of dealing with uncertainty, taking responsibility, operating holistic management systems and coping with substantial degrees of customer dependence. In the environment there are problems that arise in respect of the control over resources exercised by the Mafia and racketeers, and there are still great difficulties in respect of the regulatory environment for small businesses which does not provide encouragement for their legitimization. Finally, there are problems in re-allocating the 'social aspects' of the business to local authorities because of the absence of funds for these purposes.

The reconstruction of parts of large companies into small businesses, although arguably necessary if substantial job losses are to be avoided and if a balanced economy is to be created, is therefore full of major difficulties. There is, moreover, an absence of sustained expertise in consultant, advisory and training organizations geared to this process. Western support for privatization has been substantially associated with developing mechanisms for the privatization process rather than for the management of restructuring. The process of Western management education support (much of it provided under bilateral funding programmes) has been predominantly one of knowledge transfer via broad business school-type education rather than programmes focused on needs arising from the management of the reconstruction and change process. As a result there is an absence of models to manage the process over time. There is the model of the rapid downsizing of a large company to a core viable business referred to above. But the planned disintegration of a company via a process of establishment of small businesses will take a much longer time. It will continue to demand support from the centre for the acquisition of resources funding and management, and will necessitate a gradual process of transition, perhaps via the large state company playing a 'transitional holding company' role. It might also involve some planning (not always a popular word).

Restructuring large into small in practice—the Prompribor example

The (former) State company Prompribor in Chuvash in Russia in 1989 was a typical state-owned company with over 3000 employees. Its core business was electrical actuators and electronic devices used in automatic control systems for power generation, metallurgy, chemical and other industries. In practice, it was a conglomerate of manufacturing units producing a wide range of domestic and industrial products, with little common market focus. It had become like this because, after the Second World War, the company, like most similar companies in the USSR, needed to make all kinds of components, tools and packaging and distribution equipment in order to solve problems in getting adequate state supply-sector response under the old Ministry central planning system. For example, it introduced electrical motor repair facilities; it made instruments and tools, packages and boxes for distribution, conducted civil engineering work, made maintenance equipment for the building industry and even microcircuit assemblies. There were therefore some obvious internal interconnections in terms of component supply, the transfer of parts and of finished items and the use of services between many of the individual producing units.

The chief executive in 1989 (and currently Chairman of the Directors' Board of the present company) is the co-author of this chapter. His overall objective was to retain the viability of as much of the business as possible under the new market conditions (although privatization was still then a little way off) and thus retain employment. If the objective of more fully utilizing the 30 per cent excess labour in the business was to be achieved, the only option was to encourage parts of the business to grow to take up the slack. The challenge was to provide a means of assessing the total production and market capacity and also the speed of changes in the environment, and to recommend the most effective restructuring programme to this end. It was agreed at the onset that this might potentially lead to the establishment of many small and medium companies that would ultimately operate independently. These new companies could be divided into four major groups:

○ companies producing final products (as before) but with improved marketing logic;
○ companies making components or providing services that could be sold to the core business but also to other customers;
○ companies making new products for new markets using existing production possibilities;
○ self employed and sub-contracting businesses.

The underlying objectives of the reconstruction process were to: improve the efficiency of the business, in particular the core business, by means of pruning ineffective linkages; enhance the capability of the business to adapt to quickly changing environments; increase utilization; increase quality; increase the motivation and commitment of the work force; and find new customers outside for existing products and services. In this process five key issues needed to be addressed. The first was that of ownership (the degree of freedom in controlling conditions of transfer and investment) of capital in the subsidiary companies, in particular the position of the new 'private' owners. The second was that of the character of economic interrelations to be established between the core company and the subsidiary companies that were to be created during restructuring. The third was the need to examine the constraints and opportunities presented by the existing economic and legal environment together with a view as to how these might change. The fourth was that of the degree of autonomy to be given to 'subsidiary' companies, covering in particular the choice of the related management functions. And finally, there was a need to raise the motivation of employees, particularly the key managers holding shares in the new firms. The choices available for establishing new small businesses out of the large organization were those of: a completely independent company (bought out by the workforce); an independent company with the state company as a minority shareholder; an 'independent' company with the state company as the majority shareholder; a subsidiary of a state company but with a high degree of autonomy; and a complete subsidiary with rather more limited independence.

Managing the process—the problems to solve

The process of managing this reconstruction was complicated by the absence of a local, regional or indeed national capital market and adequate banking system, the lack of personal wealth and savings, exacerbated by the then emerging inflation, and the restrictions imposed upon the state company, leaving little room for manoeuvre. There were also many problems remaining in respect of ownership laws, particularly relating to land. The state company had the option of choosing different structures for different businesses as identified above, dependent upon the stand-alone capability of the potential small business units within the present environment, their scale and resource needs and the degree of linkage/dependency upon the state company as customer, supplier or provider of 'know-how'. 'Temporary' options to be explored included the establishment of a holding company which might in turn finance an 'internal bank' for business development.

Other issues that have had to be considered in respect of linkage relationships include: the price of supply from, or supply to, the core firm; capability of small business managers to run their business; the degree of prioritization of supply/demand relationships in respect of the core business (compared with others); constraints arising from the scheduling of supply; the degree of freedom to buy and sell, from and to, alternative suppliers and customers; the influence of small business activities on the work of the core business; the nature of any leasing arrangement of machinery and premises from the core firm; the proportion of payment of overheads to the core firm (where relevant) and the calculation thereof; and the responsibilities for the social and welfare provision for workers. Of

44

critical importance also were the nature of incentives and degree of ownership to be given to management and workers. At the time the management structure of the company was complicated, the accounting and control system inadequate, there was low motivation of labour and an absence of financial responsibility and autonomy of managers.

Managing the process—solving the problems

The options for restructuring at the beginning were limited by the fact that the company was a state company and there was, as yet, no privatization law. Notwithstanding this, the early actions revolved around determining which parts of the business could stand alone and, indeed, appraising those who might make both new 'autonomous' managers and ultimately entrepreneurs. Such was the degree of ambiguity in respect of property ownership at the time between Moscow and the Republic that the managing director's activities were pursued at some considerable personal risk to his status and career. It was recognized, however, that no matter what the ultimate ownership, restructuring would have to take place because objectives for survival could not be met in a situation where the command/administrative system was being quickly destroyed.

Internal discussions, seminars and informal workshops focused the managers on parts of the business that might be restructured. Visits were made abroad to analyse Western disaggregated business models. The Russian Small Business Law and the Privatization Law conditioned the subsequent response to the important resourcing issues. The major initial problems to be overcome were access to resources for the new 'companies' and the lack of personal capital of managers (and workers) for participation in the capital of the business. The answer was to turn the main (core) business into a holding company. Initially the state company took up to 99 per cent ownership of any subsidiary and the managing director of the new (autonomous) company was given one per cent. After one and a half years his share and the share of employees was raised to ten per cent. Gradually, via profits and borrowing money from friends and outside investors, the ownership of private co-owners was extended. The holding company was able to provide development finance and also could assist with material and equipment supply and marketing. Thus the core business was turned into a financial/production/sourcing holding company.

By December 1992 fifteen independent companies had been started. These included companies making wooden boxes; casings, tools by metal casting, boat propellers; alarm devices; electronic micro chips; and coffee grinders, mixers and household appliances, among others. In addition there was a repair and maintenance company providing services to the core firm. And in the following years new companies were created not only by 'transfer out' but also by joining departments in the firm with outside companies to create, for example, agricultural enterprises, power engineering services and a Moscow technical consultancy. The selection of the managers to run the new units was facilitated by a great deal of training. During the early years the team of would-be managing directors met every Tuesday and debated learning needs and the problems of the companies. A lot of attention was given to improvement of the accounting system. More formal training programmes followed using Russian consultants—learning was focused on solving and strategic planning.

The present situation

The Prompribor Association in mid-1994 consisted of 25 linked companies, of which 22 are located inside the main plant. The holding company owns between 3 and 95 per cent of the capital of these companies. The smallest company has seven employees and the largest 130. As a result of the privatization of the core company, it is now owned 60 per cent by workers and pensioners, 5 per cent by the management team, 1.2 per cent by the chairman (and co-author) and 4 per cent by others. This picture is a result of the gradual erosion of the state share. The holding company still, however, does not have the right to buy the shares of other companies and has set up a bond/stockholding independent firm to trade in shares. By August 1994, as a result of several cash and voucher auctions as well as investment tenders, the ownership structure was over 90 per cent private with 63 per cent owned by company employees. Changes in shareholdings are accelerating because of the revival of regional share markets. The company managers are showing interest in extending their ownership.

In all, only 200 jobs have been lost in the process. Many of the smaller units have expanded and operate autonomously. The core company now concentrates upon new products, know-how, staff training and developing basic technologies. It also looks for external investors not only for itself but for the 'subsidiary' companies. The resource problem still exists but is much less of a problem than previously. The new companies are small and need only small amounts of resources, and purchase part of their materials through the supply services of the core company. Because of the breaking-up of dealer and supply networks in the CIS, the company has set up agencies in CIS countries, often (as in the case of Ukraine) to barter in kind because of currency problems. Companies have been organized in Moscow (to train production personnel of those who buy the core company products) and in Ukraine, Latvia, Kazakhstan, and Belarus to organize sales, service and supply. These companies may ultimately set up production units.

In general, there are still problems in certain industries because of the old 'association' control of trade and there are constraints on managers, particularly financial, because of the lack of alternative funding for the former 'social' responsibilities of enterprises. The monopoly state system still survives in practice (if not in theory) and presents major problems to the development of certain parts of industry. In conditions of high inflation there is still a major lack of money for restructuring and, by and large, Western capital is not interested. Inflation rapidly depletes cash reserves and many of the small firms are still struggling for survival. Moreover, competition is emerging, particularly from military conversions. Interest rates are impossibly high (for industrial investment), although it is possible to deal successfully with the banks in some of the other CIS countries. Most new projects still therefore need to be part financed by the holding company and profits can be accumulated into a common 'development account'.

The former director of the state company has acquired share holdings of the holding company and retains his position as chairman and executive director. As in normal Western practice he is responsible to the shareholders via a board upon which sit workers as well as external representatives. His reward package includes salary, related to the average salary of enterprise employees, and to profit, state pension arrangements and share options.

The ownership and dependency factors considered above will obviously dictate the scope for holistic management and total management responsibility. It is envisaged, however, that responsibility will grow over time and that the market place will become freer to allow individual companies to develop their own marketing and resourcing strategies. For some time in the future, however, the 'spun-off' small firms will be dependent and therefore limited in managerial scope. The major aim in the short run, therefore, is to maximize the potential for independent decision-making and responsibility, taking into account the constraints of the environment. Here, even now, the main problem seems to be that of culture, in particular the absence of a culture of entrepreneurial behaviour, of a sense of ownership and of ultimately taking total responsibility for decisions.

Implications for Western (management) development assistance

The experience of Prompribor is not unique, but arguably it is rare in its early vision and action. The case is important in that it demonstrates clearly the relationship between small business development and large company restructuring; the importance of restructuring *before* privatization and the importance of leadership and chief-executive vision.

The company now feels:

that creating small businesses out of the body of the core company is the most preferable path to the acceleration of small business development as well as: creating the necessary environment for business activities; accelerating the process of change of management and worker mentality; creating responsibility; widening the

range of manufacturing production in Russia; raising the capability of large structures to respond dynamically to the changing environment; and accelerating the
process of restructuring of the economy without state money; and saving jobs.
(Interview with the Chief Executive, Moscow, April, 1994.)

The implications of this for development support now are important. The
priority should be to support those programmes that concentrate on the
process of management of change and preparation for restructuring. These
programmes should concentrate on the 'how to' rather than the 'what' and
should focus on 'total project' as opposed to functional management. They
should be geared to action learning and strongly focused on the view of
ultimate customer satisfaction as the major determinant of success. They
should begin from where the managers in the organization already are (and
their vision) as opposed to where the Western 'presenter' is.

The key priority arguably ought to be how to teach managers: how to
review the structure of their businesses; how to make decisions on what
needs to be pruned and disaggregated; what are the main actions that need
to be taken to do this; what skills, attitudes and motivations will be needed
to manage this; and how they themselves might develop suitable programmes and activities to meet these purposes. The main points in the
curriculum should be: creating vision of what the organization might be;
developing capability to convert this vision into practice; developing capability to prioritize decisions and manage the restructuring process and the
change in culture.

Because of the difficulties involved in SMEs and sub-contractors being
able to stand alone, managing partnerships and alliances should be a part
of this curriculum. The programme will need to use appropriate technology. Sophisticated analysis of financial ratios will be less relevant if basic
systems are not established. Marketing concepts have different shapes in
economies where there is, as yet, a major focus on marketing and selling
through personal networks rather than by more formal sophisticated and
expensive means. Of the above perhaps the most important is developing
capability for strategic thinking and vision. Experience would indicate that
it is undesirable for Western lecturers or consultants to impose strategic
development plans on the staff of companies, or indeed on any form of
public or private organization, where they (the staff) themselves cannot yet
see the horizons (or have not internalized them).

What kind of actions are needed by the West

If it is accepted that one major focus for small business development work
might be concentration on downsizing and disaggregation of large state
companies to small and medium enterprises then the priority will be to
create *ongoing* local capability for local support for this process. In practice
this means:

○ training teams of local consultants to go into large companies to undertake a downsizing/restructuring audit and a 'management of change' needs analysis;
○ training trainers to take enterprising and project-based business development approaches linked with needs identified above;
○ identifying key 'train the trainer' organizations and systematically developing the staff of these organizations;
○ focusing on how to deal with immediate problems and opportunities of survival, and in some cases, liquidation;
○ developing enterprising modes of teaching focused on action learning and starting a continuous and efficient training process;
○ focusing on issues relating to ethics and morals in business and the responsibilities of directors of companies in this respect.

Overall, given that managers learn better from each other than from lecturers and are motivated to learn by the examples of their peers, this means a focus on a number of companies who will in the locality provide role models for the future.

Conclusions

This article has sought to illustrate the potential in using large company restructuring as a base for creating small and medium enterprises. It has argued that, in the CIS in particular, many small and medium enterprises have been internalized in large firms as a result of the previously prevailing political ideology of communism. It is also argued that privatization mechanisms themselves may not be enough to ensure a smooth transition to the market economy without the development of associated management of change models. It has identified the problems and opportunities that arise in approaching large company restructuring, with reference to a case in Russia. Finally, recommendations have been made as to the means by which a local capability might be developed via the training of consultant and trainer groups in the management of downsizing and the development of a number of effective role models which might be used as a basis for wider dissemination. In this respect it seems important to support a range of pilot projects in different regions and industries.

There is already a wide variety of activity in the area of privatization and restructuring, much of it led by financial aspects of restructuring. The article has underlined the primacy of management development (not just training) to the restructuring process and its planning over time. Above all, it leads to the conclusion that any training that is pursued must have a sound, conceptually based relation to the 'management of transition' process and use staff who have some proven insight into this process. This is as much a challenge to the West as to the East.

References

Boeva, I. and Shironin, V., (1992), 'Soviet arms manufacturers in the summer of 1991', Unpublished paper, Working Committee for Economic Reform, Moscow.

Charap, J., (1992), 'Entrepreneurship and SMEs in the EBRD countries of operation', Published paper, European Bank for Reconstruction and Development, London.

de Melo, N. and Ofer, G., (1994), 'Private service firms in a transitional economy. Findings of a survey in St. Petersburg', Studies in economies in transformation, World Bank, Washington.

European Network for SME Research, (1994), 'The European Observatory for SMEs Second Annual Report', Netherlands.

Gibb, A.A., (1993), 'Key factors in the design of policy support for the small and medium enterprise (SME) development process: An overview', *Entrepreneurship and Regional Development*, 5:1–24.

Harrison, B. and Maryellen, R.K., (1993), Out-sourcing and the search for flexibility', *Work, Employment and Society*, Vol. 7 (2):213–235.

Kayser, G., (1991), Privatisation and re-privatisation in the new German States', Paper to the ICSB World Conference, Vienna.

Kupserberg, F., (1992), 'Bandits and Bureaucrats: the law of entrepreneurship in the transition from Socialism to Capitalism', Seventh Nordic Conference on Small Business, Turku, Finland.

Webster, L., (1992), Preliminary findings from a survey of manufacturers in St. Petersburg', World Bank, Washington.

Williamson, O.E., (1985), *The Economic Institutions of Capitalism*, Free Press, New York.

Small and medium enterprise development in Belarus

A. KOMSA AND P. MERKULOV

WHILE THE number of small and medium-sized firms in Belarus has risen in recent years, particularly in the service sector, their overall significance, both in terms of employment and output, remains relatively small. This contrasts sharply with the position in western Europe where, in recent years, SMEs have been the main source of employment growth. In Belarus, however, there is a growing recognition within government of the role that could be played by SMEs, and increasing attention is being given to legislation and measures which would support their emergence.

Under the State Programme for Supporting and Developing Entrepreneurship, approved in November 1992, particular emphasis was given to support for small firms. The programme called for the creation of a chain of commercial centres for the support of small businesses. In 1993, additional legislation was passed, providing for the setting up of entrepreneur support centres. The Anti-Monopoly Ministry (AMM) has overall responsibility for regulating the activities of the centres. We carry out this function in the context of our lead responsibility for policy in support of the demonopolization of the economy.

The centres are the main vehicles for providing practical support to emerging new firms. This chapter describes some of the key issues and problems which have been encountered in developing the centres, many of which are common to other countries.

Fourteen entrepreneur support centres have been approved to date. The majority of the centres are located in and around the capital, Minsk. In order to gain official authorization, a centre must have the support of one of a number of recommended sponsor organizations, which should be represented on its Board. These organizations include local government, three unions covering both SMEs and larger firms, and the Fund for the Financial Support of Entrepreneurs. This fund has been set up with government support to assist SME start-ups. Loans at preferential rates from the fund are available to entrepreneurs during the centres' first two years of operation. Interest earned on credits provided by the fund represent the major source of income to the centres.

A. Komsa and P. Merkulov are with the Antimonopoly Ministry of Belarus in Minsk.

It is clear from the centres' performance to date that they are making strenuous efforts to provide the core services required under their terms of operation, covering loans and loan guarantees, information provision, training, the provision of material, technical equipment and advice. At the same time, it must be recognized that the development and operation of the centres is being constrained by a number of factors, which can be summarized as a lack of funding, resources, premises and experience.

Finance represents a major constraint. At present, the only source of external funding is via the Fund for the Financial Support of Entrepreneurs. As a result of a funding shortfall, centres are engaging in activities which are revenue generating, but in many cases somewhat secondary to their intended focus of supporting new small businesses. Many of the training programmes offered by the centres at present fall into this category.

As a result of their financial difficulties, the centres often lack sufficient basic equipment to carry out their business support functions (e.g. photocopiers and faxes). Most importantly, they experience major difficulties in finding and paying for suitable premises. Finally, while the centres' staff show a high level of commitment, many have relatively little familiarity with market economics or providing business information or advisory services. There is a clear need for staff development, and this is particularly the case for provincial centres where staff training is a major priority.

In response to these issues, a major SME development project is about to be launched, supported by the European Union's TACIS programme. Under this programme, project work will be undertaken to provide business planning support and training to the centres, and to assist central government in developing overall SME policy. This work will be conducted using management consultants from Coopers and Lybrand.

Preparatory work on this project was undertaken in 1994, again with TACIS support and the involvement of consultants from Coopers and Lybrand. The work focused on three specific areas:

o the development of our objectives for the centres;
o our role in administering and supporting the centres; and
o developing and conducting a process to identify centres which will be the primary beneficiaries of the business planning and training support which will be provided under the forthcoming TACIS SME development project.

As part of this project, staff of the Anti-Monopoly Ministry had the opportunity to visit a number of SME initiatives in EU countries in order to learn from their experience. The study tour covered SME initiatives in the United Kingdom, Ireland and Belgium and concluded with meetings with TACIS officials in Brussels. The visits were of immense help in developing ideas for Belarus's own centres. The main observations can be summarized as relating to the institutional support framework for SME development;

the development of policy relating to SMEs; and the centres' aims and activities, their administration and monitoring, and their funding.

The institutional framework for SME support

In European Union countries there is a well-developed institutional framework which supports local economic development, including SME assistance. At present, a number of central government departments in Belarus are engaged in SME-related activity. These include the Ministries for State Property, Employment Services and the Economy, in addition to the Anti-Monopoly Ministry. It is essential that the involvement of all central government departments engaged in creating and supporting SMEs is harnessed and directed towards the achievement of agreed common goals.

To this end, the Anti-Monopoly Minister has recently proposed the formation of a body which will co-ordinate all the activities of the various departments of government, which play a role in supporting SMEs. This recommendation has been incorporated into a draft executive order which has been submitted to the President for approval.

Developing policy

The assistance to be provided through the centres needs to be delivered within the context of an overall SME strategy for Belarus. During the course of the forthcoming TACIS SME Private Sector Development project, a long-term adviser will assist the Anti-Monopoly Ministry to develop this overall strategy further. The strategy should have a regional dimension, with each region developing a plan for SME development which fits into the national strategy.

Key areas where specific measures should be developed are: encouraging more people to start businesses; assisting the formation of new businesses through industrial restructuring; and continuing to reform the legal and fiscal environment in which SMEs operate. In addition, there is an urgent need to improve advisory and information services to new businesses.

The centres' objectives

Turning to the centres' aims and activities, the work carried out to date has suggested the following conclusions:

o The main focus of the centres should be on assisting new start-ups and helping recently established businesses. They should take the lead role in delivering assistance to these target groups.
o The centres should work with other agencies in assisting SMEs created as a result of restructuring. These are likely to have different needs from

53

the straightforward business start-ups, and require specialist skills which the centres are unlikely to have in their early years of operation.

o The centres will be the main vehicles for delivering SME support programmes and assistance measures funded by central and local government, and international agencies, aimed at new and recently established small businesses.

o The centres should provide services for persons wishing to start a new business. In addition, they may have special programmes aimed at key target groups.

It is vital that the focus and operations of the centres are geared specifically to local circumstances. To achieve this, the centres need to produce an operational business plan which includes an economic analysis of the circumstances and needs of the centre's local area.

In addition to the centres' core functions of business advice, information and training, particular importance should also be given to two further potential service areas: premises and finance. The centres should make every effort to be located in premises which also provide accommodation for small firms. In addition to meeting an acute need to enlarge the availability of SME premises, particularly at affordable rents and conditions, this would allow centres to provide on-site business counselling and advice; and to generate revenue through rental income and the provision of business services, such as a reception, meeting room hire, photocopying and other administrative support services.

The Anti-Monopoly Ministry has recently made a number of recommendations to the government covering these issues. First, it has proposed that government ministries and departments and local authorities should be required to draw up inventories of surplus premises and equipment, and allow SMEs to bid for them at favourable rates. Second, the Ministry for State Property, together with other relevant committees, should develop a procedure for transferring production premises and equipment to SMEs on a competitive basis.

Monitoring the centres

As a result of the study tour, the importance of monitoring and evaluating centre operations became very clear. Formal systems will need to be developed to do this; and in connection with monitoring the setting up of a computer network to provide information to, and receive data from, the centres could be very useful.

Effective monitoring systems are essential in order that: resources can be managed and allocated efficiently by centres, and performance can be measured against plans. It is also advantageous if centre performance can be reviewed, and resources allocated between different centres.

Programmes also need to be evaluated and lessons incorporated into future actions.

Funding

Funding the centres is perhaps the most challenging issue to be faced. There is little value in assisting the formation of centres if they have no prospect of generating sufficient income in the future to cover their ongoing operations. Centres in EU countries receive funding from external sources: usually this is provided to deliver specified services on behalf of central governments or European institutions, often on a contractual basis.

A market solution in Belarus is likely to prove difficult, since many of the activities to be undertaken by the centres, such as promoting positive attitudes to self-employment, assisting the unemployed and helping new businesses, involve persons who are unable to pay. Moreover, there is no tradition of paying for such services. Exploring the avenues for funding the SME programmes delivered by the centres is a priority task. In the current economic circumstances, it is not easy to find a solution which is dependent on government funding, and there is a clear need for additional support from external donors.

At the same time, there are steps that can be taken within Belarus to improve the financial viability of the centres, and the Anti-Monopoly Ministry is promoting such actions. In particular, legislation has recently been proposed to allow voluntary contributions to the Fund for Entrepreneurs and to Entrepreneur Support Centres to be offset against taxation.

A tender has recently been launched to select centres that will receive support through the TACIS 'SME Strategy Project' which will start shortly. In order to select centres the following principles have been adopted. One centre in each province should be selected, except Minsk, where two centres will be set up, reflecting the relatively large volume of demand for SME services likely to be encountered there. While the aim will be to achieve this geographical coverage, centres must reach certain minimum standards in order to be selected. Centres are being chosen by strict and fair procedures described in the detailed invitation to tender.

In assessing submissions from centres, equal weight will be given to the following criteria: the centre's performance to date; the centre's analysis of the needs of SMEs in its area; the centre's director and staff, including experience and qualifications; and the centre's ability to generate income and resources, including links with and support from other local bodies and institutions.

The submissions have now been received, and initial evaluations have started. The results will be announced in the very near future. This will mark the launch of the next phase of the Anti-Monopoly Ministry's efforts to strengthen the SME sector.

Conclusion

In Belarus there is a clear commitment to SME development as a means of supporting transition to a market economy, and to achieving enhanced economic prosperity and employment opportunities. In order to support such development, entrepreneur centres have been established as a key part of the SME strategy, with very helpful assistance being provided under the TACIS programme.

A great deal of work has already been carried out and the key issues have been identified that need to be addressed in order that the centres are successful. Solutions to these issues have already begun to emerge. It is recognized that there is much that can be achieved by drawing on local resources, but at the same time it is clear that additional external support is needed.

Support for small and medium enterprises in the Slovak Republic

JOSEF BRHEL AND JAN FOLTIN

THE DEVELOPMENT of small and medium enterprises is regarded as a key factor in the economic development of the Slovak Republic and in different resolutions of the government dealing with the SME sector support. Even in the main programme declaration of the government great attention is given to the SME sector development and to the creation of a positive entrepreneurial environment in the Slovak Republic.

The National Agency for the Development of Small and Medium Enterprises (NADSME) is the most important institution for SME development in the Slovak Republic. It was established in January 1993 as the result of a joint initiative of the European Union's PHARE project and the Government of the Slovak Republic (SR). The NADSME is a foundation set up by the Ministry of Economics of the Slovak Republic, and is an independent institution controlled by a managing board which represents both public and private interests.

The Agency's aim is to enhance the development and growth of existing and newly established small and medium enterprises in the Slovak Republic. The Agency provides for the co-ordination of all activities supporting small and medium enterprises in the Slovak Republic, on an international, national, regional, and local level.

Among other responsibilities, the Agency:

○ recommends to government the policy and strategy needed for the development of the small and medium enterprise sector;
○ identifies and analyses barriers to enterprise development and suggests ways to eliminate them;
○ co-operates with financial institutions to develop credit and guarantee schemes;
○ supports Regional Advisory and Information Centres (RAICs), co-operates with Business Innovation Centres (BICs) and other business advisory centres in the Slovak Republic, to help develop the managing, marketing, financial, and technical skills valuable in small and medium business;

Josef Brhel is State Secretary in The Ministry of Industry, Slovak Republic, and Jan Foltin is Director of the National Agency for the Development of Small and Medium Enterprises, Slovak Republic.

- o promotes enterprise awareness through marketing campaigns, the publication of information and the organizing of conferences, seminars, and exhibitions;
- o manages European Union aid to the SME sector in the Slovak Republic; and
- o acts in co-operation with domestic and foreign sponsors on behalf of small and medium enterprises in the Slovak Republic.

Policy and programme development

The National Agency co-operates in the field of policy and strategy with state ministries, especially the Ministry of Economics. The NADSME prepares for the government annual and semi-annual reports on the state and development of SME in the country. An important appendix to the report are strategic and short-term tasks in the field of legislation, support for SME access to capital, training and counselling and the increase of information for SMEs.

The National Agency co-operates with associations and unions of entrepreneurs and traders to improve communication between the government and entrepreneurs. This co-operation and support helps to build structures with clearly defined objectives and strategies.

In co-operation with entrepreneurs' organizations in Slovakia, the National Agency has defined the main barriers to the development of SMEs. The government's legislative plans are working towards the removal of these barriers.

The National Agency has also worked with state ministries in the preparation of the legislation for SME state support in the Slovak Republic, which has been approved by the government and will soon be submitted to the parliament for approval.

Counselling and training for SME

NADSME provides advisory services and training for SMEs through a network of Regional Advisory and Information Centres (RAICs) and Business Innovation Centres (BICs), supported by the Agency. The establishment of the RAICs was started by the Government of the former Czechoslovakia, the Slovak Republic, and the European Union within the framework of the Small and Medium Enterprises Programme for CSFR, signed in October 1991. The centres were established as non-profit organizations, associations of legal entities which represent both the public and private sectors. Thus a complete network of 12 RAICs has been established.

The main task of the RAICs is to provide all existing and potential small and medium entrepreneurs in each of the regions with advisory, consulting and information services. The RAICs are supported by PHARE.

Business Innovation Centres (BICs) are also assisted through the PHARE programme. BICs have an important role in the SME support system and focus on innovations in all fields of business development. BICs provide these innovative firms with special long-term care (2–3 years). In addition to advisory services, the BICs provide new firms with an 'incubator environment'. Thus BICs help lower the start-up costs for a firm. BICs mediate contacts between Slovak firms and firms within the EBN, the European Business and innovation centre Network. BIC Bratislava is a full member of the EBN. At present the BIC network consists of a pilot BIC in Bratislava and satellites in Prievidza, Spisská Nová Ves, and Kosice.

RAICs and BICs have been building up satellites and supporting local initiatives as part of a project to cover all of Slovakia with a comprehensive system of services for SMEs.

RAICs and BICs provide a broad range of high-quality consultation services to entrepreneurs interested in the start-up and growth of small and medium enterprises. In 1994 the RAICs and BICs expanded both the number of services provided as well as effecting improvements in the quality of services provided to their clients. Some services increased by over 100 per cent and others by more than 200 per cent, due to an increased awareness of the centres within the regions and more clients using the services. 'First-line consultancy' is very important for new entrepreneurs, and involves RAICs and BICs providing information on business possibilities in the region, as well as legal, financial, tax, accounting and other entrepreneurial information.

The most important step in starting a business is the development of the business plan. The business plan states the probability of success for the business and estimates the returns on the investment, time and capacities. The 'expert consultancy' provided by the RAICs and BICs focuses on leading the entrepreneurs step by step through the process of writing their business plans. The RAICs and BICs also help to evaluate business plans where these have already been prepared by the entrepreneurs.

An important condition for business plan implementation is the accessibility of financial resources. RAICs and BICs assist entrepreneurs in applying for commercial loans. An important help in this respect for SMEs are the financial credit schemes developed by the NADSME, in which RAICs and BICs play an important role. Employees of the RAICs and BICs ensure that the entrepreneur has a viable plan by evaluating and making recommendations on the plan and ensuring all conditions of the financial credit scheme are met.

The RAICs and BICs thus assure both efficient utilization of the financial credit scheme and that the business will be viable when considering the economic needs and potential of each region within Slovakia. Business plans in 1994 focused primarily on the textile and clothing industries, fruit and vegetables, the wood industry, tourism, printing, metal-work, energy, glass making and replacement, stone cutting, building, services and trade.

Another important component of RAIC and BIC activity is training for entrepreneurs. The RAICs and BICs provide training on the development of business plans, and in other areas such as legislation, tax, and accounting. Special courses were organized for the unemployed under the title 'Establishing small companies in self-employment' in RAIC Povazská Bystrica and RAIC Trencin has a special project in co-operation with a French organization.

In addition to the activities listed above, the RAICs and BICs also performed individual activities arising from the specific requirements of their respective regions. The results of this activity are:

○ the activation of local entrepreneurial potential;
○ the development of new enterprises;
○ the creation of jobs; and
○ the support of existing enterprises to meet their business goals.

In the near future, in addition to the current advisory services and training provided to entrepreneurs, the centres' activities will focus on development trends and issues of SMEs, such as:

○ company strategies;
○ growth and organizational structures;
○ human resources development;
○ payroll systems;
○ price policies; and
○ promotion and marketing.

Participation in bilateral programmes is the main trend in counselling and training, especially in programmes from Germany, the Netherlands and Austria. Co-operation with Germany focuses mainly on: seminars and counselling for start-ups; education and training of sector advisers and the development of sector counselling; and initiating co-operation among associations of entrepreneurs.

The main object of the bilateral programme with the Netherlands is to design an operating system (including software) for writing business plans and to implement this system in the NADSME network.

Financial support

Access to financial resources can be decisive for the development of small and medium-sized enterprises. New entrepreneurs must create facilities for production, either by upgrading their existing assets or through the purchase of large enterprises and factories (through the privatization of such companies), which requires large amounts of initial finance.

There is a lack of financial resources in Slovakia because of the history of the last 40 years. Funds, both domestic and foreign, play an important role for entrepreneurs. Entrepreneurs can obtain capital either through commercial loans from financial institutions or through state financial support programmes. They can also ask for help from foreign programmes and institutions, such as the PHARE programme of the European Union, the EBRD, the Export–Import Bank of Japan, EIB and from various grants from bilateral sources.

Since it was established in 1993, the NADSME has been making tremendous efforts to establish and implement financial support programmes through loan and guarantee schemes, and most recently the seed capital fund. The main purpose of establishing these programmes is to create good conditions for entrepreneurs to obtain a loan or a guarantee. In the beginning the funds were provided through the PHARE programme, but later also through the state budget. In 1994 three commercial banks participated in one of the projects.

The loan and guarantee schemes for SMEs are designed to help restructure the economy and to support the development of targeted areas, mainly manufacturing, services, crafts and tourism. For this reason the funds are allocated for the purchase of machines and equipment; the construction and reconstruction of work facilities; as well as for the purchase of basic supplies and raw materials for further processing.

Guarantee schemes

Guarantees for small and medium-sized entrepreneurs are disbursed through the Slovak Guarantee Bank, a state monetary institution. In August 1992 an agreement had been concluded with the Slovak Guarantee Bank under which 2 million ecu were allocated to its Guarantee Fund from the funds of the PHARE programme, currently managed by the NADSME. The bank added an equivalent sum in Slovak crowns representing the participation of the Slovak Government in the project, which created a guarantee fund. In March 1993 an additional 1 million ecu from PHARE were allocated to the Guarantee Fund. Because of the poor response to this programme (no applications were made) these sources have now been merged into one Guarantee Scheme. The number of approved applications within this programme has reached 53, totalling 97 million Slovak crowns. The average credit guarantee accounts for 62 per cent of the total credit raised.

All guarantee programmes, including those of the NADSME are implemented through the Slovak Guarantee Bank. This bank has implemented the following programmes in 1994:

o to support SMEs in industry and services;
o to support SMEs in agriculture; and
o to support the construction and renovation of small hydro-electric power stations.

In 1994 there were 375 applications, and guarantees amounting to 766 million crowns were approved. In addition, the Slovak Guarantee Bank also has development programmes aimed at: tourism, the development of industrial production based on domestic raw materials, economic activities leading to energy conservation and the reduction of imported raw materials, agriculture, and the reduction of wasted domestic energy. In 1994 the amount of the state contribution towards a subsidized interest rate was 74 million Slovak crowns.

Small Loans Scheme

In 1994 the NADSME implemented its first loan programme called the Small Loans Scheme. This scheme was fully financed by the PHARE Programme with 1 million ecu; and the loans were disbursed through the Slovak Savings Bank. The maximum loan amount was 800 000 Slovak crowns for one entrepreneur (the current exchange rate is 47 crowns to £1). The business had to employ fewer than 25 persons and be engaged in manufacturing, services, crafts or tourism. The rate of interest was 14.5 per cent, which was very advantageous when compared with the commercial rate of interest. The loan maturity was five years. There were 223 applications for this programme and, after evaluation, 80 loans were disbursed to the entrepreneurs, who employed a total of 296 workers. The businesses were engaged in small construction, manufacturing, wood processing, services such as the maintenance of sports facilities and cars, cleaning services and tourism.

Support Loan Programme

In 1994 a new Support Loan Programme was established, which enables rather large SMEs to access loans and overcome initial financing problems. There were 600 million Slovak crowns available for this support scheme: 200 million from the state budget, 200 million from the PHARE Programme (through the National Agency) and 200 million from three participating banks, the Slovak Agriculture Bank, Slovak Savings Bank and Tatra Bank. This programme targets SMEs with a maximum of 500 employees in manufacturing, services, crafts and tourism.

By the end of 1994 more than 980 requests for information were sent in by entrepreneurs. The NADSME and Regional Advisory and Information Centres and Business Innovation Centres received a total of 511 loan applications, 466 of which met the eligibility criteria and were recommended to receive a loan. Commercial banks evaluated the business plans in accordance with good banking practice and made the final loan decision. By April 1995 more than 400 million crowns were disbursed. The loans are divided proportionally by region, but the number of applications varies. On the basis of experience with the Small Loans Scheme and the Support Loan

Programme it would seem that one in four business plans is approved and provided with a loan through a commercial bank.

Seed capital

At the end of 1994 the Seed Capital Company was established to help SMEs overcome a lack of initial capital. Entrepreneurs are very interested in this type of funding. At the present time, 38 investment applications have been submitted. The proportion of submitted plans by industry is as follows: manufacturing 63 per cent, construction 3 per cent, agriculture 10 per cent, services 21 per cent, and trading 3 per cent.

It is expected that these funds will be increased as more donors participate (including state banks, commercial banks, and financial institutions).

Information and contacts

EICC (European Information and Correspondence Centre). The chief objective of the information centre is to respond quickly to both domestic and foreign entrepreneurs' requirements, from questions of a legislative character, and problems concerning financial and banking operations, to direct requirements for identifying partners for various types of co-operation.

The Centre makes use of the accessible commercial database of Slovak enterprises both in printed and electronic forms, as well as the VANS network system through which it has been interconnected to other information centres in Europe, as well as to its headquarters at the EU Commission in Brussels.

It also organizes Slovak entrepreneurs' participation in sub-contracting exchanges, and domestic and foreign exhibitions and fairs, such as Europartenariat. Apart from responding to specific requests from particular information centres of the network, the EICC is also linked to the BRE system (Bureau de Rapprochement des Entreprises).

The EICC provides information on European Union activities, such as:

○ advice for small and medium enterprises in business activities with foreign partners;
○ basic information on EU legislation concerning entrepreneurial activity;
○ information on support programmes for SMEs.

The EICC also has its own library and information system based on materials from the Directorate General and its own data bases monitoring entrepreneurs in Slovakia.

Building an Enterprise Information System (EIS). NADSME has started building an information system, by gathering information concerning SME development from the network of regional centres, on a case-by-case basis, depending on the specific requests of government institutions, foreign partners and SME clients. The EIS will obtain and provide access to the following information: country and regional SME databases, and graphic desktop mapping to enable the visual, analytical and statistical presentation of SME data for public purposes.

Powerful hardware and software will speed up communications and data and information exchange between the NADSME and regional centres, making more effective use of sub-contracting and other services.

Enterprise fairs. NADSME organizes the participation of Slovak companies in business events abroad, such as the Europartenariat and Interprise. Both fairs were launched by the EU as part of its regional and enterprise policies and are designed to stimulate the less economically developed regions by encouraging small and medium-sized companies to receive all forms of business communication. Slovakia's participation has steadily grown in the last three years. Slovak delegations to Europartenariat in Scotland, Poland, Spain and Germany have been organized with financial support for participants through the PHARE Programme.

Sub-contracting Exchange of Slovakia (SES). Slovakia has a highly skilled labour force and labour costs are relatively low. It is already known that in the many traditional areas of Slovak industry, small and medium enterprises could represent excellent partners for joint ventures with foreign companies.

The Sub-contracting Exchange of Slovakia, set up in October 1994, has tried to take advantage of this situation. SES acts under NADSME, and is supported through the PHARE programme. This has enabled the start of the UNIDOSS project which is implemented through SES with the assistance of UNIDO. The French Government has supported a team of technical advisers to collaborate with SES, PHARE and UNIDO.

The main tasks of the SES are as follows:

o To utilize the software and database of UNIDOSS to search for corresponding industrial information and to make the best choice of possible sub-contracting partners in Slovakia that meet the requirements of main contractors both in Slovakia and abroad.

o To provide advisory and consultancy services in important aspects of subcontracting operations, such as offers and demands formulation, quality assurance and certification, export, and joint ventures for SES members.

o To provide promotional services, such as the organization of participation in sub-contracting domestic and international fairs, and the preparation of promotional material with details of its members.

o To prepare a qualified analysis, relating to the industrial development of small and medium enterprises and to build up the direct influence of the government's supporting programmes for development of the entrepreneur's area.

From January to March 1995 more than 50 companies in the industrial sector became members of the SES. The network of external experts of the SES ensures helpful feedback between the SES and members.

PART II

Financial Assistance

The Ostrava Regional Development Fund of the Czech Republic

GIJS BOOT

THE OSTRAVA Regional Development Fund (RPF) was founded because of the concern of the Czech Republic to stimulate the development of small and medium-sized companies by introducing venture capital, particularly in the Upper Silesia and North Moravia region. The RPF was created with financial help from the European Union, which started it as a PHARE pilot project. A similar pilot project is running in the Slovak Republic (Želina).

North Moravia and Upper Silesia were chosen as the region partly for political reasons. The Czech authorities had been concentrating mainly on the development of Prague, Pilsen and Brno. The Ostrava region is about 400 km away from Prague and is seen as a 'difficult' region. Out of the many interviews carried out it was clear that people in the region felt themselves 'forgotten by Prague'. The North Moravia region was historically a trade region. Ostrava is situated on what was once the trade route from the Baltic Sea to the Mediterranean, and was a trade centre until about 220 years ago when coal was discovered and mining began. Steel factories were developed, and nowadays the region is dominated by the two industries of coal mining and steel. The mining company had about 135 thousand employees and the two steel companies each about 55 thousand employees. Recently the mining company went down to 60 thousand employees and the two steel companies each reduced to approximately 25 thousand: the employment in these basic industries was more than halved. Nevertheless the average unemployment rate in this region, although it is the highest in the Czech Republic, is only 7 per cent.

The idea behind RPF's founding is that the key to the development of a thriving environment for SMEs is the creation of an appropriate climate and the structural factors favourable for investment. The European Venture Capital Association (EVCA) shares this view, based on the experiences of its members.

In December 1993, after a selection from five short-listed consortia, a Dutch consortium (NEHEM/ING) was contracted to provide the technical assistance to create RPF. Unlike normal technical assistance contracts, the

---

Gijs Boot of the Netherlands is Director of the Ostrava Regional Development Fund, Czech Republic.

consortium not only provided technical assistance as a consultant, but also took full responsibility for running the programme in the first three years.

The first half year was spent on the creation of the institutional framework (establishing the limited company), the selection of the key persons (the staff and board of directors), and the practical aspects, such as finding premises, information sources, local consultants and of course publicization within the region about what venture capital (VC) is and how a financial instrument like VC can benefit SMEs in the region. In the first half year, in more than 30 information sessions organized for groups of entrepreneurs, regional institutions, banks, and so on, RPF was able to publicize its products and objectives, and more than 140 key persons in the region were personally informed of the aims of RPF.

RPF held its official opening ceremony on 23 June 1994 in the presence of Minister Dyba and a number of other dignitaries, as well as entrepreneurs, intermediaries and fellow venture capitalists from Prague.

Establishing the institutional framework

RPF was created as a venture capital company operating on a fully commercial basis within the framework of regional development. It seeks to invest in regional companies offering the prospect of an attractive commercial return on investment. Venture capital is a temporary capital resource provided in return for a share in the equity of a company. It has a strong risk-bearing character, and focuses on companies with a high growth potential. A venture capital company not only provides capital for promising projects, but enters into partnership with the investee company and advises its management, if necessary. Venture capital will always be provided in addition to financing by the company's own bank. In addition to straightforward equity finance, venture capital can be provided in the form of subordinated loans (which may be convertible into equity under specific conditions).

Usually, a venture capital provider will only take a minority share in the company, and will sell his stake once the corporate objectives have been achieved. Providers of venture capital do not expect interest on the funds made available for equity, but rely on the prospect of capital gains when they sell their holdings.

In the Czech Republic, any entrepreneur can approach the RPF for financial support who can demonstrate that:

- he or she or the management team have the skills to run and develop the business successfully;
- the market shows a (potential) demand for the product or service offered;
- the business plan is complete, with an analysis of viability and including details on promotion and marketing, operations and financial projections;

○ there is a clear profit potential; and

○ he or she is willing to accept a partner.

RPF was originally founded as a limited company; however, neither the EU nor the Czech Government were legally permitted to become shareholders of such a company, therefore a Foundation was created. The Foundation for Regional Development has the following members: Czech Authorities (Václav Kupka, deputy minister of the Economy CR), the EU (Giorgio Ficcarelli, EU Delegation) and the EBRD (Kurt Geiger). The EBRD is involved as a professional observer on the board of directors of RPF on behalf of the Foundation. All finance was provided by the EU, a total of 8.2 million ecu, to be allocated to the RPF only and for technical assistance. The Foundation was created in order to provide further SME support. Recently it founded a new venture capital company in Prague, focused on start-up and early stage finance. It is also expected that the Foundation will prove very useful for the next stage of RPF.

RPF itself was founded as a limited company, because the procedures were shorter than for establishing a joint stock company. It will be a joint stock company in the future and from the beginning we took this into account. The articles of association were drawn up, and a board of directors chosen, which is not usual for a limited company. The creation of a Board of Directors was not very straightforward. First of all, the name Regional Development Fund was found to be misleading, as it suggested public investment: the municipalities found it very confusing, so the name was changed to the Regional Entrepreneurs Fund.

Nevertheless, many organizations wanted a position of influence on the board of directors, and this was considered to be unworkable. Many potential board members were proposed and several possible members with an entrepreneurial background were selected. Finally, there were more than 20 potential board members and after 12 of them were interviewed by a selection committee from the Foundation, four people were chosen. None of the selected persons had any experience or knowledge of venture capital; neither was any of them a representative of any organization: all were chosen for their experience. In Central and Eastern European countries, people with recognized qualities should be chosen to make sure that political influence is minimized. Three of the board of directors members are running a company, and one was the founder-dean of the Silesian University, the only university that focuses completely on management, marketing and business administration. As is usual in the Czech Republic, the Chief Executive is also a board member. The board consists of five persons, and since its start there have already been two quite intensive board trainings.

The board of directors is of great importance, due to its regional knowledge. The chairman of the board is crucial to the operations of RPF. His personal involvement and willingness to learn as much as possible is a great support to RPF.

The selection of the staff was also crucial, since with venture capital the human factor is very important. Past experience suggested the need for ambitious successful managers, speaking English and having some economics background. The deputy director of the local airport, who had been asked to be the managing director of the airport, developed a great interest in venture capital and the new fund. When he was offered a job with the RPF he finally decided not to become the MD of the airport but to join the RPF. From advertisements in the regional newspapers and direct contacts within the growing network two more investment officers and an office manager were chosen.

The present team consists of nine people in total and attention has been given to team-building and training. Furthermore, students from the Silesian Mining University are employed part-time for labour-intensive research. The main success factor of a venture capital company is good staff, and this has been borne out by the RPF staff.

Top-quality staff in the 'region' is more difficult to find than in the big cities (Prague, Brno, Pilsen). Due to their knowledge of English one tends to choose younger academics, but it is advisable to look for more experienced persons for the position of investment manager. Subsequently, younger, less experienced staff members can be added as support to the investment officers.

The support structure for SMEs

RPF has given a lot of attention to improving the SME support structure. Since financial engineering as such was unknown, the instruments were not understood. From the start RPF had to train its staff in financial engineering and the use of venture capital as a financial instrument. The support structure for SME development consists of the following organizations.

The Regional Development Agency mostly concentrates on financial support for individual companies. There are also the Regional Advisory and Information Centres (RAICs), of which there are five in the region. RAIC's are commercial consultancy firms, which receive financial help and training to give some 'first-line' consultancy. Although the RAICs have existed for some time in the region, very few SMEs know of them, since there has been little promotion.

The Technological Information Centre (TIC) Ostrava is an incubator centre focused on innovative companies, and is owned by Vitkovice, Moravia Banka, a RAIC, the CoC and the Municipality. Also providing support for SMEs there was a Consultancy Centre for Entrepreneurs, which is an American-financed organization to support entrepreneurs with the preparation of business plans, market research and so on; this was a good initiative, but in 1994, after its founding it was also closed down. In addition, the Chamber of Commerce has offices at Ostrava and Opava in the region; the Czech Moravian Guarantee Bank supplies commercial banks with guarantees for loans under certain conditions, and there are commercial banks, private consultancy firms, and accountancy firms.

When activities were started in December 1993 it seemed surprising that there was no official BIC (Business Information Centre). The Technological Information Centre was started in Vitkovice, but had never had the opportunity to become a real BIC; since it was focusing on being a good landlord to the incubator. Recently it was decided to accept TIC within the network of BICs in the Czech Republic, next to Prague, Pilsen and Brno.

At RPF experience shows that in the first- and second-line consultancy BICs can be very helpful in the pre-selection of venture capital companies. Within most banks at the beginning of their existence, the procedure for providing loans was lax, with many loans being given to 'a friend of a friend'. It took some years to fully realize that this criterion was not the best way to assess a bank loan, and in 1994 the first banks went into bankruptcy. The result of this period of poor assessment was the adoption of a very conservative attitude on the part of all banks. Collateral is required for a loan in the form of a pledge of buildings and ground of more than 160 per cent of the value of the loan.

For companies which survived their start-up period and began to grow, further finance is needed, and together with the changing attitude of the banks, there have been huge liquidity problems for potentially sound firms. And although new financial instruments were coming on the market, bank staff were not able to use them. Even within the Guarantee Bank, at first staff were only trained to follow the rule book when they were authorized to give guarantees for bank loans. The Czechs are used to 'procedures' and the Guarantee Bank was an institution following procedures rigidly at first. Entrepreneurs were so used to such procedures that in many of RPFs presentations they raised the question: 'Can you give us the enquiry list and criteria to fill in, so that we can be sure to get the money from you?!' However, a venture capitalist cannot select a partner from information on paper.

For RPF it is very important that the funders of potential RPF customers understand venture capital and have knowledge of financial engineering in general. RPF went to some trouble in getting all the intermediaries together over two days, and together with Ladislav Macka, the director of the Guarantee Bank, and a financial expert from England, training was provided, using many case studies, in what financial engineering is and how to use the available instruments.

'Networking', which is a little-known phenomenon within SME support in the region, was the second objective of these two days. The event was considered to be a success, and is likely to be repeated. Nevertheless, competition is keen, and co-operation is unusual, so it must be learned that there are advantages in co-operation.

71

The experience so far

It is true that in the chosen region there is a shortage of investment money in general and risk capital in particular. This concerns new as well as existing companies, regardless of their stage of development. The continuous flow of requests for capital has served to convince us that the concept of equity finance is being accepted, and that a policy of active involvement as a partner in the structure and management of a project is beneficial. In 1994, after little more than half a year of actual operation, we received 181 requests for finance, for a total amount in excess of Kč7.8 billion (the current exchange rate is Kč33 to 1 ecu). To date we have received more than 230 requests for a total amount of more than Kč9 billion. The geographic spread of the requests for capital is reasonable. Of course, most of the requests came from the capital Ostrava, which represents 30 per cent of the inhabitants of the region and is the city where RPF has its offices.

The volume of investment requests is the lowest in the region of Bruntál, due to the fact that this region is dominated by agriculture. This region has also the highest unemployment rate in the whole of the Czech Republic; and it is hard to find suitable staff in this region for good industrial projects.

The requests from businesses at the development stage vary from management buy outs and buy ins to start ups. Most of the investment requests come from the manufacturing sector and services.

Building partnership is something requiring considerable time. Unfortunately, the effects of the former system are still there, where lies and fear were commonplace. Partnership can only be based on trust, but in general the Czech is more suspicious than the average European.

The assessment of potential projects is a time-consuming activity in view of the limited availability of reliable market data. RPF's board of directors have made decisions to invest in seven companies. Even after the decision to invest, finalizing an investment takes some time. In one case the investment was abandoned. In two cases work is still going on for the finalization. The average investment amount is Kč17 million (approximately 500 000 ecu). At the moment work is progressing on four serious projects of which at least two will end up as a board proposal. Actual investments receive on average more than 300 hours of work. They also receive a lot of external help from students, consultants and consortium support. The people involved in the projects that are finally refused (of which there are more than 200) have to be treated with all possible care. A refusal does not always mean that a project is a bad one. From the beginning of RPFs contact with entrepreneurs it is explained that venture capital is just one instrument out of many, and is not suitable in all cases, and also that the composition of RPFs own portfolio must be considered. In many cases the entrepreneur can be helped further, either through suitable financial alternatives, or by introducing him to strategic partners. There is financial support to make this possible from the Netherlands Government.

It has been necessary to explain the results to the Czech Authorities, who introduced venture capital to this region with great expectations of numbers being reached. Although the Czech politicians involved were frequently informed about what venture capital can do, the expectations regarding the amount of investment was and always is much higher than can realistically be achieved. The average figure on deals in the European countries is not more than 3 per cent of all the incoming requests. The four venture capital companies in Prague together only did one or two deals. So the results of RPF in 1994 is actually very encouraging. Nevertheless, for the politicians involved the result is meagre.

To start a venture capital fund in other countries the potential numbers of companies realistically to be helped by venture capital should be made clear from the very beginning to the politicians involved. Better to start with very low expectations than too high. RPF tries to be as clear as possible about the reasoning during the decision-making process. We explain at the start how our process works and what our demands are. We give information about the sort of contracts we will pass by handing over blank contract documents, including a confidentiality agreement, followed by a mandate agreement, a provisional offer and any changes in the articles of association. Mostly RPF is involved with limited companies, sometimes in joint stock companies; and in some cases there is a need to convert an individual business person into a limited company.

How project requests are processed

Project requests arrive daily, people having heard about the RPF through television, other funders and by word of mouth. Every incoming project is allocated to one of the investment officers in order to study its suitability. If it is not suitable, the client is informed within two weeks of his application. If possible, we will inform the client that we are starting to work 'step-by-step' on our decision pyramid.

In general the projects that come in have relatively little capital. Most companies start as limited companies with a basic capital of Kč100 000 (approximately 3000 ecu). If the company started as private and is three to five years old, even if the company is developing well, the available capital will be small. In general the equity improvement during the first two to three years of a start-up company is little or even negative.

Moreover, in many cases the companies which are three to five years old have had the potential at the outset of getting bank loans. Banks have been too generous with their loans in some cases. Projects approach us with an equity of sometimes only a few per cent and bank loans of more than 80 per cent. Quite a lot of projects that come in can be considered to be technically bankrupt. The bankruptcy law is only a little more than one year old and the flexibility of banks concerning the discharge of payment is nil. Banks are nowadays very strict on repayments and instalment periods are short. Most projects come in with a clear cash flow problem. The 'account payables' are mostly far more than the 'account receivables'. A lot of the profit reduction comes from high interest rates and all profit has to be used to meet loan repayments. Little can be used for growth investment.

An entrepreneur with a cash-flow problem can waste a lot of time on this problem. Marketing activity, sales and general management become secondary to cash problems. Entrepreneurs have learned how to be 'creative' in attracting funds and this makes the assessment of projects a difficult task. Suppliers are used as financiers, a position they generally do not ask for and certainly do not want. The same can happen to tax authorities.

When the entrepreneur is considered to have some ability, the market is checked to see whether there is a potential need for his or her product or service. Mostly RPF starts with the information provided by the entrepreneur or management; after that, we do our own research, using our own capacity, students and external consultants. We spend a lot of time discussing the business plan and adjusting it where it seems to have potential. Next to the entrepreneurs' financial figures we will provide our own figures, based on our own research. We always create three scenarios, the best, the realistic and the worst. From our own financial figures we will create a deal structure, which will include bank finance, sometimes using the guarantee scheme of the Czech Moravian Guarantee bank.

The RPF invests a maximum of 49 per cent of the ownership, and in most situations will offer enlargement of the funding in the same proportion as the present equity. In some cases the value of the present company is agreed upon and RPF pays an intrinsic value. The investment request is generally more than this equity portion and therefore subordinated loans are offered, in some cases convertible to equity. RPF will always calculate the subordinated loan as fully risk money in its calculations. The full amount provided by RPF will include some provision for interest on the sub-ordinated loan (interest on the subordinated loan is higher than bank interest), and capital gain. RPF asks for an initial investment fee and a management and monitoring fee. For the calculation of the capital gain we consider the expected company value after five to seven years, (using an average of three valuation methods), and this is multiplied by RPF's percentage of ownership.

Future developments—an incentive scheme

After seven months of operation, RPF has already allocated approximately 45 per cent of its initial capital. In order not to run out of funds too soon discussions are under way within PHARE, the EBRD, some European venture capital companies and the Foundation on how to construct a scheme to attract new investors.

At the last Foundation meeting, after agreement between two major partners in the proposed arrangement, EBRD and PHARE, it was decided to create the structure, called the 'Envelope scheme'. Preparations are currently going on to finalize this structure. Investors will be invited and if the pre-discussions with potential investors are positive, this structure should be finalized soon.

Key factors for success

The success of a project such as RPF depends on a combination of factors. As a basis, a positive attitude on the part of the involved parties is necessary, including in RPF's case the Czech authorities, the EU, and all regional actors. Secondly, a regional approach is desirable, and should include clear explanations of what politicians in the involved region can expect; clear communication in the region and active promotion; and acceptance within and co-operation with the SME support structure in the region. Investment officers should have management experience, ambition and motivation; there should be a good and motivated team of local staff members, and an active and motivated board of directors, consisting of local experienced selected members; and the training of board of directors and staff is essential.

The assessment of projects needs to be of high quality, involving clear internal procedures and careful treatment of non-investments. Venture capital companies need to consider the soundness of their portfolio, in order to build up a solid track record. Finally, venture capital companies need to be active in the management of investee companies, and to continue to help manage these companies for five or more years; and this will require quality technical assistance for the companies' management and the board of directors and staff of the venture capital companies.

Financial institutional development—the case of the Russia Small Business Fund

ELIZABETH WALLACE

THIS CHAPTER will discuss the European Bank's major initiative in small enterprise finance and institution building; this is the $300 million Russia Small Business Fund (RSBF). It focuses on this key question:

Is it possible to reform existing financial institutions through training, organizational change and technical assistance so that they meet the needs of SMEs?

However, before proceeding to provide an answer, I would like to modify the question. One additional tool needs to be added, and that is finance. It is often through lines of credit provided under well-defined conditions and coupled with technical assistance that local financial institutions modify their behaviour. Of course, there is only one thing that can lead this to being sustainable over the long-run, and that is demonstrated profitability.

In many of the countries that we are concerned with, medium-term financial resources are in short supply and in order for financial institutions to put into practice at an early stage what they are learning, the capital resources should ideally be made available. Moreover, credit provides a 'carrot' to encourage financial institutions to change the way in which they do business. And, it also provides the 'stick'—in the form of possible withdrawal of a reasonably priced, relatively long-term and stable source of funds—something which is a rare commodity in the fluctuating markets in which we are involved.

In the first section, the background and objectives of the Russia Small Business Fund are presented, as well as the main achievements to date. In the second section, attention is turned to the obstacles encountered. In both sections, an overview is presented on the design of the finance mechanisms. In the final section, conclusions are drawn concerning lessons learned for other countries.

Objectives of the RSBF and results to date

The Russia Small Business Fund was initiated by the European Bank and the G-7, with contributions of $150 million from the G-7 matched by $150 million of the EBRD's ordinary capital resources. Funding was secured

---

Elizabeth Wallace is a Principal Banker at the European Bank for Reconstruction and Development, with specific responsibility for the RSBF.

initially as a result of a policy decision to support emerging private sector firms as part of the Russian reform process. As dismantling the old system was resulting in a loss of employment and income in many heavily subsidized sectors of the economy, most notably in heavy industries and those connected to the military complex, it was important to implement programmes that could help stimulate new, viable production and employment. In addition to the goals envisaged in terms of assistance to the real economy, an equally important objective was that through the RSBF, local banks could be motivated to considerably strengthen their credit analysis skills and to adopt sound banking practices.

A major objective was to bring within the scope of the formal finance system groups of customers whose financing needs had not been previously met by the banking system: Russia's smallest firms, microenterprises, and small firms requiring investment capital to go into service sector businesses or manufacturing. These firms have faced numerous barriers to obtaining formal sector finance to meet their needs—a lack of credit history, a lack of 'bankable' collateral and, for those firms requiring medium-term inputs for investment purposes, the unavailability of funds beyond a three-month time horizon.

The RSBF has two principal products: 'small Loans' and 'micro-credit'. On a more limited basis, the RSBF offers a third financial product, 'small equity', and a non-financial product, 'business advisory and training' services which are meant to work alongside the finance components. The RSBF has recently expanded operations from three to eight regions, some of which are now in the training phase. A total of 10 banks and some 30 branches are now participating.

Russian banks seek RSBF partnership for a variety of reasons; some are at first attracted by the prestige of participation in an international programme—possibly not fully realizing how much commitment is demanded. Others participate in order to (i) train their employees in sound credit analysis, (ii) diversify their portfolios away from reliance on large enterprises, many of which are now failing, and the state sector, (iii) support economic development in their regions, and (iv) move into a profitable and growing area of business. Through the RSBF they receive extensive training, management information systems, full-time expert advice for two years and a source of medium-term funds for on-lending.

Because there is rather favourable risk-sharing on investment between the EBRD and the G-7, and substantial technical assistance funds are available, we have been able to focus on institution building and work through bank-to-bank loans. While there is higher risk to the EBRD in lending directly to local banks, particularly given low levels of capitalization and a fragile regulatory environment, there are also very clear advantages. Local banks have a substantial stake in the success of the portfolio as a result of carrying the loans on their books and bearing the risk. This heightens the responsibility felt by the banks. Bank-to-bank loans also allow the EBRD to take a more commercial approach and to avoid substantial delays which sometimes plague programmes requiring governmental approvals. Most importantly, it has allowed the bank's experts to have a more direct and effective impact on institution building.

First results. Implementation of the RSBF began as a pilot project in two regions in early 1994 with the small loans component. The first loans were granted in March 1994. In June, training for credit officers for the micro-credit component commenced in three regions; by September, the first micro-loans had been extended. In December a management agreement was signed for an additional financial component, the Small Enterprise Equity Fund, which currently operates in one of the pilot regions. Over 500 micro- and small loans have now been disbursed, and the first equity investment has recently closed.

Small loans. The small loans component provides medium-term dollar and dollar-indexed finance up to $75 000 for production and service sector firms. Loans average $50 000 and are typically for firms with up to 50 employees. Ninety loans have been granted. The arrears rate is 20 per cent, and there has been one loss. It is too early to detect what percentage of arrears will translate into losses. Most of the arrears are due to delays involving receipt of equipment that has been purchased with the proceeds of loans, and problems with non-payments by some of the firms' primary customers. In most instances, this involves late payments by state enterprises. Production firms in an unstable environment such as in Russia are of course vulnerable to the whims of the market, far more so than are trade firms with a quick turn-over. In addition to training loan officers to analyse projected cash flow under different scenarios, they must also be taught to judge the entrepreneur's capabilities to adjust in the event of either an up-turn in the market, which could stimulate new entrants into what may previously have been a monopolized niche, or a downturn.

While there are inevitably risks in lending to small production firms, the contribution of these firms to economic transition is important. The following projects provide an indication of the types of firms that have received loans. Employee numbers are given for illustrative purposes only:

○ A metal foundry received $75 000 to purchase new equipment and to upgrade purification systems. Employment increased from 59 to 120.
○ A food processing and wallpaper producer received a $50 000 loan to purchase new equipment. Employment increased by 50 persons.
○ A small high-technology firm which produces laser lenses, received a loan of $50 000 for new equipment and working capital. Employment increased from four to eight persons.
○ A clothing manufacturer received a $30 000 loan for equipment. Employment increased from four employees to 25.

Micro-loans. In comparison to the small loans component, the micro-loans scheme concentrates on enterprises with up to 20 employees and provides rouble finance. The target group is extemely large and growing. Almost always the micro-loan is the entrepreneur's first formal credit transaction. Loans are for up to $20 000 in rouble equivalent and the average loan size is currently $2000. Loan proceeds are predominantly used for trade activities, although there are also a number of loans for food processing, services and manufacturing.

The borrower's first loan is generally very small, with a term of up to six months; size and term increase once a credit history is established. Demand for this product is strong even in the unstable Russian environment. Although these firms are very small and often comprise the poorer end of the spectrum, they are opportunistic and can quickly adjust to changing market conditions, they often make high profit margins and can afford to take loans with high interest rates. Therefore, even given the transaction costs of making very small loans, these loans are profitable for local banks. A major contributing factor is the credit technology that is being implemented. This has served to lower both the direct cost of extending credit and the cost in terms of potential loan losses. Thus far the credit technology has yielded a portfolio that has only 4 per cent arrears, and no losses have been suffered. Since the start of the programme, over 400 micro-loans have been disbursed. This number is expected to grow quite markedly as partner banks have been eliminating some of their more onerous procedures that have slowed down disbursements.

The repayment record of both the small and the micro-credit components stands in sharp contrast to the high level of non-performing loans— often in excess of 70 per cent—which are often familiar to Russian banks. While initially banks were reluctant to enter into micro- and small enterprise lending, the strongest commercial banks in Russia are now requesting participation in the programme. Another major step forward in recent months has been the request by Sber Bank, the Russian Savings Bank, for the programme to work with its branches throughout the country. The RSBF is at an early stage of formulating a programme that could make at least a small contribution to transforming this 4000-branch bank. This could potentially provide many micro and small businesses with access to finance.

Small equity. The Small Enterprise Equity Fund is a $5 million fund that provides four to five-year capital for small enterprises, ranging in amounts from $25 000 to $200 000 with a targeted investment average of $75 000. The fund operates in one region and we have plans to expand to one more this year. CARESBAC is implementing this for us, based on their experience with small enterprise funds in Poland, Bulgaria and St Petersburg. Although we have recently closed one investment and there are 20 under consideration (with probably four to six having good investment prospects), entrepreneurs' fear of outside ownership and the web of bureaucratic and regulatory obstacles has caused work to proceed slower than anticipated. One of the main objectives of this fund is to develop equity and quasi-equity formats that can work in the given environment.

Barriers

The major problems that the RSBF has experienced in the start-up phase with some partners have been procedural red tape, the reluctance of some bank managers to accept the target group or to delegate authority to loan officers, and the tendency in Russian banks to rely on collateral-based decision-making rather than credit decisions based on cash flow, debt capacity and management characteristics. From the outset, these problems were expected and they are among the main reasons why the programme was designed with substantial technical assistance. It should be noted that these problems are not universal, and some of the banks can be considered model partners.

For many small enterprises, in particular microenterprises, the time it takes to obtain credit is one of the most important factors to the borrower. The reason behind this is simple: enterprises want to take out loans as business opportunities arise—when they are neither compelled to take loans too early, and therefore hold liquidity that is rather expensive if not quickly invested, nor are they forced to miss opportunities while awaiting a lengthy credit process. One of the key elements which distinguishes the methodology that is being implemented from the traditional approach of partner banks is that it is rapid. A thorough analysis is undertaken, but the entire process, from analysing the client to bringing loans before the credit committee for a final decision, is nevertheless swift.

One of the problems that our programme faces in Russia is the myriad of procedures and documents required of borrowers *after* loan approval. When our first micro-loans were approved in Siberia, in one of the banks we were working with 27 documents had to be provided—many requiring notarization—before funds could be disbursed. Most of the requirements are within the domain of the banks and can be addressed through general institution-building efforts, while others must be tackled with regional and national authorities.

The impact on the programme of over-bureaucratic procedures is that the loan portfolio handled by each credit officer is smaller than would otherwise be the case, because time that is spent processing documents is time that cannot be spent on generating, analysing and monitoring loans. The overall costs to borrowers also increase because of time lags and because of various fees, many of which are excessive, that might be levied for notaries and other documentation. In one region, a number of clients rejected approved loans by one bank when requirements were disproportionate to loan size, and they

80

took their loans to another participating bank which offers disbursement upon loan approval. The contrast could not be sharper—between November and April, one bank extended three loans while the other extended 79. If one takes into consideration that a commercial relationship is being formed between client and bank that should continue over the years, this kind of difference can have a significant impact.

Another barrier is that some managers will not delegate decision-making to lending staff or will not devote enough staff to the programme. In the micro-loans programme, new loan officers are hired and trained specifically for the programme, so this has not been a problem. This is now being instituted in the small loans programme. Far more attention is now being placed on training managers and other bank staff who are influential in the success of the programme and the overall strength of the bank.

When we started the programme, most of the partner banks were unduly conservative about collateral, while overlooking the financial viability of a project or the debt capacity of the entrepreneur. Consequently many firms were handicapped by their inability to provide very high levels of collateral. Convincing banks to be more reasonable in the amount and kinds of collateral cover which is acceptable, and to rely primarily on sound analysis and relevant information, is one of the major areas in which work with bank managers is crucial. While substantial gains have been made with respect to improved credit analysis, this does not always translate into a reduction of excessive collateral requirements by some of our banks.

Earlier in the programme many of the bank managers simply did not believe that microenterprises and small firms would repay, or there were prejudices inherited from prior times about the validity of small business activity. This is not generally a phenomenon we face any more. Initial reticence about repayment has generally been overcome because of the demonstration effect that has ensued from the high level of repayments. If ideological problems exist, or if a bank does not see part of its future as being with microenterprises and small businesses, then the main answer is competition. As indicated earlier, we work with several banks in each region and the banks that are the most receptive to the credit technology and the clientele will capture the market. The banks that do not perform to a certain level, and which over time continue to be unwilling to change, will be told they are no longer welcome in the programme. Of the 30 or so banks and branches we are now working with, this will be a likely outcome for only one small bank in the coming year, and possibly for one branch of a major bank.

Lessons learned and recommendations for other programmes

In answer to the main question posed, 'Can existing financial institutions be reformed to meet the needs of SMEs?'—the answer is 'yes: with well-defined and flexible technical assistance and finance'. Can all? The answer is of course not. But it must be said that even with all the pitfalls of working in Russia, a country in which banks have traditionally channelled funds from government to large enterprise and where small business was illegal until fairly recently, there are banks that are committed to learning new techniques that will allow them to lend profitably to microenterprises and small businesses. Transforming institutions is rarely an easy process; it takes working day to day in the banks and it takes training a new generation of loan officers, but from the perspective of the RSBF it does appear possible to build a permanent capacity in existing banks.

In addition to a well-designed programme, what are the key ingredients for success? We would say that it is the attitude of management and the standard set for the bank, or the branch. If the management shows commitment and is open to new ideas and new markets, the programme should succeed.

The RSBF's experience is still limited; we continue to improve the products, the way in which we implement the programme, and the incentive structures with the local banks, all with the aim of creating self-sustaining microenterprises and small business lending programmes in the banks. Although we are still at an early stage, we are nevertheless frequently considering questions of replicability. The project has recently moved from a three-region pilot to an eight-region operation, so we have already been testing replicability in Russia. We are also interested in lessons for replication and adaptation in other countries. What are the major lessons learned?

First, it is important in terms of SME operations that we recognize that in many of the countries which we work this is not a matter only of encouraging good, well-trained, organized banks to go 'down' to a new target group and loan size. It is an institution-building effort and banks often need to be 'upgraded' in terms of their organizational structures and credit process before they can be considered successful participants in our programmes. In addition to providing finance, technical assistance focuses on training loan officers, advising management on the organization of micro and small loans departments, and introducing management information systems to achieve these objectives. The end result—in our view—should be that institutions are capable and willing to provide firms with permanent access to finance.

Second, upgrading banks requires significant technical assistance. Downgrading a bank so that it efficiently lends to small borrowers also requires substantial technical assistance. Even the best banks will need special MIS and credit procedures if they are going to be competitive and profitable in working with small clients. They may also need to hire and train new staff. Aiming to make 30 loans a month is a different matter to making 30 loans a year. It requires staff that can generate and oversee sizable portfolios. It also requires that management delegates decision-making downward to *skilled* credit officers.

Third, the learning that takes place in Micro- and Small Loans programmes has broader application to other areas of the local banks' activities; these

externalities should be factored in when judging the success of programmes.
For example, few of the RSBF partner banks had a formal credit committee before joining the programme. This is something we insist on for our sub-loans for the purpose of transparency and as a forum for discussion. We encourage that the practice becomes adopted for the entire bank.

Fourth, liberalization alone in the financial sector will not be enough to push the frontier of formal finance downward so that it reaches small borrowers—or at least it will be a rather slow process. Technical assistance and incentives are required. When providing these, staying close to private sector norms is important. If during start-up some degree of subsidy is necessary while banks are learning and building up portfolios, this should be in the form of covering cost for new systems and training, and possibly for hiring new staff. A time-line for the removal of the subsidy element should be clearly explained and applied. However, sufficient time should be given.

Fifth, in the RSBF programme, we see the differences of working directly with the banks rather than through a government unit. Technical assistance is far more effective if it is direct. There is no one between us and the banks to moderate our actions and there is more room for manoeuvre with various incentives. It allows for more accountability by ourselves and part-ner banks. If we had to reach a consensus with other agencies before taking actions, or rely on others to take actions—or if we had to deal with certain banks for political purposes, or exclude others—the programme would be adversely affected. This is not to say that we oppose sovereign-backed lending—it is to say, however, that it must be structured so that the experts work directly with banks. In this case it can be successful.

Sixth, it is very important to work with more than one bank in each region. If one bank is resistant to change, having a more receptive bank nearby provides a model and helps assure that there will be at least one bank that is willing and capable of providing finance to the target group. Competition is also important in terms of pushing banks to compete on interest rates and to be more cost efficient.

Finally, it is our experience that on-the-job training is extremely important. There is no better way to teach organizations how to lend to small busi-nesses than actually to work with clients and make loans; the same applies to loan monitoring and setting up new small business departments. With-out the funding to provide loans (either from the bank's own resources or from external sources), theory is not turned into practice and assimilation of methodological and other change is likely to be limited.

Conclusion

The Russia Small Business Fund demonstrates that existing financial in-stitutions can be responsive to the financing requirements of SMEs. They can also be motivated to work with the smallest segment of firms:

microenterprises. Appropriate design, meaning the right incentive structures and relevant training, are key factors that contribute to the success of programmes. Flexibility is of course important, as adjustments and improvements may need to be made on a fairly constant basis. Equally critical is the human element. Some bank managers will be convinced by a programme that is, arguably, financially sound and helps to diversify and increase their client base, but others may prefer not to change the way they do business. Neither the target group, nor the methodology, will appeal to all banks. However, for banks that are sufficiently interested in microenterprises and small businesses as clients, we believe that mechanisms can be designed for reaching the target group while at the same time contributing to the strengthening of the bank.

Micro-lending in the Russian Federation

CLAUS-PETER ZEITINGER

SINCE EARLY 1994, the IPC has been heavily involved in the 'Russia Small Business Fund', a project initiated and sponsored by the EBRD and the G-7 nations. It co-operates with existing Russian banks in several regions of the country. The RSBF aims to encourage and enable the participating banks to serve a clientele which until now has not had access to formal credit, it can be called a 'downgrading project'. So far, IPC's main activities within the programme have been in the areas of institution building and the introduction of an innovative micro-lending technology at the level of the individual banks. This chapter concentrates on the experience gained in the introduction of this technology.

The target group

In general terms, the Russia Small Business Fund helps to provide loans to microenterprises and small businesses. The distinction between small businesses and microenterprises is based on the number of people working in the borrowers' firms. Small firms are those with 20 to 50 employees; they may obtain loans of between US$20 000 and US$50 000; and these loans are provided in US dollars. Micro-businesses are those with fewer than 20 employees. They may receive loans, denominated in roubles, of up to the equivalent of US$20 000. The average size of micro-loans granted to date has been US$2500. This fact alone indicates that the programme is indeed directed towards, and actually reaches, a target group of very small businesses.

As expected under the conditions of a transitional economy, most micro-loans finance trade. This is primarily a result of strong pent-up demand which was unmet during the ideologically motivated tendency of the former system of economic planning to concentrate on production and to neglect the tertiary sector. The growth of private trading activities has also been fostered by the almost total collapse of the state-run distribution system, as well as by an expansion of the range of goods available. Given that the initial capital input needed to set up a trading business is quite small, a large number of 'new entrepreneurs', many of them women, see trade as an opportunity to secure quickly a livelihood for themselves.

Claus-Peter Zeitinger is a consultant from Interdisziplinäre Projekt Consult GmbH (IPC), Frankfurt, working with the EBRD Russia Small Business Fund.

Furthermore, trade, more than any other sector, can react flexibly to what is a rapidly changing business environment. Trade is the first and most elementary form of private market-oriented economic activity.

The typical micro-borrower is a trader with 1 to 3 employees. Most trading is conventional retailing, being undertaken either out of a kiosk located at a fixed site or as a mobile trade operating from a truck or simply with a person standing at a market place. The nature of these activities is the reason why the target group or the borrower clientele is interested more than anything else in very fast decision-making and disbursement procedures.

Some of the projects being financed are, however, productive ventures, which often emerge from trading or other service activities. Small traders in Russia seem to find it increasingly attractive also to produce some of the goods which they offer for sale. This backward integration seems to be the second step in the process of establishing a private market-based economy at the small-scale and micro-level of economic activity.

The financing of productive projects concerns micro-producers who are also engaged in service provision or trade (the direct sale of their own food produce, the installation of spare parts they built themselves, and so on). This represents the second step in the establishment of small-scale private enterprise: the entrepreneur shifts from trading purchased goods to selling his or her own products.

The credit technology

Any credit relationship is characterized by an asymmetrical distribution of information between the borrower and the lender. Usually, this problem is solved by the borrower providing the kinds of data on his or her business— balance sheet, profit and loss statement, business plan and so on—which a bank needs to determine creditworthiness, as well as bankable collateral. However, small business people and microentrepreneurs are seldom able to furnish the requisite information, or what is considered to be adequate collateral.

The credit technology which IPC has worked on in Latin America, and is now introducing to Russia, takes this into account by implementing a credit analysis that makes extensive use of information which the responsible loan officer has gathered by surveying the applicant's business and household. Thus, the credit technology rests on information-based rather than document-based analysis.

The IPC also asks borrowers to pledge assets as collateral which they can easily provide and which they would find particularly problematic to see taken away, including items used in their households. The use of this kind of loan security has above all a signalling and an incentive effect. It serves to demonstrate clearly that the banks take their insistence on repayment very seriously; and it helps to increase the incentive of the borrowers to repay their loans on time. In contrast, the credit technology attaches little importance to the salvage value of the pledges. It is of less relevance how much of the money owed by the lender can actually be recovered in the case of default and foreclosure.

Careful credit analysis and the policy just described of securing loans are supplemented by the application of a graduation principle. By initially granting relatively small, short-term loans, but then gradually increasing the volume and the maturity of the loans it offers, the bank builds a relationship of trust, increases its information about the borrowers and, last but not least, establishes a strong incentive on the part of the borrower to safeguard his or her continuous access to credit by establishing a credit record as a reliable borrower.

Representing the bank, the loan officer cultivates a personal relationship with his or her customers. The loan officer is not only responsible for selecting customers and granting loans, but also for loan recovery and follow up. By having general responsibility for a given client, a loan officer is able to accumulate information over time. This increases the efficiency of his or her operations and enables the bank to make very quick decisions on applications for repeat loans. At the same time, making a single staff member responsible for each borrower, renders it possible to introduce a performance-based pay scale and an appropriate incentive structure.

Finally, very rigorous credit monitoring procedures are an important element of the credit technology. As soon as a given borrower misses a payment, he is contacted by his loan officer. This quick response to arrears problems underscores the seriousness of the institution's commitment to recovering the loan and enables it to eliminate default due to a simple unwillingness to repay loans.

The use of this lending technology is supported by an appropriate computer software package which IPC has developed for micro-business lending. It serves as a credit and management information system for the entire process of credit analysis, credit granting, and credit monitoring and recovery. The use of this software package reduces administrative costs greatly, and helps the participating financial institution to make its micro-lending activities profitable.

The partners and the TA package

In order to reach as many microenterprises as possible, the Russia Small Business Fund is currently spread over seven Russian regions, where the programme is co-operating with several private banks and the state-owned Sber Bank. The partner banks were selected by the EBRD. At present 10 local banks are participating in the programme, but the group is growing all the time. A number of the partner banks have been subjected to a thoroughgoing audit within the framework of the World Bank's Financial Institutions Development Programme, while others are small regional banks which the EBRD has screened.

The partner banks are expected to set up distinct micro-loan departments of their own in order to provide the organizational facilities which are needed for handling a large number of micro-credits. A major part of this exercise is the recruitment and training of loan officers for the micro-credit programme. In this area, the banks receive strong support from EBRD experts. First, future loan officers undergo a training programme lasting several weeks to prepare them for their new tasks. They then begin to carry out their first credit analyses under the guidance of a foreign field expert. This on-the-job training lasts roughly one year and is financed entirely out of funds provided by the programme. The goal is to enable the banks to build qualified staff and a sufficiently large loan portfolio so that— after a little over a year—they will be able to cover all the administrative and risk-related costs themselves.

Special software, the IPC-loan package, is installed on the computer systems of all the partner banks. This allows the loan officers to keep a day-by-day check on all outstanding loans with regard to maturity dates and any arrears which may have occurred. The software also includes numerous evaluation menus for an *ex-post* performance analysis, and serves the loan officers as an aid to credit analysis and the preparation of loan contracts. In each region, one long-term field expert is on hand to advise the banks on reorganization necessitated by the project, and to help ensure that the new loan officers are integrated into the overall framework of the bank's operations. In addition to the long-term training measures for bank employees, the programme also offers training courses and seminars aimed at middle management and at the senior executives of the partner banks.

Banks which show an interest in participating in the micro-credit component of the programme start by extending loans out of their own funds using the new credit technology, including the IPC software package. Very soon, however, the EBRD makes the banks an attractive offer of funding, which is a financial inducement to motivate the banks to become active small-scale lenders. The EBRD concludes a loan agreement with the participating banks that meet the qualifying criteria. The initial amount is US$200 000, only half of which is disbursed. Once 80 per cent of the funds received from EBRD is outstanding in the form of loans to sub-borrowers, the bank may call on the second tranche or, after this, conclude a new agreement with the EBRD for the provision of additional funds.

Results to date

The selection and training of the first loan officers began in June 1994. The credit extension process itself got underway in September of that year. The programme has only been operating for quite a short period, therefor, and one should be cautious when assessing the results. In all, 344 loans have been granted during this period. In order to narrow the field down to this number of loans, roughly three times as many applications had to be analysed. As of 30 April, 1995, the loan portfolio of the micro-credit programme stood at US$410 000. Thus, given that 214 loans were outstanding on that date, the average size of an outstanding loan was US$1900. The average size of loans granted during the observation period as a whole was US$2500, while the average maturity was 4.3 months. Unlike the situation with most of the other loans in the partner banks' overall portfolios, the repayment performance of the microentrepreneurs was remarkably good. And here it should be emphasized that all micro-loans are repayable in equal instalments with no grace period; in other words, it is virtually impossible for 'hidden arrears problems' to accumulate undetected.

At the end of April, 90 per cent of all outstanding loan contracts exhibited no repayment problems whatsoever, 6 per cent of the clients were between 1 and 15 days in arrears, and in a mere 4 per cent of cases were payments more than 30 days overdue. Even if this repayment discipline were to deteriorate slightly, it would still deserve to be regarded as remarkably good, and is comparable to the record of similar micro-loan programmes in Latin America.

The profitability of the programme

Given the labour-intensive analysis involved, micro-lending will only be economical for a bank if it succeeds in realizing sufficient interest margin on a large micro-loan portfolio. The interest margin for micro loans realized by the banks participating in the programme has averaged 2 per cent per month. The other key factors in determining whether or not the operation is profitable are the costs incurred, the capacity of the individual loan officers and the size of the individual loans.

Is cost coverage achievable? The following assumptions appear realistic in the present context in Russia and at the present stage of the programme. The average loan size is US$2000; one loan officer administers a stock of 16 micro-loans or, more precisely, 16 micro-business clients; the direct salary costs plus general administrative costs per loan officer come to US$450 per month; annual loan losses are assumed to be in the range of 6 per cent. Thus, the break-even point will be reached when the average loan portfolio per loan officer stands at US$32 000. According to our projections, this point will have been reached throughout the micro-credit programme by the end of 1995, though individual partner banks should be able to achieve this sooner.

This forecast is based on comparatively conservative assumptions, since over time one can expect to see not only a slight increase in the average loan amount but also, and in particular, an increase in the number of clients that each loan officer will be able to handle. We anticipate that two years after completing their on-the-job training at the latest, the loan officers' capacity will settle in at a peak level of around 50 clients. If we also assume that by this time the average size of each outstanding loan will have risen to US$3000, one loan officer will thus be managing a portfolio worth US$150 000. This provides both an attractive business opportunity for the participating banks, and leaves room for reducing the effective interest rate for the clients.

Problem—the business and legal environment

The lending process is being impaired by the fact that Russia is still in the throes of transformation, and by the general climate of bureaucratization inherited from its past as a centrally managed economy. This situation manifests itself in the changes that are constantly being made to the legal framework, and in a legal system which is scarcely able to meet the demands of a market economy. As a consequence, problems have arisen when designing the loan contracts, especially with regard to stipulating collateral. Vast amounts of red tape, coupled with the uncertainty of whether the agreed terms can actually be enforced, may cause considerable delays in processing loan applications. Furthermore, loan contracts have to be designed with extreme care in order to avoid having to resort to legal channels.

Russia's monetary situation places a further handicap on credit extension. The inflation rate may fluctuate violently within short periods, and there is virtually no way of predicting the extent and direction of these fluctuations. Yet in order for credit extension to function properly, borrowers and lenders must be able to conclude firm contractual agreements regarding the repayment schedule and the rate of interest. The combination of a fixed rate of interest on loans and an uneven inflation rate has produced wide fluctuations in the real interest rate. This poses a problem to the individual borrower, and not merely in phases of falling inflation. It adds to the cost of borrowing in general, since the banks make an additional charge to compensate for assuming the inflation risk. Thus, on average, borrowers face very high interest rates, a problem which traditionally hits the manufacturing sector particularly hard. Due to all of these uncertainties, it is virtually impossible to enter even medium-term contractual commitments, let alone long-term ones. This is reflected in the short maturities of rouble loans extended by the banks.

Problem—the real economy

The year 1994 saw industrial production and investments decline by more than 20 per cent. Many enterprises are paying reduced wages, or have stopped paying their workforce altogether, and this is having an adverse impact on demand for consumer goods. It is via these multiplier effects that the recession eventually hits even members of the target group, from traders to small producers, who have otherwise remained unaffected by it. Even now, four years after the reform process began, gross domestic product still appears to be on the decline, although the pace of contraction seems to be slowing down.

Conversely, services and trade are growing in importance. Many employees are leaving their poorly paid jobs to start up their own businesses. Thus, in 1993, the number of self-employed people rose by almost 50 per cent. In the meantime, their overall share of the total number of people in work has probably risen to well past the 10 per cent mark. Empirical research conducted in the cities in which the Russian Small Business Fund is active confirms the growing importance of the target group as a provider of employment and incomes in the region. Therefore, while conditions in the real economy remain as adverse as ever, our surveys are a clear illustration of just how important it has become to ensure that micro-businesses have access to reliable sources of finance.

Problem—the banks

Right from the outset, the project ran into problems with numerous partner banks; some of these difficulties have still not been completely resolved or are taking a very long time to overcome. The problem areas are, on the one hand, the organization of the banks' operations, and on the other, the banks' lending policy, and in both areas the problems relate both to the general situation and to micro-lending in particular.

Most of the Russian banks with which the programme is co-operating serve only a small number of borrowers; this is true even of the branches of several big banks with which we are collaborating. Their portfolios contain on average no more than 50 to 200 loans. However, the individual loans are very large. With such a small number of borrowers, relations with each client are relatively easy to organize, and can be handled by the manager or one or two well-qualified staff members. The other bank employees are effectively no more than support staff, as is reflected in their low level of pay. The introduction of micro-loans entails making fundamental changes not only to a given bank's previous lending policy, but also to its organizational structure, which in turn has significant implications for its salary structure. The micro-loan officers maintain constant contact with the borrowers, prepare analyses for the credit committee, take care of the administrative banking tasks involved in disbursing the loans, and are responsible for monitoring and recovery in connection with their particular clients. The integral method inherent in this credit technology contrasts sharply with what has until now been the banks' standard practice, which is characterized by a greater division of labour but also by a more hierarchical structure. The performance-based pay scheme for loan officers, as required by the programme, the frequent meetings of the credit committee and the necessarily short processing times from submission of application to disbursement of the loan, all present a challenge to the bank's present organizational structures and their management personnel, a challenge which some have been unable to meet.

In the first phase of economic reform, many Russian banks pursued a lax credit policy and some of them sustained heavy losses as a consequence. Now, most have gone over to an extreme form of collateralization policy, whereas hardly any have adopted a policy of conducting detailed credit analysis. Furthermore, some Russian banks wrongly assume that small businesses and microenterprises are not capable of surviving, and therefore demand particularly high levels of collateral from this target group. This practice conflicts starkly with the credit technology which the EBRD programme sets out to introduce. Although this technology also makes use of collateral wherever feasible, the main focus is not on loan security, but on creditworthiness assessment and follow up.

So far, the micro-credit portfolios of the participating banks have been growing slowly but steadily. Complex learning and adjustment processes are involved here, yet once they have been successfully accomplished, the way will be open for the extension of micro-loans on a massive scale. The institution-building process currently taking place is a comprehensive one which, as has been said, goes beyond the narrow confines of micro-lending itself. It affects, and changes, the entire bank. For example, the head office of Kussbazosbank has decided that all of the assessment forms used in the context of micro-lending are henceforth to be used in the regular credit business of all its branches. The same bank has also expressed a strong interest in introducing throughout its network the software package for monitoring outstanding loans. And Sberbank has issued new organizational guidelines for its entire nationwide network of branches based on the new organizational processes which the programme introduced in connection with micro-loans.

The role of the EBRD

Despite the problems I have outlined, the Russian Micro-credit programme is a unique and path-breaking project. Above all, the EBRD has departed from the mistaken strategies of old-style development finance and has put improved contract and incentive structures in their place.

For this programme, the EBRD has chosen not to finance state-owned development banks, people's banks, co-operatives or NGOs, but instead has aimed the programme at ordinary commercial banks, following the 'financial sector approach to micro-finance' which is now beginning to gain widespread acceptance.

In extending credits to Russian partner banks, the EBRD is operating without any form of sovereign guarantee. In this respect, the Russia Small Business Fund differs markedly from similar programmes run by the World Bank, the IDB or bilateral institutions which insist that governments secure their credits, thereby inviting the kind of political influence which can water down such programmes or even cause them to fail altogether. By engaging in direct lending at its own risk—and thanks to the generous provision of risk funds by the G-7 nations—the EBRD is undoubtedly incurring a higher level of risk, yet at the same time it is securing for itself the opportunity for direct communication with the partner banks, and for intervention in their operations. Experience has shown that this kind of unmediated contact—and mutual dependence—between the lender and the borrower can induce the partners to take a more understanding and responsible attitude toward one another than they would in the context of a sovereign-backed programme. If a partner bank shows by its behaviour that it is willing to co-operate, the EBRD also has the option of acquiring an equity stake, which in present-day Russia would undoubtedly be perceived and valued as a substantial boost to the prestige of the partner institution.

Aside from a very small number of activities, such as arms production, the EBRD's Micro-credit programme offers to finance any kind of economic activity by an enterprise. In this respect, it also sets itself apart from many targeted lending programmes, which are usually aimed exclusively at the manufacturing sector. Especially in transitional economies, i.e. where most of the new small businesses that are gradually beginning to emerge are operating in the trade and service sectors that were neglected under socialism, it would be totally inappropriate, both from a political and from an economic standpoint, to discriminate against precisely these sectors. Furthermore, the programme does not insist on linking credit to training courses for the borrowers. On the contrary, it respects the investment decision of the autonomous enterprises, just as it respects the lending decision of the partner bank which bears the risk. Although the Micro-credit programme is certainly target-group oriented, it is by no means a targeted lending programme.

The EBRD makes no stipulations regarding the interest rates which the partner banks may charge on the loans they disburse within the framework of the Micro-credit programme. Aside from reaching the target group, a prime concern of the EBRD is that the partner banks regard this lending activity as a profitable business and therefore make an effort to establish themselves in this market, regardless of whether or not funds will continue to be provided by an outside organization in the future. This policy also takes account of the—now generally acknowledged—fact that where relatively small, short-term loans are concerned, the rate of interest is of no more than secondary importance. Rather, the key factors for successful micro-lending are an efficient credit technology, a swift and unbureaucratic credit extension process, and low transaction costs for the borrowers.

Alongside its general orientation toward the target group, the EBRD's Micro-credit programme places the partner bank and its institutional and technical development at the centre of attention. The rhythm of the activities is determined not by the desire to see a fast flow of credit funds to the target group, but by the exigencies of building a financial institution that is target group-oriented, certainly, but also efficient and profitable. By offering a complex technical assistance package, giving temporary financial support to specific institution-building processes that need to take place at the lowest levels of bank branches, the EBRD underscores the seriousness of its commitment and provides an essential complement to institution-building processes that are taking place at the level of the central bank and the development of the financial sector as a whole.

Conclusions

Neither in Russia nor in any of the other CIS countries will micro-loans have a decisive effect on economic developments. Viewed in isolation, each micro-loan has only a very minor impact on growth and employment. Nonetheless, by sheer weight of numbers they begin to acquire a certain significance. Thousands of these loans mean not only a corresponding number of jobs saved or created, thereby compensating for the loss of jobs in the old large industries and bureaucracies; they also convey the message that entrepreneurship is being taken seriously, and that every enterprise can gain access to the services of a financial infrastructure. And finally, the extension of micro-loans also means that the participating banks have the opportunity to diversify, to reduce the risks of maintaining a highly concentrated loan portfolio and to open up a comparatively safe market segment with which they will be able to establish lasting business relationships and which in the future may form one of the cornerstones of a healthy lending business. To achieve both of these effects together is the purpose of target group-oriented financial institution building.

Regionally oriented financial instruments in Poland

MAREK KOZAK

THE POLISH AGENCY for Regional Development (PARD) is the Treasury foundation set up in 1993 in order to stimulate and support economic initiatives in the regions, as well as cultural, social, administrative and organizational objectives. Economic development is particularly needed in underdeveloped regions, in areas that require structural reconversion and also in regions threatened with high unemployment. PARD also promotes the spread of information, advisory services and training programmes, as well as market ideas and technical development concerning assumptions, methods and forms of regional development. Finally PARD is involved with setting up and participating in the establishment of financial institutions for regional development.

PARD is responsible for the implementation of the largest assistance programme in Central Europe, which is aimed at the provision of a complex set of instruments to support regional development in six selected provinces of Poland; as well as to transfer and disseminate methods and techniques of regional development. The main source of funding is the PHARE programme of the European Union.

PARD also administers the Polish–Swiss Regional Programme, which aims at economic development of rural communities, by offering loans and technical assistance to mainly family businesses in agriculture, agribusiness, forestry and the construction industry.

Although the Polish–Swiss programme has achieved a considerable success, this chapter concentrates on the PHARE–STRUDER Grant Scheme. Other financial instruments, such as the Guarantee Fund and venture capital Regional Investment Companies are dealt with in other chapters.

Background

There is a perception, even a misconception, in many quarters that the Programme for Structural Development in Selected Regions in Poland (STRUDER), which is implemented by the Polish Agency for Regional Development (PARD), is solely an SME grant scheme. It is important to

---

Marek Kozak is the Director of the Polish Agency for Regional Development.

realize that the grant scheme is only one element of the programme, and it has to be seen in the context of the programme as a whole, and not looked at in isolation. It is perhaps useful to give a brief overview of the programme, its objectives and the role of the grant scheme in the achievement of those objectives.

The objectives of the programme are:

o to develop measures and basic structures for regional economic restructuring;
o to mobilize local resources for the promotion of new economic activity and employment;
o to provide financial and other supports for SME creation and development; and
o to develop the methodology and techniques that can be used by the Polish Government in a general regional development programme.

To achieve these objectives, the programme consists of four main components: support for regional structures and institutions; training and advisory services; regional financial measures, and small infrastructure projects.

The grant scheme is one of four elements under the heading 'regional financial measures', the others being a guarantee scheme, regional investment companies, and technical assistance to the banking sector. From this it is clear that the scheme is only one of the financial engineering techniques supported by PHARE under this wide-ranging programme which provides support for regional and local development in selected regions in Poland.

In answer to the question, 'Why a grant scheme?', it might be said that, at this stage in the development of the SME sector in the less developed regions of Poland, a relatively straightforward grant scheme is the most appropriate mechanism with which to start financial engineering for SMEs. Furthermore, in comparison with some of the other options, for example, interest relief grants, it is probably more attractive to the entrepreneurs, since it offers an immediate investment capital with the minimum of regulatory requirements.

The grant itself takes the form of a non-repayable grant of up to 25 per cent of the cost of investment in mainly fixed assets with a minimum of 20 per cent contribution from the entrepreneur's own resources (a minimum of 15 per cent for projects over 200 000 ecu) with the balance coming either from more of the entrepreneur's own resourses or from bank credit. The maximum level of grant for any one project is 100 000 ecu. The other eligibility criteria which are applied may be summarized as follows.

Grants are made only to private sector manufacturing, or service activities including transportation, tourism and agribusiness. Investment (fixed assets only) must be located only in the region. Businesses must have no more than one hundred employees. Suitable businesses must also demonstrate sound management and evidence of project viability; and there should also be no tax or social security indebtedness.

As well as the broader programme objectives, the scheme also attempts to address some specific issues which have been identified as inhibiting SME growth. Among these are a lack of domestic capital institutions and instruments; high collateral and guarantee requirements by banks; and also more generally underdeveloped banking services and banks are risk averse. In addition it is recognized that entrepreneurs are reluctant to invest in fixed assets.

By and large, these are the same problems which face SMEs everywhere and to a certain extent we would expect that a capital grant scheme would impact on most of these. The other elements of the regional financial measures component outlined above would, however, impact more selectively on these issues.

Implementation of the grant scheme

The implementation of an SME grant scheme in Poland addresses exactly the same issues as any other grant scheme, whether in Eastern, Central, or Western Europe. Of course, the implementing agencies will vary from country to country, but there are certain basic tasks which have to be carried out.

The application process. In order to ensure a regional dimension to the scheme (and the grant scheme is only one part of a wider Regional Development Programme), Regional Development Agencies (RDAs) in each of the six regions were selected by PARD to receive the applications and to check their eligibility against the detailed criteria set out in the Grant Scheme Regulations. The role of the RDAs at this stage is to confirm that the application is complete (i.e. that the application form has been filled out, a business plan prepared and documentary evidence provided in compliance with the eligibility criteria), and that the project is eligible. The RDA may reject any project deemed to be ineligible, in which case the entrepreneur may appeal to PARD to review the case. The RDA is not required to make any judgement about the feasibility or viability of the project: their task is to verify that it fulfils the eligibility criteria.

The appraisal process. Once satisfied with the eligibility of the project, an appraisal must be carried out to determine its viability before any decision is made. For this purpose PARD has engaged the services of two separate categories of organizations. The first of these is what is known as accredited banks, which have been selected and accredited by PARD on the basis of their financial standing, their regional branch network and their willingness to offer services to SMEs.

Where projects submitted for grant assistance are funded in part through a loan provided by an accredited bank, the decision on whether or not to approve a grant will, in general, be taken on the basis of the project evaluation carried out by that bank. Where the balance of project funding comes either wholly from the entrepreneur's own resources or in part from a bank other than an accredited bank, PARD has engaged the services of separate external financial institutions to carry out the project appraisal. The financial institutions selected at present are the Polish Development Bank and the Bank for Socio-economic Initiatives (BISE).

Where the total project investment is greater than 200 000 ecu, and where the entrepreneur's own contribution is below 20 per cent, then the opinion of the financial institution will be sought, regardless of whether or not an accredited bank is involved with the project.

The approval process. Once the project has been appraised, a decision on whether or not to approve a grant is taken by a panel set up by PARD. The panel consists of representatives of PARD, the RDAs, the banking sector, the PHARE-SME Development Programme, and the Polish Chamber of Commerce. In general, the grant panel is expected to endorse the opinion of the appraising institution, but it may, in the case of projects appraised by an accredited bank, seek a second opinion from the financial institution before making a final decision.

Clearly a negative opinion from the appraising institution will result in a rejection from the grant panel. The decision of the panel is final and there is no appeal against it; the applicant is however, given the reasons for the refusal to approve the grant. In such circumstances, the applicant is, of course, free to submit a revised proposal, taking into account the reasons for the rejection of the original one.

The award. Once approval has been given, a mechanism has been established for the award, or payment, of the grant. The first step is a contractual agreement—the grant agreement—between PARD and the entrepreneur, which sets out the level of grant approved and awarded, and the terms and conditions upon which it will be paid. In general, the grant is paid in instalments in order to ensure that the amount of grant disbursed at any stage is proportional to the level of expenditure from the entrepreneur's own resources or bank loans associated with the project.

For the moment, the mechanism chosen for the actual payment of the grant is to use either an accredited bank, if one is associated with the project, or else the financial institution which carried out the appraisal. In either case, it is their responsibility to verify the invoices, bills and other documents relating to the investment project to ensure that the expenditure being made is in line with the proposed investment outlays of the project, as set out in the original application.

Administration. The overall responsibility for the administration of the SME grant scheme rests with PARD. Clearly PARD does not have the staff resources to monitor and review every project, and yet the verification and monitoring of expenditure is a critical area. It rests with the disbursing entities—the accredited banks and the financial institutions—to monitor the implementation of the projects to ensure that the original investment is being carried out. PARD has retained the power to cancel any grant agreement, and to seek repayment of any amounts already disbursed, if serious irregularities are detected by either the accredited banks or the financial institutions.

Results

In evaluating the results of the grant scheme, there are two issues: output and outcome. By 'output' we mean data such as the number of companies assisted, value of grants awarded, and so on. By 'outcome' is meant, what has been the impact of the scheme on the achievement of the objectives set out earlier. Before starting to consider these evaluation issues, it is important to realize that the grant scheme has been in operation for only 12 months, and the results have to be seen in that context.

Taking 'output' first, at the end of April 1995 the grant panel had approved grants for over 200 projects, totalling nearly 7 million ecu. This represents total investment by the SMEs involved (all of which employ less than 100 people) of almost 30 million ecu in the preceeding 12 months in some of the most disadvantaged regions in Poland, which must represent a significant success in quantitative terms. Turning to the question of the impact of the grant scheme the wider objectives have to be considered.

Lack of capital. Clearly a 25 per cent contribution to investment costs has the potential to make a significant impact on the level of capital available for SMEs. A total inflow from the grant scheme of almost 7 million ecu would suggest that the scheme has made some positive impact.

High collateral requirements. One of the less tangible benefits of the scheme is the fact that, by contributing 25 per cent to the cost of an investment project, the level of risk has been reduced and thus helped entrepreneurs to obtain bank financing for their projects. This will in turn reduce the overall level of collateral required.

Weak/risk averse banking sector. The accreditation process referred to above, as well as being an integral part of the scheme in terms of appraising projects, has also achieved a secondary objective of helping to strengthen the capabilities of the banking sector in terms of project and risk assessment. The accreditation scheme has contributed to helping the banking system meet the needs of the developing SME sector, although not every bank has responded to the same extent.

Lessons

There is now in Poland for the first time an effective means of providing direct financial assistance for SMEs. There are lessons to be learned from this experience, and what follows is a reflection on what has been learned and how things may develop in Poland in the future.

Timing. It is important to realize that before PARD was able to launch the scheme in April 1994, it had already spent six months in conjunction with Portuguese consultants, IAPMEI (the Portuguese Institute for support to SME), preparing the regulations which set out the detailed eligibility requirements, and drawing up the procedures by which applications are to be processed by the RDAs, the banks and by PARD. When dealing with public money, whether EU, national, regional or local, proper systems have to be in place to ensure accountability at all times.

As well as these technical and procedural matters, there was also the task of training the RDAs to help them develop their capabilities for working with local entrepreneurs in order to encourage them to come forward with investment projects which could be supported under the scheme. There was a very steep learning curve for everyone—the European Commission, PARD, the RDAs, the banks and the entrepreneurs themselves—and one should allow at least 12 to 18 months for the initial planning and implementation period, should a similar scheme be launched elsewhere.

Flexibility. The parameters of our scheme were tightly defined by the terms of the Programme Financing Memorandum. One consequence of this, for example, is that the scheme appears to be overly bureaucratic for the smaller investment projects. At the other end of the scale, it might be preferable if the upper limit for employees was higher than the 100 persons which it is at present.

Any regulatory system should be kept as flexible as possible so that the scheme can be adapted to meet the actual needs of SMEs, rather than rigidly trying to meet the needs anticipated at the outset.

Flexibility should also be maintained in terms of offering a variety of instruments, such as training and advisory services (both on the side of businesses and financial institutions) and help for various business support institutions.

Region-specific approach. It is clear that the needs of regions vary and this differentiation is well reflected in the mix of instruments and financial disbursement outlays provided to individual regions. There are regions in Poland which enjoy 30 per cent growth in GDP per annum. They generally have a rich and heterogeneous industrial structure, a well-developed financial institutions network, a high proportion of university graduates, a favourable location on main transport routes and high levels of investment. These are the regions where one would prefer to do business in Poland. Certainly, one cannot forget that this 30 per cent growth rate is in part possible because of the low starting point.

Bearing in mind the limited resources that can be used for the development of less developed regions, the earlier descriptions have been related to the support which can be offered to backward regions. In such regions (mostly rural) venture capital would probably not be a great success. It can prove its efficacy in high growth-rate regions where, as the financing is more easily available, the grant scheme would seem to be unnecessary and perhaps even have a destabilizing effect on the local financial markets. So the general lesson would be to ensure that the mix of assistance on offer fully meets the characteristics and needs of the target group.

The success of the regional development programme implemented in Poland stems to a large extent from the fact that local communities led by democratically elected governments enjoy autonomy in financial terms. They, SMEs and regional development agencies, are real partners. Local governments should be considered as a prerequisite of local and intra-regional development. The alternative is centralized government policy which is a memory from the past.

The future

At present in Poland plans are being made for future support for regional and local development. It is essential that such support includes a range of financial engineering techniques in order to provide as broad-based support as possible for SME development in the less-developed regions. Such financial tools might include a grant scheme, much as described above.

There would, of course, be some differences and it should become easier for the smaller entrepreneur to benefit. The administrative procedures should be simplified so that the time taken to process applications is as short as possible.

Overall, the scheme is soundly based and as such will continue to play a role in the economic restructuring and development of the SME sector in less developed regions of Poland for some time to come.

Equity and venture capital financing in countries under transition

THOMAS C. GIBSON

SMALL ENTERPRISE ASSISTANCE FUNDS is a not-for-profit organization which provides financing, in combination with business assistance, to SMEs. SME, as we use the term, refers to private enterprises which, generally, employ 15 to 150 people; have annual revenues of between $250 000 and $2.5 million; and have assets, prior to our investment, of $25 000 to $250 000. While SEAF's four funds have been operating for an average of less than two years, we have now invested approximately $6.5 million in some 35 businesses, at an average investment of about $185 000 per investee.

SEAF is majority voting shareholder in three locally registered investment funds: CARESBAC-Polska in Warsaw, CARESBAC-Bulgaria in Sofia, and CARESBAC-St Petersburg in Russia. We also manage the newly formed Small Enterprise Equity Fund in Nizhny Novgorod, Russia, for the European Bank for Reconstruction and Development (EBRD). In addition to EBRD, SEAF's principal funders include the US Agency for International Development (USAID), the US Department of Agriculture (USDA), and the Overseas Private Investment Corporation (OPIC).

SEAF's investment funds provide direct financing to enterprises with majority local ownership, typically to SMEs engaged in agribusiness, light industry for export, and essential business services. Investments generally range from $25 000 to $300 000 and are made through combinations of minority equity participations and long-term loans. All investments are made through local offices in the country of investment, operating according to commercially sustainable principles.

Each of SEAF's funds is staffed primarily by local young professionals trained in finance, working under the direction of an experienced expatriate financial executive. SEAF staff provide assistance in management and business planning as they structure commercial investment instruments which best fit the needs of the investees. Although SEAF operates its funds on a for-profit basis, we have pledged that returns on SEAF's shares will remain in the country of investment to be used for further SME financing and the support of social, economic, and environmental programmes in the country of investment.

Thomas C. Gibson is President of Small Enterprise Assistance Funds, a USAID-supported financing programme for SMEs.

We anticipate that by late 1995 the total commitments of capital to be invested under SEAF's management will be approximately $45 million. We hope to have these funds fully invested within the next three years as we establish new funds, not only in Central and Eastern Europe and the former Soviet Union (hereinafter, the 'region'), but also in Africa, Asia and Latin America.

SMEs, the missing middle

SEAF's initial research into SMEs showed that, in comparison with micro-enterprises and large firms, SMEs bring proportionally greater benefits to a local economy. For example, in most countries, SMEs generate more jobs per unit of investment, generate greater social benefits in relation to investment, reinvest proportionally greater earnings in the local community, and introduce a greater variety of new goods and services. SMEs are also more flexible in responding to dramatic market changes and economic shocks. Recent advances in technology have made it possible for SMEs to engage in highly profitable new sectors and to expand their markets. In Poland in 1990, voters who saw their incomes dwindle, prices explode, and nearby state companies close or lay off legions of workers looked to the success of the local small entrepreneur to provide the most convincing evidence—sometimes the only evidence—of the benefits to come from economic reforms.

Nonetheless SMEs appear to have fallen through a great gap between donor-supported NGO development programmes and the investment objectives of private sector and development finance institutions. Many charitable organizations assist microenterprises with small loans of a few hundred, or a few thousand, dollars, and multilateral and private investors provide capital in the tens of millions of dollars to large-scale industry. Meanwhile, the SME sector is largely denied access to long-term financing.

In studying the performance of virtually every SME equity-financing scheme implemented in a developing country between the mid-1970s and 1990, we found that few, if any, had been both successful and true to their original intentions. In almost every case, one of the following three situations had occurred:

○ The programme had closed, faced with the improbability, or impossibility, of becoming profitable. Operating and transactions costs, in relation to the size of investment, had been too high, particularly when financial professionals from outside the country were flying in and out.
○ The investment criteria had changed. The fund which started out to make average investments of $200 000, soon turned to projects of $500 000 to $2 million, often not only to diminish risk and increase returns, but also to protect the reputations of the fund managers from the very risks they were intended to take.

○ The investors had turned almost exclusively to debt financing, although the original intention of the fund had been to invest half or more of its capital in equity, partly for the purpose of assisting capital market development. Debt was simpler, safer, less time-intensive, and more secure.

During the past five years, SMEs, their needs and their benefits to economies, have risen appreciably in the consciousness of the development assistance community. The problem remains, however: donors—private or public—are not eager to see subsidized or grant funds go into commercial businesses where, for example, the owner is sufficiently affluent to drive a recent-model automobile. At the same time, investors who expect to get their money back are, in varying degrees, averse to the risk entailed in investing in SMEs in transitional or developing economies. SMEs remain in the 'missing middle' between subsidized micro-lending and commercially attractive investments.

The role of publicly funded financial institutions

The role of SMEs is too crucial, however, to wait until SME investment is attractive to private risk capital. And risk capital from an equity partner is precisely what SMEs need. Bank lending in the region is almost invariably short-term, high-interest, and highly collateralized. Moreover, credit institutions do not bring with their financing the kind of experience and transfer of know-how which the venture capital investor provides.

During this period of transition in the region, which will surely not be over soon, the SME sector will need public funds in order to grow and become attractive to private capital. There are numerous commercial funds for purchasing equity through voucher systems and emerging stock markets, primarily targeting equity in larger, privatized firms. Those few funds financing SMEs are almost exclusively supported by bilateral and multilateral institutions. Many development finance institutions, however, have a mandate to invest on commercial terms. One way of making smaller investments for a reasonable return is to work through NGOs whose cost structures are lower than commercial fund managers.

Whatever the vehicle, investments of public sector funds in SMEs must be made according to good business sense and, most importantly, in ways which are economically sustainable. Only by making a positive return to SME investments, and making them on commercial terms, can publicly funded investors prove that the SME sector makes sense for private capital.

Development venture capital for SMEs

SEAF's task is to assist SMEs to become profitable and grow. At the same time we owe it to our funders and investors, and to the reputation of the

104

SME sector, to produce a reasonable return on the capital we manage. This means we must supply our investees with what they need to be profitable, while keeping our operating costs low. Venture funds normally look for returns of between 25 and 35 per cent. In high-risk situations, such as that of SMEs in the region, commercial investors would normally look for even higher projected returns on investment, say 35 to 45 per cent. In industrially developed countries, venture capital companies normally incur annual operating expenses of 2–5 per cent of total capital. A 1992 study by the IFC found that the annual cost to capital ratio of venture capital companies in developing countries ranged from 4 to 9 per cent.

In SEAF we generally go by a formula wherein we look for an average return on investment of about 18 per cent, maintain an average annual cost ratio of no greater than 8 per cent, and look for a return of around 10 per cent over the 10 to 15-year life of each fund. The development financing of SMEs must take into account that operating cost ratios will be higher, and that rates of return across the portfolio will be lower.

SME investment: what's working

The following are elements of our practice that we would recommend to other SME investors. In general, our mistakes have been made when we departed from these prescriptions:

Be an active partner who contributes more than money. All SME entrepreneurs need more than money from a partner. The successful ones know it. Their lack of access to capital is generally no greater handicap than their lack of business training and experience within a market system. The provision of technical assistance and business support is a central element of the SEAF model.

Business assistance is as crucial at the time of initial negotiations as it is during the life of the investment. One might reasonably expect that an SME entrepreneur will oppose selling a part of his or her business. It is essential to convince the entrepreneur that the investor intends to do more than come by to monitor books and collect dividends. An essential part of the negotiations is to work with the entrepreneur in business planning and to show specifically where the investor will supply assistance in areas like marketing, cost accounting, materials sourcing, and the selection of equipment. When entrepreneurs understand this, then a patient explanation of terms will normally reveal the attractiveness of equity. We have purchased equity in all but one of the more than 35 companies we have financed, and we have lost few prospects because they were unwilling to part with a proportion of the ownership.

Business assistance at the outset may allow us to purchase shares in the SME, but only ongoing assistance will define us as a true partner. With limited staff and diverse portfolios, we have had to look beyond our own staff for technical expertise. However, neither we nor our investees can normally afford paid consultants from outside the country. The use of voluntary and publicly supported business assistance programmes is an integral part of the SEAF model and it is unlikely that we would exist without these programmes.

For almost every investment we have made, we have called upon organizations like the International Executive Service Corps (IESC), AGIR, the Citizens Democracy Corps (CDC) and the Volunteers in Overseas Co-operative Assistance (VOCA) for *pro bono* business people to work with the investee enterprise. The investee may need only a short consultancy to assess what equipment is most appropriate for the new stage we are financing. Or, it may need longer-term attention. Recently, an IESC volunteer, a Polish-speaking former chief financial officer of a major multinational firm, spent two to three days with each of our investees in Poland performing diagnostic surveys of existing management information systems and cost accounting practices. As a result of his work, a number of businesses shifted the focus of their accounting from exclusively reporting functions to greater service in controls, management, and forecasting. Similarly, we have engaged a consultant from AGIR to work with a number of our agribusiness investees in assessing and revising their marketing strategies. In many cases, after an initial on-site consultancy ranging from a week to two months, a volunteer consultant will keep in frequent touch with an investee by phone and fax over an extended period of time.

Invest through local operations. This means that investment analysis and investment decisions should be made in the country of investment. Negotiations with SME proceed iteratively and require a series of decisions. Most SMEs are in need of relatively immediate financing to meet deadlines for new orders or seasonal operations and sales. Involving professionals from abroad can cause repeated delays and, in the light of the size of the investment, prohibitively high transaction costs. Above all, SME investors must be flexible with both their schedules and their terms to meet the legitimate needs of SMEs. Headquarters involvement jeopardizes this flexibility. Each SEAF fund has a local chief executive with a clear mandate and a well-defined investment policy. Generally, investment decisions which are made within these guidelines receive automatic approval from an executive of SEAF in Washington, serving as a member of a predominantly local supervisory board.

The majority of SEAF staff are host-country nationals who understand not only business and finance, but also the cultural, political and economic circumstances which have shaped the attitudes of the investees. At present, each local chief executive is an expatriate with extensive business and financial experience, particularly the experience of having been held accountable for investments prior to joining SEAF. Local people with this kind of experience are still rare and generally outside our financial reach.

Our expatriates are as responsible for training local staff—almost invariably young, virtually bilingual, and exceedingly bright—as they are for directing the structuring, nurturing, and exiting of investments. To accomplish this, they must be in full-time residence.

Take minority *equity positions.* This may appear contrary to conventional wisdom. Most investors in the region insist that unless you have majority rights, you lose virtually all control as well as your fair pro rata financial benefits from an investment. This may well be true for larger investments. The SME, however, is both owned and managed by an entrepreneur who may have waited long years to control his or her own business and for whom ownership is fundamental to having a strong incentive to succeed. It is difficult to control or monitor such a business from the outside. Inevitably the entrepreneur will control the business and its accounts, particularly in an environment in which enforcement of shareholder rights through the courts is a long, expensive, often impossible task. We would rather earn and enjoy our rights as a minority shareholder, than lose them as a majority shareholder.

Invest in combinations of debt and equity. At present, about 80 per cent of our investments have both loan and equity components. There are four principal and compelling reasons for this:

○ *Flexibility.* Take the example of a printer who has built a business and a customer base using older, locally made equipment. The current equity of the company is $100 000 but the business needs a new $150 000 piece of equipment. If we invest the entire amount through equity, we become the majority shareholder. Instead we invest $90 000 in equity for 45 per cent of total equity, and lend $60 000 to the business for the remaining capital requirement. The combination of debt and equity also permits us to structure payments of interest, dividends, and principal in a manner which best suits the needs of the SME and our own. Furthermore, as opposed to dividends, interest payments are tax deductible for the investee.

○ *Rights and controls.* As a minority investor we have certain voting rights but the extent of our control is largely dependent upon good faith. As a lender, however, the law permits us separate and additional rights such as collateral security. Debt is also an effective monitoring tool for an equity investor, in that debt service payments are predetermined milestones in the performance of a business.

○ *Current and long-term income.* As an equity investor we look to capital appreciation for the majority of our income and, on average, anticipate selling our shares no sooner than the fourth or fifth year of investment. Interest and principal payments on debt provide us with income for our operating costs during the years preceding the exit.

○ *Avoidance of conflict with banks and banking laws.* We are not a bank and do not wish to be. Local laws in the region do not permit non-bank institutions to be straight lenders. They do, however, allow for share-holder loans. If a business wishes to borrow money from us, we must be a shareholder in the business.

Avoid start-ups. There are far more good SMEs in business in the region than there is sufficient capital to finance their growth. In general we invest in situations where the entrepreneur has already put his or her own time and financial resources at risk and where some track record has been established. Start-ups are not only higher risk than even development finance can afford to take as a regular practice, they are also extremely time-intensive for staff.

Identify 'pre-screened' investments through a network of referrals. An unsolicited application for financing does not always make for an auspicious start to a partnership and rarely supplies significant useful information. Rejected applications—or worse, unanswered applications—send a message to the community of private entrepreneurs that an investor is 'not serious'. Thus, we have started each of our funds with a low public profile and looked to reliable referrals to identify good prospective investments. Our best source has been the many business assistance organizations who supply non-financial assistance to SMEs, particularly volunteer programmes such as CDC and AGIR and official assistance programmes, such as the Polish Business Advisory Services, the Small Business Centres managed by the PHARE and the US Peace Corps, and TACIS. Projects identified through these programmes have already demonstrated an ability to listen, provide accurate information, submit to analysis and work with outsiders before we see them. Working with these programmes saves time and mitigates risk.

Exits

An equity investment ends not with a closing of the transaction, but with the sale of the investor's shares after years of a partnership. SEAF's first investments are less than three years old and it will be at least another year before we begin to exit from those. Nonetheless, we began to learn lessons about exits from the moment we introduced them in investment negotiations. The greatest of these lessons are these:

Be flexible. Typically, we have a provision in the investment agreement for the investee to purchase our shares during the fifth year of the investment. Such 'puts', however, are rarely exercised simply according to agreement. This is the case in most developed free-market countries and puts are even less likely to be exercised as planned in the region. We therefore look for one out of a number of exit strategies to emerge during the life of the investment. We anticipate using a variety of valuation formulas, including percentage of sales, multiple of cash flows, discounted cash flow, multiple of sales, appraised value and fixed cash amounts. The specific formula, however, will most likely be determined during the later years of the investment, even when we have established at the outset a right to sell our shares according to a predetermined formula.

In general, we anticipate that about half of our investments will be bought out by management or a combination of management and employee stock purchases. Another quarter will be purchased by strategic outside investors, more often than not, as part of the purchase of a majority of the business. Due to the small size of our investments and the slow establishment of equity markets. it will be surprising if more than a quarter of our investments are sold in public offerings. Whatever the exit from the investment, it is unlikely that we will have the luxury of establishing a specific, assured exit as we enter the investment.

Be a partner, not a banker. Although we have found that most SMEs are willing to part with minority shares, this does not mean that they have fully understood and agreed to the difference between debt and equity. If we invest our $100 000 for 35 per cent of equity in year one, and the value of the business is $1 million in year five, will the entrepreneur feel, after his or her years of late nights and headaches, that we are entitled to $350 000 of the money he or she has earned? Nor unless we have helped earn that money. Recently we have reassessed our record for either supplying or arranging for assistance to investees and looked for new ways to increase that assistance. This is not only to help the businesses grow, but to demonstrate that we will deserve our share when we exit.

SME investment: the real 'bottom line'

A recent issue of *Business Central Europe* focused on venture capital in the region. Its lead article pointed to certain misconceptions about venture capitalists. 'The first' it said, 'is that they exist to support budding entrepreneurs, when in fact their *raison d'être* is to buy into a company cheap, add value over a period of years and sell off their shares for a fat profit.' We would obviously agree on the adding of value over a period of years, but it is not likely that any portfolio of SME investments, at this time and in this region, will produce a *fat* profit. For these two reasons, the public sector and the not-for-profit sector must work together to 'support budding entrepreneurs' and to build bridges between SMEs and private sector investors.

The promotion of private small and medium industrial enterprises in Kyrgyzstan

P. LINDLEIN

AFTER THE DECLARATION of political independence of the Kyrgyzstan in 1991, the young state had to face a whole raft of economic problems: interstate trading was disrupted, soon output was shrinking, and inflation and deficits were rising. Reforms were involved, and liberalization and privatization were on the agenda. This political top-down approach soon had its partners at the bottom level. In the summer of 1993, more than 3700 enterprises, about 200 of them in the industry category, were considered to be private companies, although the legislation for privatization was far from being complete. In January 1992 a privatization law had been adopted by the Kyrgyz Parliament, subsequently supplemented with a number of additional laws, decrees and regulations. A new privatization law was on the agenda for the autumn of 1993 and the government was discussing the drafts with legal and economic experts. Production had to go on, however, and technicians, engineers and managers of state-owned enterprises found themselves challenged by the constantly changing situation.

It was the first period 'for promoters' in a new economy. As a German I cannot forget that the economic miracle of Germany after World War II had its 'magicians': people who invested money they seemed suddenly to draw out of nowhere.

When the directors of KfW came to Kyrgyzstan to discuss the project ideas for German financial co-operation they used the opportunity to visit a few of these new enterprises in old factories. They saw people toiling with outdated machines in inappropriate buildings, nevertheless producing goods competing with imports and serving the local population.

They also talked to the new entrepreneurs, who were mainly people who in former times had the responsibility of making decisions and now saw the opportunity to gain the benefit for the risks they were taking. Of course, these profits would not be only for their private benefit: they would also create job opportunities, satisfy local demand, earn some foreign exchange in the regional markets of Central Asia and some would even pay taxes.

However, the most important impact at this crucial stage is the demonstration factor of success. This would provide support to the whole reform

P. Lindlein is a managing partner and consultant with ICEE Consult GmbH in Dusseldorf, Germany, now working with the KfW-supported (Kreditanstalt für Wiederaufbau) project in Kyrgyzstan.

process. Everybody involved knew that many obstacles would appear on the way, but the people involved thought it would be worthwhile to promote these private businesses and the Kyrgyz Government and KfW agreed to allocate a credit of DM10.0 million.

The entrepreneurs

Although Kyrgyzstan has no tradition of creative entrepreneurs, not even before communism, it developed some competitive industries such as textiles and clothing. The managers and technicians of state-run companies knew very well their suppliers, their customers, the products and their deficiencies. In this way they had gained sufficient practical experience to start their own businesses and that is what some of them did at the first chance.

The typical entrepreneur is about 40 years old, has a high level of technical education, and belongs to a small informal social group, often linked by relationship or long-term friendship, which provided him or her with the funds to start. Such entrepreneurs bought or leased used equipment, rented a building and started at a small scale, for example in clothing with about 30 employees (above the micro-level). They soon achieved some success and their companies were expanding, satisfying the demanded quantity. With liberalization they faced stronger competition from abroad and the consumers' demand for better product quality.

It was clear to such entrepreneurs that they would have to improve substantially the equipment in their factories, and they had tried to get credits for the import of modern machines from the local banks, but

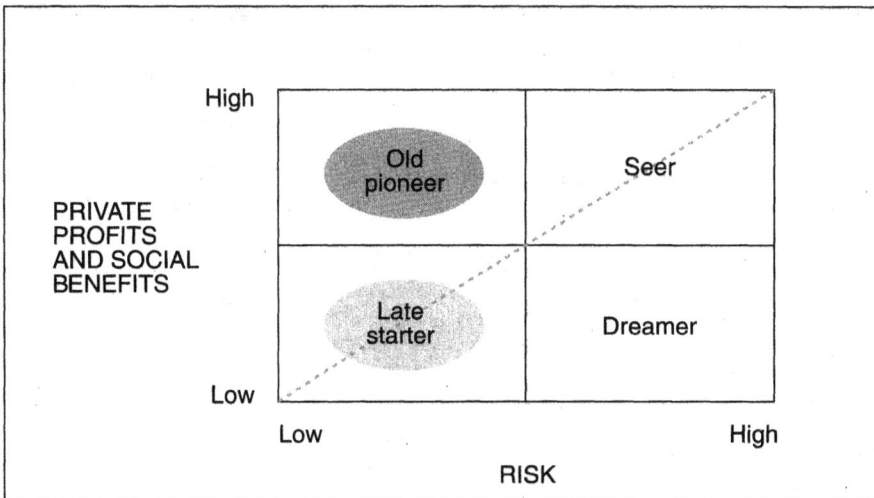

Figure 1: The creditworthiness of entrepreneurs

111

without success, due to a lack of funds. These entrepreneurs have emerged as ideal partners for KfW to help promote the private sector.

There are also potential entrepreneurs, who gained experience in the trade working in one of the state-run or sometimes even in one of the already privatized companies, and who want to start their own business, even if they are not the first in the field. Besides these late starters are the people who want to do something completely new in their life. Some of them may have visionary power, but most only have illusions. We can summarise this view in a simplified graphic of creditworthiness (see Figure 1).

The bottlenecks

These different groups of entrepreneurs share the general problems of the Kyrgyz economy, but depending on their background, experience and state of preparation and execution of the project, they face a different set of problems. A simplified scheme gives us an idea of their typical difficulties (see Table 1).

Even this simple overview gives us an idea of the enormous challenges for an entrepreneur at the beginning of his or her project. In such a context there is always the paternalistic temptation for donor organizations to look for the standard solutions to these problems, as donor experts are not only used to designing, but also to executing these projects. However, in the case of the promotion of private industry, the entrepreneurs themselves are the heart of the project. So the job is to find these entrepreneurs and to help them, not to replace them.

This does not exclude broad and deep programmes with long-term training measures within the framework of technical co-operation. At the beginning of the programme of financial co-operation in Kyrgyzstan there was no time to wait for the results of such an ambitious technical programme.

Table 1. Typical problems for the different groups of entrepreneurs

	Old pioneer	Late starter	Seer
1 Management and organization		☐	☒
2 Juridical questions		☒	☒
3 Staff/qualifications	☐	☐	☒
4 Production process	☐		☐
5 Product quality	☒		
6 Information about competitors		☐	
7 State of equipment	☒	☐	☒
8 Information about suppliers	☐	☐	☒
9 Funds for start and expansion	☒	☒	☒
10 Collateral	☐	☒	☒
	☒ major	☐ minor problem	

In the meantime the programme is also responding to new starters; however, typically very small projects have to tackle a lot of technical, economic and juridical problems and do not only need credit, but also a degree of systematic mid-term technical assistance. This is provided by a team of experts under German technical co-operation with Krygyzstan, who started their activities recently. This team is also responsible for the allocation of individual sub-loans of up to DM100 000 from a fund of DM 2 million, which was reserved for this target group. The rest of this chapter deals only with the programme of financial co-operation, however.

The promotion approach: division of labour

In developed market economies, private banks assist entrepreneurs and business founders, offering them long-term credit on commercial conditions, sometimes helped by governmental promotion programmes. Although there were a lot of financial institutions in Kyrgyzstan, they lacked the funds and the experience for this kind of project financing. Regarding the state of preparation of the projects, there was no time to wait for assistance from one of these banks. So the Kyrgyz Government and KfW appointed a consultant to study the creditworthiness of the project proposals and limited the role of the local bank purely to the financial administration on a trustee basis. GoskomInvest, the state commission for foreign investment and economic assistance, is responsible for the selection of the projects. A German consultant is assisting the working group of Goskom-Invest during periodical stays in the capital, Bischkek.

It was then that a stringent selection process began. It was a period with some success, more hope and even more disappointment for the Kyrgyz applicants. The first state of the evaluation consisted of three steps. Firstly, a multiple-choice questionnaire helped the applicants to check the state of preparation of their project and to present it to the evaluation team. Then, depending on the quality of their proposals they were invited for detailed discussion. Finally, a visit to the site of the project ended the first stage.

Only when there was a general positive view after these steps did the consultants help the entrepreneurs to solve the remaining problems of the project preparation. At the same time the working group forwarded a detailed sub-loan proposal, including the definition of the prerequisites for the first disbursement, to KfW for final approval. After that a sub-loan agreement was prepared and signed, enabling the entrepreneur to proceed with his or her project.

The credit scheme

The companies receive the sub-loan credits on the following terms and conditions. The annual rate of interest is 9 per cent, and is for a duration of 4–7 years, depending on the characteristics of the project, with a grace period of 1–2 years. Amortizations and interests on the sub-loans can be paid in DM or in the local currency. In the latter case a compensation to offset the effects of Kyrgyz inflation has to be paid by the sub-borrower.

The main criteria for eligibility of the project and the financing under this programme are:

o The owner structure and the management of the enterprise have to be predominantly private, for example, private individuals and the employees having at least two-thirds of the shares.
o In view of the intention to create employment opportunities, small and medium enterprises are defined as firms with up to 500 employees.
o Individual project cost, including investment cost and adequate working capital, in general should not exceed the amount of DM2 million.
o As medium- and long-term credit is scarce in general, local costs can also be financed.
o Sub-borrowers are expected to make all efforts to use their own funds to finance at least a part of the project cost and own property to provide guarantee for the sub-loan. However, in view of the special circumstances, this is not always possible. In these exceptional cases, guarantees are limited to pledges on the new equipment.
o The minimum criterion of profitability for a project to be eligible under the programme is an internal rate of return of 15 per cent per annum.

For the financial administration of the programme the local bank receives a fee of 1 per cent to be paid out of the repaid debt service, which shall not exceed 2 per cent of the paid annual interests on sub-loans.

The response

About 200 applications requesting a total credit amount of DM140 million were presented in the first six months. Meanwhile seven sub-loans with a total amount of DM7 million were approved by KfW and credit proposals are under preparation for the rest of the credit line. They mainly consist of lending to 'old pioneers' and the purpose of investment is to modernize and extend adequately their equipment to be competitive with importers and to be able to offer their products in the neighbouring countries after the *de facto* liberalization of foreign trade. Most of the proposals are within branches of the food industry, like bakeries, butchers' shops and mini breweries, and textiles and clothing, especially knitwear. The average credit amount is about DM800 000. The first equipment has been installed recently and production has started. Some are faced with teething difficulties, others show sales above expectations, but it is too early to talk generally about the results of these investments.

The first experience, lessons learned and the next steps

The response to the programme by the entrepreneurs and potential business founders was good, showing the need for long-term financing with adequate commercial conditions. The quality of the project proposals, however, and the experience of the applicants were very mixed, as had been expected. So the low number of approvals is no surprise to the donor (who reserved an appropriate amount for the programme, which is now almost fully allocated), but it is of course a disappointment to many of the applicants, who expected an immediate positive response to their project idea.

Although there are some projects in an advanced stage of study, it is clear that during the next stage applicants will need more technical assistance in the preparation of their projects. They will need more information and better help to get the same knowledge of the market, for their products and for the investment goods, that the entrepreneurs of the already approved projects had because of their commercial experience and visits abroad. This will expand the role of the consultants involved. Up to now they had to fulfil mainly the task of a conservative banker, selecting promising projects and clients. In the next stage they have to be more active, supporting the potential entrepreneurs, but avoiding the risk of displacing the entrepreneur from the driver's seat. The first stage of the programme can be considered a partial success despite all its possible shortcomings, because with its pragmatic and moderate approach it was possible to turn the elaborate proposals of private entrepreneurs into reality. Some of the approved projects might need more assistance than was expected. Nevertheless, the programme has provided some good examples, motivating the other potential entrepreneurs to develop their ideas and projects to overcome the problems of the transformation of the Kyrgyz economy.

115

The Romanian Loan Guarantee Fund

SORIN COCLITU AND TATIANA BRATESCU

IN 1991, THE ROMANIAN GOVERNMENT embarked on an ambitious programme of economic reform which was designed to move toward and ultimately create a market-based economy. One of the principal elements of
that reform process concerned the privatization of housing, agriculture and
the ownership and operation of commercial companies. The latter had
specific objectives with emphasis not only on the privatization of state-
owned enterprises, but initiatives to support and encourage the creation of
a privately owned profitable small and medium-sized business sector.

The National Agency for Privatization recognized that in order for this
to happen, there would be an increasing need for medium and longer-term
capital financing for the emerging small and medium-sized enterprises. The
Agency also recognized that the Romanian Banks, for a variety of reasons
including limited capitalization, inexperience, collateral requirements and
inflationary uncertainty, would not be able to respond adequately to the
SME's future needs. It was against this background that a decision to
establish an SME Guarantee Programme was made by the Agency.

The outcome was that the Federal Business Development Bank
(FBDB) with the support of the Canadian International Development
Agency (CIDA) was asked to provide the National Agency with the
technical assistance to set up the legal and organizational framework
to create and launch the Romanian Loan Guarantee Fund for Private
Enterprise. The second phase of the FBDB's assistance was to help the
fund fully implement and operate its programme in an effective manner.
This assistance continued until the end of 1995 with a full-time FBDB
adviser at the fund. Assistance was also received from the Austrian
Burgesforderungs Bank, who financed the acquisition of a computer system for the fund.

The Romanian Loan Guarantee loan fund

Objective. The fund is a joint stock company and was established as
a public intermediary financial institution to support the economic
restructuring and privatization process by helping SMEs attain access to

---

Sorin Coclitu is President of the Romanian Loan Guarantee Fund. Tatiana Bratescu is
Executive Assistant to the President.

116

medium and long-term financing for the purpose of establishing and expanding their businesses.

Ownership. The principal shareholder of the fund is the National Agency for Privatization with minority positions held by the Romanian Bank for Foreign Trade, the Romanian Development Bank, the Commercial Bank of Romania and the Bank for Agriculture. The fund's initial capitalization was 5065 million lei (US$1.87 million).

Target markets. The guarantee fund is for Romanian SMEs, both natural and legal persons engaged or prepared to start in business. SMEs seeking assistance from the fund must be appropriately supported by owner's capital and be able to demonstrate that profitable operations have been achieved or are in prospect. Eligible businesses may be organized as a sole proprietorship, general or limited partnership, joint stock or limited liability company.

Project preference. The fund gives preference to the guarantee of loans for viable projects which will produce added value, increase exports, replace imports, generate foreign currency inflow, improve the infrastructure of Romania and improve productivity. Guarantees for loans made to effect changes of ownership through the purchase of shares or assets are permitted, provided the business will benefit from the new ownership and all other criteria are met.

Type of assistance. The fund provides assistance by way of loan guarantees to commercial banks in support of medium and long-term loans granted to SMEs who could not otherwise obtain such loans. The fund restricts its guarantee support to loans for capital projects. It does not guarantee loans for working capital, the restructuring of debt or for other short-term operating needs. The fund can also provide consulting services to its clients.

Risk sharing. Guarantees provided to the banks address the loan principal amount only on an 'ultimate loss basis'. The fund's guarantee support is restricted to a maximum of 70 per cent of the loan principal which may remain outstanding after all collateral and guarantees provided by the borrower have been liquidated and the proceeds applied to the bank loan. The fund's risk-sharing policy is based on two factors. Firstly, the degree of risk assumed by the fund must be such that the administration costs plus the losses experienced can be covered by the fund's fee structure without causing fees to be an undue burden on the borrowing SME. Secondly, the level of risk assumed by the lending bank must be at an appropriate level to ensure that the fund will not be expected to guarantee loan proposals that involve unacceptable risks.

Fees. The fund's mandate requires it to recover all its operating and guarantee loss costs, show a profit, pay profits taxes, declare dividends to its shareholders and protect its capital. Therefore, a fee structure is in place to meet these objectives, as follows.

- *Study fee.* One per cent of the amount of the guarantee approved is applicable and payable when the analysis is undertaken. If the guarantee is not approved or taken up, the fee is retained to cover the fund's costs.
- *Guarantee fee.* Three per cent per annum of the amount of the loan guarantee outstanding is payable in advance in January of each year, based on the outstanding guarantee commitment as at the preceding 31 December. New guarantee commitments made during the year are subject to payment of the 3 per cent per annum fee in advance, but on a pro rata basis for the balance of the year.

The fund's activity

The capital was fully subscribed in early 1994 and the fund was then in a position to start operations. By early 1995, 21 businesses had been assisted with guarantee commitments totalling some 7.3 million lei (US$2.7 million). These guarantees supported loans of some 11.4 million lei granted by commercial banks, which in turn financed capital projects totalling 13.3 million lei. The assisted companies are expected to generate some 70–80 billion lei in activity in 1995 and create or maintain 684 private sector jobs.

Fee income, together with interest earned on invested capital, permitted the fund to report a profitable operation in its first year. At year end, the fund's capital totalled 7.8 billion lei, plus a 2.7 lei general reserve fund for future losses. No specific losses on guarantees had been incurred by early 1995.

Challenges and lessons learned

The Romanian Loan Guarantee Fund has been launched against the background of a strong governmental commitment to help the development of private sector in Central and Eastern Europe. There is a corresponding need for understanding of such programmes from the local banking community. In this respect, in Romania a major role was played by the National Bank of Romania. In order to make the best use of this programme, the technical assistance delivered through governmental donors or international institutions must be of a high quality.

In addition, a suitable legal framework and regulations are needed for sound financial operations in non-typical financial institutions to be achieved (for example, tax and VAT exemption should be agreed for fees collected from the entrepreneurs). A positive goal achieved was that all the companies guaranteed by the fund could not have accessed their long-term financing without the guarantee scheme's help.

A negative aspect of our operations is that it is too much tied to the banking community. Although the fund is independent as a company, its operation relies a lot on the banks who send the clients. In this respect our expectations exceeded the banks' willingness to work with us on a profes-sional basis.

The fund's experience of working with the banks is affected by the following factors:

o the still monopoly situation of the state-owned banks in the market, although in the last five years a further 23 banks with private share-capital structure have started operations;
o a poor capital and savings market;
o a lack of experience in analysing proposals for longer-term investments;
o methods of committing money based on collateral, versus review of cash-flow or the ability of the business to pay back its debts;
o the entrepreneurs' poor experience in working with the banks;
o a lack of experience of how to present a business plan or a feasibility study.

A look to the future

The business development profile of the Romanian Loan Guarantee Fund shows that the fund at this stage has two main choices. It can either consoli-date its position in the market or it can consider further expansion through the development of new products or markets. In order to increase the financial efficiency of the fund, after one and a half years of experience, the conclusion is that there are opportunities to fill gaps in the marketplace based on the growing need for SME financial and management support. Choosing the latter option (but not ignoring the need for consolidation), the fund has therefore developed a strategy to pursue additional capital investment; to seek to identify and develop new SME market needs; and to introduce various types of indirect and direct financial instruments; and to work in close co-operation with others.

Conclusions, and advice to others

Guarantee funds can play an important role in the establishment and growth of SMEs; however, for them to work, some of the key ingredients for success should be considered.

o The banking environment and the role to be played by the fund must be carefully evaluated, defined and understood.
o In order to be developmental the guarantee fund may have to play a proactive role in the marketplace, identifying financing opportunities independently and pursuing them, rather than simply reacting to com-mercial bank requests.
o The fund should be prepared to act on its own due initiative and back potential winners; i.e. help those businesses that can demonstrate good prospects for success.

○ The fund will need to be properly capitalized to allow it to assume risks and fulfil its mandate.
○ The fund should operate in an efficient manner and be seen as efficient by the SMEs it serves.
○ The fund should have the resources to provide training and counselling to its clients.
○ The fund must be able to promote itself to user banks as a valuable risk-sharing agent.
○ The fund must make itself known to its clients as a helpful resource.

The fund's services must be known, accessible and affordable to its clients.

PART III

Training and general support projects

The experience of the ROM-UN Centre in Romania

JOHN ALLEN

THE PRIVATE SECTOR was reborn in Romania in December 1989. Since then, it has had an impressive growth.

By the end of 1993 the private sector was providing jobs for 43.7 per cent of the total active labour force, and was covering 56 per cent of the total retail sales; its contribution the GNP was approximately 32 per cent. By the end of February 1995 there were 441 600 entirely private commercial companies, representing 97.9 per cent of all the existing commercial companies in Romania.

The government reform programme

During the five years 1990–5 the legal economic framework and most of the institutions specific to a market economy have been established. Reforms in the financial and banking fields are ongoing, and privatization of the state enterprises sector has started.

The continued development of the private sector is one of the main objectives in the government reform programme. The strategy is based on a three-way approach:

○ to remove obstacles to private sector development and to create a more favourable market environment;
○ to create a 'level playing field' between private, state-owned and foreign enterprises;
○ to provide support and incentives to developing new small and medium-sized private enterprises (SMEs) and to privatized firms.

The Romanian Development Agency (RODA), the central body directly subordinated to the government's Council for Co-ordination, Strategy and Economic Reform, has been assigned to co-ordinate activities related to SME development. The institutional framework also comprises the National Agency for Privatization, the State Ownership Fund and five Private Ownership Funds, all involved in restructuring and implementing the large privatization programme.

John Allen the UNIDO Technical Adviser with the ROM-UN Centre for the Promotion of Small and Medium Private Enterprises in Romania.

Private business support infrastructure

There are several assistance programmes for the support of small and medium private enterprises, some of which are co-sponsored by the Romanian Government. The main donors are: (multilateral) EEC, UN, World Bank and (bilateral) British, Canadian, Dutch, German, USA governments, and some foundations established with private funding and donations from different foreign NGOs.

The private business support infrastructure created with Romanian and foreign funding currently comprises: 27 business development centres, some incipient business incubators, and two loan guarantee funds. Business or management training is provided (usually on a paid basis) by Romanian and foreign universities, training centres, and some of the consulting centres.

Regarding financial support, there are very few programmes. In fact there is only one subsidized credit line for SMEs, funded by RODA. EBRD, EIB and the World Bank have some credit lines available, mainly for private exporters and farmers; in addition, PHARE (EU) has developed a 2.4 million ecu grant scheme. The scene is completed by various volunteer consulting organizations providing free services in different specialized areas.

The first directory of sources of assistance for the private sector was recently issued by a USAID-funded programme. The directory includes the Romanian Government, non-government organizations involved in supporting private sector development, most of the foreign-aid assisted programmes that are currently operational in Romania, and other relevant information.

The ROM-UN Centre

The ROM-UN Centre was the first consulting centre for SMEs established in Romania in 1991, to assist in the development of the SME sector. It is a project jointly funded by the Romanian Government and UNDP, with additional contributions since 1994 by the Dutch Government, and from 1995, by the British Know-How Fund. The executing agency is UNIDO, and the government counterpart is RODA.

The centre provides confidential and impartial consulting, training, and information services to private entrepreneurs. It also provides feed-back to the government on the current problems and obstacles in the development of the private sector and suggestions on effective ways of improving its environment. It is involved in implementing the government's programme of developing a national network of business centres for SME.

Since its start in 1991, the ROM-UN Centre has assisted over 1700 existing and potential entrepreneurs; and has provided practical, topical training seminars for entrepreneurs. It has published two issues of the book entitled the *Entrepreneur's guide*, selling 50 000 copies; and has developed a database with technical information for entrepreneurs. The centre has assisted in the establishment and start-up of ten autonomous county business development centres; and has provided training seminars for a pool of 60 SME counsellors, including those working with other programmes (such as the PHARE-funded centres of which there are five for SME and three for restructuring). Staff at the centre have prepared various papers for RODA and other government bodies; and have undertaken surveys related to private sector development for national and international organizations. The centre has also widely co-operated with other bodies, missions and programmes supporting private sector development.

A few figures from the ROM-UN Centre's annual report in 1994 illustrate the scope of activities:

○ 643 clients were assisted during 854 consultations;
○ 91 loan applications were processed, worth US$ 33.6 million, out of which 36 loans were approved, worth US$ 6.1 million, plus 4 projects financed through equity funds worth US$ 1.1 million;
○ 27 series of seminars were arranged on various topics, and were attended by 617 persons, including: existing and potential entrepreneurs from nine counties, members of different minorities and NGOs, SME counsellors, and other specialists from government institutions and banks;
○ seminars for Women in Business were undertaken, funded by the British Government through a UNDP programme, Women in Development, and these were very well received.

Through the work undertaken, the centre has gained a good reputation nationally and internationally.

Assistance in establishing local business centres

The role of the centre in this respect is to communicate the experience gathered by the ROM-UN Centre and to act as a methodological co-ordination unit, rather than a hierarchical control and co-ordination body.

Our assistance proceeds in the following manner. Contact is made with potentially interested entities (local authorities, chambers of commerce, SME associations, and so on) and the local business community, to explain the advantages that such an initiative can bring and to describe the centre's approach. The centre then provides assistance in creating an interested group to establish a local foundation, i.e. to ensure initial operational funds and appropriate premises, to register it as a legal entity, and to start the personnel selection process. The centre has some involvement in the selection of personnel; and it stipulates, as an essential condition, that this is a transparent process and undertaken by a panel.

Three weeks' intensive training for local counsellors and administrative staff is provided in Bucharest; followed by assistance in implementing all internal organization structures and information flows, including the computerized client-reporting system. The centre also provides all written support material used for consulting sessions and training seminars.

The centre's counsellors deliver a series of seminars for local entrepreneurs, aimed at attracting clients for the new centres and passing on practical experience in undertaking seminars. This is followed by the same seminars, delivered by the new counsellors with our assistance. Direct assistance is provided by one of the centre's team members at the new centre location for four months; and further support and assistance is available on request.

This approach has had several advantages. Assistance has been provided by trained personnel who were able to pass on their experience; and materials that had already been developed and tested in practice were made available to the centres. The approach has also developed a sense of unity among the centres; and has created the premise for further improvement and strengthening of these activities within a national network.

Further development plans

The centre's services are in increasing demand, by national and international clients and organizations, including those with investment funds. In order to strengthen and further develop a network of business development centres, a new foundation was recently established: the Foundation for the Assistance of Romanian Enterprises, FAIR. The founding members are the 10 local business development centres assisted by the centre, as well as others.

This new foundation has a bottom-up structure, initiated by the local centres, and a representative management (the local centres have a majority of seats on the Board). This ensures that the needs of the counties are met.

The foundation will be open to co-operation with other bodies and projects involved in supporting the SME sector. The aim is to ensure a nationwide spread of information, an effective use of available assistance sources, and synergetic development of the support infrastructure.

Key points for success

The most significant points for success are the following.

Dynamic, effective management is a prerequisite. In this respect, objectives, activities and success criteria (written into the project document) are periodically reviewed and adapted to changing needs; and services are widened and developed according to the centre's developing experience. Since starting, the centre has continually improved the distribution of tasks and developed clear monitoring systems (including a computerized client-reporting system), and workable internal flows of information. Attention is paid to the stimulation of personal initiatives and responsibility.

Continuity of management. Just one expatriate consultant acting as a technical adviser for the whole duration of the project enabled a better understanding of the situations specific to Romanian conditions. International experiences and models were adapted to improve continually the centre's methods and to develop its areas of involvement.

Quality and practicality. Professional ethics, confidentiality and impartiality are the most important characteristics aimed for by the centre's staff. All 'products' (books, papers, seminars, advice to clients, and so on) are practical, and easy to understand and implement.

Cost-effectiveness based on the multiplier effect. The project has been very cost-effective, with a total cost of US$ 1.5 million over five years. This was possible (among other reasons) because of the multiplier effect the centre aims to produce. All the material prepared, all the information gathered, all the knowledge acquired is passed on to the other centres in the network, and to the other counsellors. So the centre continually builds and expands on national resources and only utilizes international expertise in specific areas.

People. The centre relies on the quality of the people who are in the team, and this is achieved first of all through careful selection, based on a structured open selection process. Clear and comprehensive job descriptions are compiled for each position; including decisions on the education, experience, and personality characteristics required for these positions. Advertisements are placed in national newspapers; and a selection is made from the CVs received of those that correspond to the centre's requirements. The interviews themselves are usually organized in two or three stages and include structured questionnaires and practical professional tests; and the interviewing panel includes experienced members of the team.

Attention is also paid to relevant personnel training. All counsellors attend an intensive three-week training seminar at the beginning of their work to introduce them to counselling techniques, basic business knowledge, finance, marketing, and other related issues. The new counsellors in the local centres are directly assisted by an experienced counsellor from the ROM-UN Centre for four months. Also, after several months of activity most of them benefit from an attachment to similar western professional bodies, having the opportunity to gain further practical experience.

The centre's personnel are periodically involved in in-house training programmes, when they share experience and test their seminar material before delivering them to outsiders (entrepreneurs and specialists). The centre also tries to see what the needs of the sector will be and seeks out training for its staff to meet those needs.

Motivating the team is important. Attractive salaries are necessary, otherwise the time and money spent for selection and training are lost, as people move to better-paid jobs in the private sector and in foreign organizations. Material motivation is doubled by moral and professional satisfaction for effective and appreciated work. The management pays much attention to stimulating personal initiative and responsibility.

In addition, it is not enough to have good specialists; it is equally important that people are able to develop as a team. Those who cannot fit into the team have to find jobs elsewhere, for the benefit of all parties.

Finally, all local centres hire local people, since they are likely to be the best position to know local needs and resources. They are also able to carry on such activities on a self-sustaining basis.

Ideas for the development of business support infrastructure in Romania

From practical experience and direct contact with SMEs, the following ways of building an effective business support infrastructure are suggested.

Determine the primary needs of small enterprises for advice, training and support. This is the starting point of a well thought-out approach in designing the support infrastructure, and it must take into account that the nature and content of the advice and training needed by private entrepreneurs has changed over the years. At the very beginning the focus was on how to start a business, the legal matters for registration, and rather basic business awareness. Once the private enterprises developed, their demand focused on assistance in finding sources of finance, technical information, and advice on general and especially financial management. Now there is an increased need for advice and training on human resource management, foreign trade, business planning, and so on.

Other forms of support are also required to help a rapidly growing and a healthy private sector. They consist of:

o a clear, simple, and flexible legal framework ensuring at least equal treatment with the state sector;
o reasonable access to premises, equipment, and technologies;
o financial incentives;
o finance available on reasonable terms and conditions; and
o effective and minimal bureaucracy.

This kind of support requires a structured and well thought-out government strategy, with clear medium- and long-term objectives, action plans, time scales, responsibilities and appropriate budgets. This strategy should be based on a clear political will, and its implementation should involve not only the government body directly in charge of the co-ordination of SME sector development, but also the Cabinet, Ministries and other state bodies, in a co-ordinated national effort.

Different support activities within this strategy should be implemented by relatively small autonomous, decentralized organizations. The business

128

development centres we have assisted in starting-up in ten counties are legally non-government, non-profit, independent foundations. The involvement of local business community representatives, NGOs, and regional government authorities in establishing these foundations should ensure that their activities correspond to local needs and make the best use of local resources.

The entrepreneurs themselves can influence the delivery of support services through their professional associations who are founding members of these foundations.

The business development centres which are specialized local bodies are now in the process of interlinking in a national network. This will enable them to share experience, information and other resources. The nation-wide co-ordination and control of support programmes should be organized by the government body in charge.

Self-sustainability is necessary for these independent foundations. From the experience in Western countries and from our own findings it is clear that any consulting, training or other support service centre should be subsidized at least in its establishment (to cover the initial minimum equipment) and at the beginning of its operations. It will therefore have the opportunity to build its reputation on quality professional services.

All the local centres are currently charging for some of their services (such as financial business plans and seminars) and provide other services free of charge (such as basic advice and information for entrepreneurs). After several months of operation they were able to cover their operational expenses from their own income.

There is a continued need, however, for some free and subsidized services, which would require government subsidies, as occurs in many of the 'free market' countries.

Conclusions

The success of programmes is related to the environment within which they operate. This environment is created at all levels by the government, and is influenced by other organizations established to help the private sector, and by personnel who are carefully selected and trained.

At the regional level, activities should be autonomous, and the assistance bodies established should have self-sustainability as one of their aims. Local representatives of government, business, and other relevant organizations should be involved in proposing and implementing initiatives according to local needs and resources. However, there is also a need to co-ordinate regional initiatives in order to provide effective assistance and to make the best use of resources available nationally.

Future activities should be developed building on current achievements, national personnel, and within the framework of a clear government strategy in the support of the private sector.

Supporting the Roma ethnic minority in the development of small ventures in Hungary

ANDRÁS BÍRÓ AND ANNA CSONGOR

AUTONÓMIA ALAPÍTVÁNY (AA), the Hungarian Foundation for Self-Reliance, was founded in 1990. It has been funded by US private foundations since then, and recently the EC has joined the donors with funds earmarked for local and regional projects. The budget in 1995 amounted to one million dollars.

The five years of AA's existence are special years in the history of the country, marked by a radical transition from dictatorship to democracy. During these years the non-profit, philanthropic sector developed dramatically. More than 30 000 new associations, charitable organizations and civil groups came into life during this period in Hungary, 10 000 of which are foundations.

The main objective of AA is to contribute to the development of civil society in Hungary by financing projects by voluntary organizations in the fields of:

o poverty and ethnic (Roma or 'gypsy') minorities;
o environmentally sustainable development; and
o the development of the voluntary sector *per se*.

The foundation has assisted more than 400 grassroots organizations in the country to realize their projects. In respect of support for the most discriminated and poorest community, the Roma, AA has been the only private foundation in Hungary to fund about 200 subsistence and development projects.

The rationale for combining these three apparently unrelated fields lies in the appalling legacy of the previous regime concerning the state of the environment; in the growing discrimination and marginalization of the Roma communities, the unemployment-fuelled dramatic growth of impoverishment among the non-Roma poor as well, and finally, the state in which the Hungarian civil society has found itself after 40 years of dictatorship. We decided thus to focus on the depressed social groups, and so to contribute to the overall process of the democratization of society. It can be said now, that AA has played an important role in all of these areas during its half decade of activity.

András Bíró is the Executive Director and Anna Csongor is in charge of the Roma Programme of the Autónomia Alapítvány (AA), the Hungarian Foundation for Self-Reliance.

The aims of the Roma programme

The Roma, who comprise approximately 5 per cent of the population, or about 500 000 people, are the poorest, the most undereducated and the community that has suffered the most discrimination in the country, with no political support from abroad unlike the other national minorities living in Hungary. While the unemployment rate among the non-Roma population is 15 per cent it is 48 per cent among the Roma. The Roma programme became the spearhead of the activities of AA, not only in terms of the number of projects and the amount of funds disbursed, but also because of the uniqueness of approach and scope. AA has been a pioneer in funding income-generating projects, since if in the past assistance has reached the Roma communities it has been exclusively in the field of social and educational policies or cultural and folk programmes and projects.

The AA programme consists of offering grants and interest-free loans to Roma grassroots organizations in order to:

o produce enough food for self-sufficiency (survival projects);
o engage in production for the market (development projects); and
o train Roma entrepreneurs in modern marketing and management techniques.

As many as 200 projects have been financed during the last 5 years, of which 80 per cent are agricultural, the remaining 20 per cent industrial. The large share of agriculture among the projects shows that numerous local rural Roma communities recognized settled farming as the only real means for survival. Generally this implies arable farmers—growing first of all maize and potato for household use, and sometimes growing watermelon, cucumbers or paprika for the market—and/also animal husbandry, which is in most cases pig breeding.

The amount granted during the same period totals $500 000 ($2500 per project). The repayment of the loans, which is the main evaluation criterion, has grown on average by 250 per cent per year, thanks to a more thorough preparation of the projects and the development of a team of monitors who use dialogue and discussion as the method of keeping track of the grantees. The projects are in the grey zone of the economy, and constitute an apprenticeship for eventual development into fully fledged small businesses.

The Roma people are famous for their good sense of business. However, this is not what is required by modern sophisticated entrepreneurship. Traditional Roma business is carried out in the informal sector without modern infrastructure: no banks are used, no taxes are paid, no outsiders are employed, and no written contracts are made. Nevertheless, the absence of regulation is risky both for the marginals and for the rest of the society as well. AA offers the possibility of joining the mainstream of the economy for those groups who are willing and able to join. This is a very long process, and as far as can be seen now only the pre-enterprise stage is in sight. At this stage some modern entrepreneurial techniques are required. AA's aim is essentially educational, by providing the Roma with the experience of social integration without assimilation.

The operation of the project

In the course of the Roma entrepreneurs' training project, financed by the Mellon Foundation for 18 months, more than 100 Roma leaders underwent an intensive training in order to become managers of for-profit and not-for-profit projects, which are so desperately needed in this community.

There is a distinction between survival and development projects. In the first case the group produces food for the self-sufficiency of the household, whereas development projects aim at the market, by producing more than is consumed by the family. The loan element introduces repayment disci-.pline and is important in both of them, though the loan to grant ratio differs in relation to the type of the project. By now it is the regular practice of the foundation to consider survival projects as a first step needing another round of funding to grow into a development project.

The repayment of loans plays a key role in the evaluation process of a project. While in the first two years the repayment ratio was very low, it has radically changed in the last two years, thanks to the more thorough preparation of the projects and the establishment of the monitoring and follow-up system.

Relations with local authorities

A significant number of applications have suggested the possibility of Autonómia and the local government co-financing agricultural projects. While AA's contacts with local authorities and the involvement of the local public have been somewhat lacking previously, new projects now seek co-financing or other kinds of support from local governments. Priority is given to projects successfully involving local resources (not necessarily cash, but land, seed, etc.). The financial involvement of the local government in our Roma projects also serves as a control mechanism, and contributes to their transparency, while their accountability improves public acceptance.

Lessons learned

In a relatively short period of time some clear lessons have been derived which will steer the future direction of the project. Firstly, it is possible to introduce entrepreneural and managerial techniques among the leaders of marginal communities, provided a horizontal rather than hierarchical relationship is established, with a basis of mutual respect.

132

Secondly, it is necessary and possible, though controversial and extremely difficult, to combine market mechanisms with social concerns when working with marginals. Also, if the initiative is not genuinely theirs, i.e. if it is imposed from above, the project will inevitably flop. The opposite is also true: if the dreams of the local leaders are not transformed into concrete planning from below, the result is the same. The establishment of a local autonomous decision-making capacity is essential, even if mistakes are made along the way. Tolerance should be extended towards mistakes, but strict discipline in the case of fraud.

Finally the grantees should be made aware of existing gaps in their technical and managerial know-how. This way they initiate for themselves the acquisition of the necessary training, instead of being passive receivers of it.

The future

The AA Roma programme, as relevant as it may be methodologically, is only as effective as applying a bandage to the crisis in which the Roma minority finds itself in Hungary. A much greater level of funding is necessary in order to start tackling this problem more fundamentally. A public foundation endowed with tens of millions of dollars should be established with foreign support, as budgetary funds are not available within the country. This foundation should start to tackle three problems:

○ Land ownership for those Roma communities which have no other possibility of survival, but—under adequate legal guaranties—will slowly change into small-holder farmers. Such a change will require the establishment of a land trust.
○ A loan guarantee scheme for those Roma small businessmen and women who will contribute to the reduction of unemployment (by self-employment).
○ An educational and legal defence trust, the aim of which would be to diminish the exclusion in society characterized now by a high dropout rate from education among the young. Adequate vocational training should be part of this programme.

Out of these plans the creation of a land trust is already in the preparation phase. After World War II Hungarian Roma were left out of the land distribution process when the rural poor acquired small-holdings to produce crops for their own household use. As a consequence of the present compensation procedure following the collapse of collective socialist agricultural system in the past five years, there is a new chance for the rural Roma to become smallholders.

The Foundation's new initiative with other funders to create a land trust would give support to those unemployed who are willing to earn their

133

living in agriculture, by helping them to become owners of land. This would help to integrate them better in Hungarian society, yet keeping their cultural identity distinct. A feasibility study will examine the possibilities of land ownership and the chances of future co-operation among the new landowners.

The integrated advisory service for private business in Romania

NICOLAE GHERANESCU

THE INTEGRATED ADVISORY Service (or IBD) programme for Romania (IBD stands for Integrierter Betratungs Dienst) is part of a worldwide proven technical assistance programme provided by the German Government in developing countries or those in transition. The programme has as its main objective the support by advisory services of private enterprise structures in the partner countries. The programme package is run by the Deutsche Gesellschaft für Technische Zusammenarbeit (GTZ) and the German Development Corporation (DEG).

The IBD aims at great flexibility and a broad range of services. In co-operation with counterparts from the partner countries, it puts together advisory packages that make possible a diversified but coherent approach to helping small- and medium-sized enterprises, and to building up economically relevant institutions and macro-economic conditions.

In addition to this integrated function, the IBD also has a guiding function: its advisers inform their counterparts about other instruments for promoting private enterprise.

The programme is already running in more than 25 countries all over the World. In Central and Eastern Europe and the FSU there are IBD offices in: Bulgaria, Kyrgyzstan, Latvia, Poland and Romania, and preparations are being made for opening offices in Lithuania and the Moldavian Republic.

In line with the basic concept, advisory services are provided for various target groups at different levels. However, the advisory services offered, even outside the direct business sector, always address the needs and problems of enterprises.

A classification of possible target groups and levels is exemplified in Table 1. The IBD runs both long-term and short-term activities.

Long-term projects. An adviser (the IBD Co-ordinator) in the host country is usually located in an agency closely related to trade and industry. The co-ordinator adopts three main functions: firstly, he or she gives advice in his or her own speciality; secondly, in close consultation with counterparts, the co-ordinator determines and defines short-term expertise requirements, calling for the relevant specialists from the support services in

Nicolae Gheranescu is a Romanian independent business consultant.

Table 1. Business consultancy available at macro-, meso- and micro-economic levels

Levels	Target groups	Consultancy fields
Macro-economic conditions	Government Various ministries Other authorities Governmental and parastatal promotion agencies	Economic system Overall economic legislation (e.g. propertly law, law on competition, fiscal law, etc.) Economic (especially trade) policy, monetary policy, financial policy Promotion instruments Administrative regulations and procedures
Meso-economic levels (self-help institutions in the business sector)	Chambers of commerce Trade and professional associations	Institutions building Improving the range of services offered by the institutions Public relations work
Micro-economic level (enterprises)	Small- and medium-sized enterprises Larger enterprise in the privatization process All enterprises in industry, trade and services sectors	Management consultancy in all areas of business activities Promotion of investment and co-operation Training and upgrading

Germany, monitoring their assignments and giving any assistance needed. Finally, the co-ordinator informs and advises counterparts on taking advantage of additional programmes of German and possibly international development co-operation for private enterprise development (from EC, UNIDO, ITC, etc); and co-ordinates these activities.

Short-term advisory services. Short-term assignments can also be implemented in countries where there is no IBD Co-ordinator yet. The main elements are: a trade and trade fair promotion programme (PRO-TRADE), a production and marketing advice programme for companies, market information, training, advertising materials, etc—all services which enable partner country companies to participate in international fairs in Germany. Advice can also be given in designing measures to promote investment and co-operation, such as the identification of enterprises suitable for co-operation and locating specific marketing partners.

The IBD project in Romania

The economic legal framework for enterprises in Romania after December 1989 was typical of an East European transition economy, the new framework was constructed in 1990–2 in a comprehensive manner in order to open the economy to private initiative, investment and entrepreneurship, and to permit commercialization and the privatization of former state-owned enterprises.

This has accompanied a rapid development of private business, especially the creation of private small companies, first in trade, then in services, and finally in productive sectors. For instance, by December 1994 a total of 226 000 private entrepreneurs (one-man or family businesses) and 422 000 private companies (limited) were registered. The number of foreign investments has reached 43 000, but the capital invested is only US$1271.7 million. About 1000 former state companies were privatized. The public and state-owned sector is represented by 80 national public companies, 400 local public companies and 8000 companies still belonging to the State Ownership Fund. The economic power of the private sector has increased to 35 per cent of the national product, which is still small compared with other former communist states (Bulgaria—40 per cent; Russia—50 per cent, Hungary—55 per cent, Czech Republic—65 per cent).

The privatization law of 1992, provides for what have become typical methods for privatization. Thirty per cent of shares of the former state companies are being freely distributed to the population through a voucher system. The rather complicated methods of the privatization law, the lack of private capital and the difficulties in dismantling the old type of state ownership institutional structures, has resulted in a relatively low rate of privatization. To date, only 1000 companies (representing a total of 350 000 employees) are being privatized from the total of 8000 companies (with a total 5 670 000 employees); the large majority of privatizations are selling the shares to the management and employees. These 1000 privatized companies are mostly small companies, with less than 400 employees, and represent sectors such as: wholesale and retail trade, construction, services, food processing, wood and furniture, clothing, and so on.

The relatively low rate of privatization and the small size of the privatized companies has resulted in the fact that a relatively small part of the state assets were in private hands at the beginning of 1995. Currently, the Romanian Government is trying to implement an annex to the privatization law, intended to increase the mass privatization against vouchers from 30 to 60 per cent in a large number of medium-sized and large companies. Unfortunately, however, the ownership structure of the privatized companies (mostly employee buy-outs and mass privatization by vouchers) will create problems in the governance of the privatized companies.

In this economic environment, the IBD programme in Romania was planned and organized in close co-operation with the Romanian partners, and governmental and non-governmental agencies and institutions. The planning was carried out at a workshop held in Bucharest in September 1994.

The main goal of the project, emerging from this workshop, is to assist private and privatized businesses in the productive sectors in order to improve their competitiveness and help their penetration of the international market.

The target group chosen consists of the small- and medium-sized Romanian enterprises, developed by private entrepreneurship, privatization or by the restructuring of former co-operatives, and some of the still state-owned companies in the final phases of privatization, all in productive sectors. The first three-year plan provides technical support for more than 90 enterprises in productive sectors such as: clothing, shoe-making, food-processing, furniture and investment goods. This approach makes the IBD Project in Romania a sector-oriented programme.

The local partner, which has to continue the activities of the project after the withdrawal of the co-ordinator (in three years, if not extended), is the Romanian Chamber of Commerce and Industry in Bucharest, in co-operation with the other 40 chambers in the main cities and counties of Romania.

The main objectives which the project is trying to achieve for the target group at the end of the first three-year phase are:

○ a databank and sector analysis for the involved sectors to be drawn up;
○ improvements to the know-how of top management;
○ improved knowledge of medium-level management in design, production, technical and commercial fields;
○ selected enterprises will have participated to international fairs in Germany and have managed to penetrate the western market with their own products;
○ co-operation between Romanian private enterprises and German or other western partners to be arranged;
○ realistic information on Romania to be made available to foreign partners, and the image of Romania as an investment centre to be improved;
○ the IBD project to be co-ordinated with other projects in Romania;
○ local consultants to be appointed on a full-time basis in such activities;
○ the Romanian Chambers of Commerce to have improved their services.

The project activities are wide, consisting mainly in: training seminars for top and middle-level managers, as well as short-term advisory assignments by German experts in Romanian enterprises. Help and financial support are provided for preparations and for participation in international fairs. In addition, specialists are trained in fields such as: design, tailoring, quality control, marketing, and purchasing. Also, fact-finding tours for managers and investors have been organized, as well as information trips to Romania for foreign journalists, and other public relation activities. Short-term consultancies have been provided for governmental and non-governmental institutions (Chamber of Commerce, State Ownership Fund, Romanian Development Agency, National Agency for Privatization, and so on), as well as organizing co-operation and partnerships between Romanian and German Chambers of Commerce and chamber associations. Technical assistance and seminars have been arranged for Romanian consultants; as well as technical assistance to professional associations in different sectors, and the organization and implementation of partnerships with equivalent German associations.

The organization of IBD activities in Romania is based on the assignment of a resident IBD Co-ordinator, running an IBD Office in Bucharest in close co-ordination with the Chamber of Commerce and Industry. The co-ordinator runs direct advisory activities in his own field (the current co-ordinator is an expert in marketing), and also calls for expatriate short-term consultancies in various fields for companies and institutions. Additionally he uses local experts both in co-ordinating and expertise activities, as assistants to the short-term German experts. He also has a counterpart in the headquarters in Germany, who is responsible for the co-ordination of all activities of the programme in Germany.

A major part of the short-term consultancies for the IBD Project are provided by PROTRADE, a special programme inside GTZ Eschborn, specializing in marketing and promoting participation in international fairs in Germany. In its activity, PROTRADE assigns more than 150 external experts from well-known consulting companies or directly from trade or industry.

Companies assisted

The typical company advised by the IBD programme is a small or medium-sized company (up to 1000 employees), belonging to one of the sectors supported, which has arrived in private ownership by one of three main mechanisms: entrepreneurship, privatization or the restructuring of former co-operatives.

Depending on the sector, a small private company created by an entrepreneur in Romania faces many problems, due on the one hand to the unstable economic environment and infrastructure, and on the other to the lack of specific knowledge at the management level of the mechanisms of the market economy. Such specific problems are:

○ a small volume of assets, and rarely own buildings and real estate;
○ lack of capital for investment in equipment;
○ the financial indiscipline of trade partners, especially in the state sector, creating a so-called financial interlocking (large-scale reciprocal indebting);
○ an inflexible banking system;

o high inflation and the consequent problems in financing working capital;
o the low buying power of the population for consumer goods;
o a lack of partners and contacts in promoting products in the international market;
o insufficient knowledge of the modern running of a company (financial management, cost management, controlling, etc);
o a poor knowledge of the design, quality and price conditions required on the international market.

The management of these companies needs to be motivated, active and flexible, continuously trying to solve these problems. Technical assistance can best be directed towards finding partners, information on the international market and eventually finding external financing.

Private companies arising from the restructuring of co-operatives have the same type of problems, but due to the still persistent quasi-statal structures, are less prepared for the operation of a competitive market. The management is overwhelmed by liquidity problems affecting the day-to-day running. Assets are underutilized and capacities are shut-down. Few of them have kept their former partners abroad and are producing in a 'lohn' system (wage payment), which is advantageous, taking account of the relatively large capacities. Technical assistance has to help the managers in their basic management concepts, has to find out if the company is irretrievably loss making and cannot be helped in its present state, and in the case of a relatively sound enterprise, to advise and assist in finding partners to help with product development, and improving marketing.

The privatized companies have a better chance of survival than the co-operatives, the screening process of privatization picking up the best units in each sector. One of the main problems faced by these enterprises is the large number of employees or public (mass) ownership. The technical assistance has practically the same objectives as for the restructured co-operatives.

Table 2. Guidelines for the selection of companies under the IBD programme

Characteristic	Guidelines for company selection
Structure of property	Private or in privatizing process.
Size of company	Small or middle size—max. 1000 employees.
Sector	According to the main target sectors mentioned.
Regional spread	If possible, a uniform spread all over Romania, with concentration on traditional manufacturing regions.
Financial state	Not too good and not too bad (the company has to be able to survive ultimately without major financial support).
Management	Open to change.
Product	If possible, with export potential.

Table 3. How IBD helps companies' marketing strategies

Action of management	IBD support activities
Market analysis	IBD organizes open seminars on actual market data and structure in Germany.
Company analysis. Analysis of opportunities and risks. Decision about entering the international market	IBD resident and short-term experts visit companies, help the management to identify their own capabilities, and the possibilities and risks of market entry.
Determination of marketing goals and target groups, Laying down of procedures, timetables and costs	IBD short-term marketing experts assist managers in planning the general goals and strategy.
Using marketing mix instruments: product, price, communication, distribution	IBD short-term design experts advise on design and style of products. IBD can assign help in technical or financial fields, in order to improve cost structures or management methods. IBD supports the participation in international specialized fairs in Germany. During the fair the same experts assist the supported exhibitors on the spot in both commercial and technical fields. IBD organizes fact-finding tours, buyer/seller meetings, searches for individual co-operation partners, etc.
Market entry. Start of sales and distribution in Germany	IBD edits and distributes handbooks and leaflets on quality requirements, German import procedures, etc.
Marketing controlling	The IBD marketing experts assist management in coaching and evaluation of results.

The company selection for the project is made by the IBD resident experts and short-term experts based on the guidelines given in Table 2.

The typical approach for technical assistance to a selected company with exporting potential follows a general marketing approach, as shown in Table 3.

The sector-oriented activity

The entire IBD project is sector oriented, performing activities with different sectors in its first year of operation.

Clothing sector. The main target was the orientation of selected companies in the production of the company's own collection, together with a gradual reduction of 'lohn'-type (wage payment) production. In order to achieve this target, general open seminars on marketing and design have been carried out in Bucharest and other important cities; in addition, technical assistance is provided to individual companies at the management level in design and styling, product development, and marketing.

Companies are also helped to participate at the main international fairs in Düsseldorf or Frankfurt/Main; and 'buyer/seller meetings' are organized with potential partners from abroad.

Technical assistance is provided at middle level by organizing courses and seminars for cutting and tailoring; and assistance has helped restructure a selected chain of agricultural and industrial companies in the production of environment-friendly garments in linen.

Finally, fashion contests have been organized with prizes for Romanian enterprises.

Each company is assisted over one and a half to two years (participation in at least three consecutive fairs). The pool of assisted companies was 20 in 1995 and will increase to a minimum of 30.

Shoe-producing sector. The overall objective is similar to the clothing sector: helping selected companies to produce their own collections. To this end, general open seminars on marketing and design are held in Bucharest and other important cities, and technical assistance is provided to individual managers in design and styling, product development, and marketing. On the same lines as for the clothing sector, companies are helped to participate at the international fair in Düsseldorf. In addition, technical assistance is provided at middle level by organizing practical courses and seminars for design and cutting at the Schooling Center Zlin in the Czech Republic; technical seminars on computer-assisted design in the cutting of leather are organized.

Each company is assisted for one and a half to two years (participation in at least three consecutive fairs). The pool of assisted companies was 10 in 1995 and is planned to increase to 15.

Furniture and wood-processing sector. The overall aim is to adapt Romanian furniture products to the style required in Western Europe, also raising the quality of products.

This is to be achieved by organizing fact-finding tours for interested German partners; and supporting participation by selected companies in the Fair in Cologne, first as visitors and finally as exhibitors. Contacts with professional associations of furniture manufacturers in Germany are also arranged. Finally, open seminars on marketing and design are organized, and the editing of a bilingual (German/English) catalogue of furniture producers.

Each company is assisted for two to three years (participation in at least three consecutive fairs). The pool of assisted companies was 10 in 1995 and will eventually increase to 15.

Food-processing industry. The aim is to promote Romanian traditional products in the western market, and improve the quality and packaging of these products. To achieve this aim, a group of wine manufacturers has been helped to participate at the Cologne fair as exhibitors, and a group of meat processing and diary enterprises has visited Cologne. Fact-finding tours have also been organized with potential customers or trade companies and joint venture partners.

Investment goods industry. The objective has been to find partners for sub-sector activities such as: cast iron and cast steel products, and welded steel structures. To this end, a bilingual (German/English) catalogue of cast-steel producers has been edited and distributed, listing 100 enterprises in 1995.

A group of cast-steel producers have been helped to participate in the Hanover fair, and an information trip has been arranged for specialists from Germany, including the visit of 16 potential buyers for cast/foundry products.

A symposium has been organized entitled: 'The metallurgical industry in Romania: partner of German manufacturers' at the Hanover fair, as well as open seminars for manufacturing enterprises at the Bucharest Fair.

General non-sector-oriented activities. The main targets have been to present Romanian companies and investment environment to potential foreign partners, and also to assist institutions involved in the reforms. The Romanian economic environment and companies have been presented in symposia organized in Potsdam, Hanover, Nuremberg, and Munich. Information tours have also been organized for experts and leaders of Romanian institutions to the equivalent institutions in Germany. Twinning partners have been sought for Romanian chambers of commerce with similar German chambers.

Handbooks have been edited and translated into Romanian on international fairs in Germany, and on the privatization process in transition countries. Local consultants have been involved in all steps of the IBD project.

Plans for the next two years

After one year of activity, the IBD project in Romania has the potential of becoming an important technical assistance tool for the development and strengthening of private business.

The project has several strengths, such as:

o The presence of a local IBD office and a resident co-ordinator provides continuity of programmes and an understanding of the local economic and legal framework.
o The links of the project to the chain of chambers of commerce and industry (41 chambers in Romania) gives optimum impact.

- The combined approach for each enterprise of successive seminars, on-the-spot training, participation in fairs, and short-term expertise, over two to three years, gives more effective help.
- The strong marketing character of the project is very suitable for the needs of Romanian companies.
- Providing financial support for participation at international fairs benefits small enterprises.
- A quick response to immediate requests in various fields is possible due to the large GTZ organization providing support.
- Action is at all levels: enterprises, associations and institutions.
- Access is available to other parallel German programmes (technical assistance and financing) which can offer supplementary tools for enterprises, and can shorten the application time.

The plan for the next two years includes increasing the number of assisted companies and diversifying the activities. The total number of enterprises assisted should reach 90, with an average of 4 short-term expert assignments per year for each enterprise; the number of fairs visited should be 8 per year; and the number of seminars organized should be 24 each year. Producer catalogues are to be drawn up for each main sector assisted. A programme for 'total quality management' was started in July 1995. The support to government institutions is to be expanded, according to the needs arising.

It is to be hoped that all these will finally contribute to the development of a truly competitive private economy of SMEs in Romania.

Developing markets for SME training activities in Slovenia

VILJENKA GODINA

EVEN DURING the socialist system, the SME sector in Slovenia employed about 7–10 per cent of the total workforce and contributed to the total GDP by some 3–5 per cent. Small private companies ('crafts'—the only legal form for private businesses in Slovenia and in the former Yugoslav economies) operated in both, in the manufacturing and in the service sectors.

However, since the first changes to the legislation were introduced at the end of the '80s, the SME sector in Slovenia has achieved fast growth. According to the data of the National Auditing Office, during a period of only three years, the number of small companies (crafts were excluded) increased from 6300 (end of 1990) to 30 000 (end of 1994). The number of private companies grew by over 80 per cent in 1991, over 60 per cent in 1992 and over 40 per cent in 1993. At the end of 1994, the total number of small private companies had reached 94 per cent of the total number of companies, and their employment contributed to total employment by about 20 per cent. In 1993, SMEs contributed to the growth of production by about 23 per cent, provided 42 per cent of total gross profit, and accounted for 11 per cent of exports. The fastest growth was in the service sector (trade, tourism, consulting and other business services). Currently, the majority of the recently established private companies employ on average less than two employees. However, some 5 per cent of the total number of companies achieved a very high growth rate (these are known as 'gazellas'). Among them, over 40 per cent operate in the manufacturing sector.

Some characteristics of Slovene entrepreneurs

In Slovenia, like the other former socialist countries, a fast growth of the SME sector has to some extent resulted from a declining state-owned sector. Slovene entrepreneurs have mostly come from three sources. The first is the former craft sector, which played an important role in the development of private SMEs during the 1980s, when the economic recession

Viljenka Godina is the Director of the Ekonomski Institut Maribor (Economic Institute of Maribor), Slovenia.

was developing, but private businesses had not yet been supported by adequate legislation.

Secondly, a large majority of the private SMEs which appeared in 1989 and at the beginning of the 1990s, were started by middle managers and highly-skilled employees who left large companies which had started to reduce their operations because of the economic crisis, restructuring, and the loss of former Yugoslav markets.

Thirdly, after the period of adjustment to the new circumstances (it took two years for the major economic legislation which provided the basis for the economic transition), several publicly owned large companies have started substantial downsizing and the first bankruptcies have already appeared. Consequently, the unemployment rate began to grow (and reached 17.3 per cent by the end of 1993). As a result, thousands of skilled and unskilled persons have been creating their own jobs by starting businesses.

The development of training and consulting activities for SMEs

Before the beginning of the 1990s, the SME support services were poorly developed. There were some publicly owned institutions which provided consulting and advisory activities to the SME sector (e.g. the group of academics at the Economic Faculty of Ljubljana, Celje Development Centre, the Economic Institute of Maribor, etc.), but their main programmes, also supported by the government, were focused on designing a suitable business environment for SME development. The formal management education systems were designed for employees rather than for employers, and provided no specific management courses designed to meet the needs of SME.

At the beginning of the '90s, the fast growth of SMEs immediately stimulated the establishment of hundreds of small private companies which have developed consulting, training and other professional assistance for SMEs. The SME 'boom' has, in fact, been to a great extent achieved by a fast development in such services. As in the other Eastern European countries, however, many of these companies developed their operations in 'financial engineering' (mediating or providing short-term financing on 'grey markets', since short-term money was hardly accessible from the banking system), but several serious training and consulting institutions have started their operations, too. Among them, GEA College, a modern entrepreneurship training centre in Ljubljana can be considered the most significant representative. Since its establishment in 1990, GEA college has developed over 150 carefully designed management training courses which have met the needs of Slovene SMEs and entrepreneurs. The seminars and workshops have been attended by thousands of participants from the SME sector.

In spite of the 'boom' in SMEs, and in spite of the supply of various carefully designed programmes, however, SME management professional assistance has not achieved the growth expected. Not only several smaller, SME-focused training and consulting institutions, but also the largest and the most popular Slovene SME management training centre have faced serious problems with selling their programmes to SMEs: soon after the first programmes were held, very few clients have been forthcoming. It seemed that further development was impossible, in spite of all the marketing instruments that were introduced to stimulate demand.

SME management skills—needs and demands

According to the experience of the Economic Institute of Maribor (EIM), which provides training courses combined with post-course consulting assistance, and runs its activities mainly in the north-east of Slovenia, the main reason for a poor market in SME programmes is not only the size of the Slovene market (about 120 000 potential clients), but primarily the gap that has occurred between the needs and the demands of SME management professional support.

The results generated from daily contacts with 'start-ups' and with existing SMEs, and from interviews and questionnaires which were used to evaluate EIM activities, have proved that almost all SME owners and managers are weak in managerial skills, starting from evaluating business ideas, defining products and markets, preparing business plans, accessing funding, to a lack of skills for the everyday managing of companies (including marketing, strategic planning, accounting, human resource management, and so on). Unfortunately, most entrepreneurs do not consider managerial skills as crucial to the success of their companies, and set their priorities for business development differently (e.g. access to cheap money has always been put first). Consequently, they are not ready to pay for management training or consulting services, and even worse, they sometimes consider attending courses or visiting a consultant a waste of time, even if services are free.

The situation can be explained better by considering some characteristics of the three main groups of entrepreneurs and some features of recent SME development.

Entrepreneurs coming from the previous craft sector, who still comprise some 40 per cent of all SMEs, are used to operating in an environment with almost no competition. Consequently, well-developed crafts (mostly in the manufacturing and construction industries) used to form a kind of monopoly in their markets. Most of them operated as sub-contractors to large companies. They did not need specific skills to sell their products, even if their businesses were not well managed (in any case, they were cheaper than large companies and provided good quality, as well). In the service sector the situation was similar: only a few companies would be operating in a local market. Thus, the competition used to be low.

Entrepreneurs who started operations at the beginning of the 1990s, faced the situation of 'unsatisfied markets': as the global Yugoslav market fell apart and Yugoslav companies disappeared from Slovene markets, Slovene entrepreneurs (mostly in the manufacturing sector) were encouraged to supply various substitutes. Several skilled employees and managers from larger companies started their own private businesses by using contacts and clients which they had developed while they were employed (wholesale and retail trade companies, various representatives and sales agents of foreign partners, etc.). These 'early starters' did not need to do much about their managerial skills: businesses started in the early nineties were filling the 'socialist black hole' and almost every business was very successful and sold well.

The third group of entrepreneurs, i.e., the unemployed population, are mostly coming from manual employment and company administration. Most of them consider self-employment the only way to ensure their jobs. However, most of them know nothing about management and are unfortunately often unable even to recognize the needs for additional knowledge. A great part of this population has always underestimated the importance of training and education, since there never used to be any need to change jobs, and has disregarded the value of professional services (influenced by a prevailing 'manufacturing philosophy').

Entrepreneurs who started their operations recently, however, have faced a different situation. Recently, some of the Slovene sectors have already started to show some features of competition. The first negative features were observed in the catering sector (small bars and cafés), and recently many small retail shops are in trouble. The negative signs are observed in the professional services, too, mostly in the companies which used to provide 'financial engineering'.

Helping SMEs to access the services

During the last five years, the government has introduced several SME support schemes with the purpose of facilitating further develoment in the SME sector in Slovenia. The range of available programmes is far too large to be considered fully in this chapter. The focus will be on programmes which resulted also in developing markets for training and consulting assistance for SMEs.

SME support schemes are provided by three Ministries: the Ministry of Economic Affairs, the Ministry of Labour, Family and Social Affairs and the Ministry of Science and Technology. While the last one supports technology transfer and facilitates the establishment of technology centres (for high-technology SMEs), the remaining two Ministries target SMEs in general. Both Ministries co-fund programmes which are developed by the training and consulting institutions and designed for specific target groups. No programme has been developed by the Ministry itself. The programmes developed by Slovene institutions are influenced by Western European and the USA programmes. Institutions which provide training and consulting programmes are invited to apply for co-funding by a published tender. The objectives and the target groups are globally defined, the share of co-funding too, while the methodology and the price are subject to competition. The programmes must meet the required criteria concerning quality, and the institution must provide experienced know-how.

Although both Ministries use similar elements in tendering the programmes, there are slight differences between them, too. The Ministry of Economic Affairs co-fund directly the institution or programme which has received an award. The tenders are restricted to the membership of the Association of SME Development Partners, established by the Ministry (the entry to this Association is free), and priority is given to individuals who have attended specific training courses for trainers (which are co-funded by the Ministry, too). After the evaluation of bids is completed by a specific SME Steering Committee and the decision on the programme or institution is made, the Ministry co-fund the programme. However, the reports on the programme execution have to be sent to the Ministry. Sometimes the evaluation made by the clients must be added to the reports, too.

The Ministry of Labour targets unemployed people and invididuals who are going to lose their jobs. The individuals are given specific 'vouchers' which have to be spent on training courses (some of them are compulsory) and on consulting assistance. The 'vouchers' are provided on the basis of a preliminary definition of a client's needs, which is done by the Ministry's staff. The providers of the training courses and the consulting assistance are selected annually by a specific committee. The individuals and institutions who compete for being short-listed as providers are invited by open public tender. No restrictions are made, but the applicants have to offer significant company experience and good CVs of the individuals who are to deliver the assistance. The clients are free to select the provider on the list or are recommended a specific provider according to their expertise.

The government co-funding schemes have substantially assisted with facilitating SME development. The individuals and SME managers are provided with a reliable service at a reasonable price, particularly because the providers and the programmes are generally carefully selected and only the best programmes are awarded. Although the complete data are not available, it has been estimated that during the last three years over 20 000 individuals and SME owners and managers have benefited from one form of government assistance or another.

Lessons to be learned: developing markets for SME training

There is another very important issue that has not often been mentioned to the public: by providing co-funding for management training and consulting assistance, the government has supported the development of institutions and individuals who design and deliver training courses and consulting assistance for SMEs. These institutions face a lack of demand for managerial training and consulting which has been affected by the impact of the small size of Slovene markets. Training and consulting companies are prevented from benefiting from a large scale: since the programmes have to be designed to meet the needs of the specific client target groups they often cannot be repeated (sold several times). The providers are handicapped by extremely high costs which cannot be covered by the normal price (e.g. market research, designing the programme according to the clients specific needs, preparing the materials, evaluating the programme, and so on). On the other hand, the price which the client could afford would be insufficient for the programme to achieve the required quality.

The aim of the government schemes is to provide SMEs with a good programme at a reasonable price and to assist the deliverers with further development of their programmes. It has been observed that the clients who have already benefited from some training or consulting assistance change their priorities in developing business activities and that they become aware of the importance of being properly assisted in developing business operations. Consequently, their (unrecognized) needs develop into real demands. The government thus helps with developing markets for management training and consulting assistance.

Although the impact of government schemes to develop training and consulting institutions and markets has often been neglected, seen from a long-range perspective this role of the government schemes will prove to have had a major effect on SME development.

The Foundation for the Promotion of Small and Medium Enterprises in Poland

KRYSTYNA GURBIEL

IN MOST MARKET-ECONOMY countries, the Small and Medium Enterprises (SME) sector provides a large share of GNP and employment. In Poland, however, its contribution to the national economy (excluding agriculture) over the past 40 years has been negligible. Therefore, the development of a strong, dynamic private SME sector is one of the key priorities of the Polish Government. To this end a special policy is being developed, aimed at making SMEs competitive in home and international markets.

Five main elements form the platform of this policy:

○ creating legal conditions conducive to the development of SMEs;
○ increasing the availability of finance;
○ enhancing the provision of know-how, training and information;
○ creating conditions to enable SMEs to upgrade their production capa-cities and the competitiveness of their products in national and inter-national markets;
○ creating conditions for consultation between SME representatives and government.

Special efforts have been made within this co-ordinated approach to define a stable pro-SME development policy and to create an institutional core for its communication, co-ordination and implementation. To this end the government has taken steps to establish the Polish Foundation for the Promotion and Development of Small and Medium Enterprises.

The creation of the foundation emphasizes that the continued deve-lopment of the SME sector lies at the very heart of the well-being of the economy and society, looking to the private SME sector as the driving force of free market development; as well as a natural cushion for some of the negative social and economic effects of the commercialization and privatization of state industry.

The Polish Foundation for the Promotion and Development of SMEs

The Polish Foundation for the Promotion and Development of Small and Medium Enterprises, which is currently in the process of being established

Krystyna Gurbiel is Director General of the Polish Foundation for the Promotion and Development of Small and Medium Enterprise, Poland.

has been given the mandate to proceed as the responsible agency for work within the sector. It has been given a high status and new priority in the government's approach to SME development. It has also been placed in direct contact and co-operation with private sector and business organizations, through a public-private foundation council and statutory commitments, forming a unique national mechanism devoted to SME growth. The foundation council has given the organization its full support in its role as the national catalyst of SME development; and the planned structure and positioning of the foundation provides the opportunity to develop partnership, rather than competitive relationships in the SME support field.

The mission of the foundation is to support the development of SMEs in Poland and to participate in the creation of a business environment and conditions conducive to this development.

Strategic and operational goals of the Foundation

The strategic goal of the foundation is to upgrade the competitiveness of Polish SMEs to levels enabling them to compete on home and foreign markets. This goal will be reached through programmes grouped around five operational objectives.

Access to an enabling environment. Creating a conducive environment for SME development is essential in those areas where the spheres of public and entrepreneurial activities meet, through institutions and organizations active in: preparing legal, political and fiscal regulations; representing the sector; and communicating and channelling information.

Access to know-how. The aim is to widen the access of SMEs to the fundamental sources of know-how necessary in establishing and developing businesses, through institutions and organzations providing services in the areas of: consulting and counselling; training; and standards.

Access to information. The access of SMEs should broaden to the pivotal sources of business information necessary for the functioning of enterprises on local and international markets, through institutions and organizations providing information services in: registering business activity; markets and certification; technology and standards; sources of finance; and aid programmes.

Access to financing. The aim is to deepen the access of SMEs to financing, through institutions and organizations providing financial resources, which will include: grants; credits and credit guarantees; other financial instruments.

Access to 'infrastructure'. The fundamental infrastructure for SMEs should be developed, especially in the areas of: access to facilities (buildings, machinery, equipment); and incubators.

Table 1. Strategic goal—the improvement of Polish SME competitiveness

Operational goal Upgrading the levels of private sector representation and acceptance of SME needs and interests	**Operational goal** Expanding the know-how of the SME sector and entrepreneurs	**Operational goal** Increasing the informational levels of the SME sector	**Operational goal** Increasing sustainability and growth of SME businesses through ensuring wider access, longer duration and lower cost of capital	**Operational goal** Improving the physical and technical capabilities of SMEs
Direct benefits o SME-aware government and public institutions o SME-aware public o SME organizations represented in government and public institutions o Business ethics and trade security established as basic reference point in doing business in Poland	**Direct benefits** o Increase in the markets served by SMEs o Viability of SMEs enhanced o SMEs potential for expansion improved o Entrepreneurs better equipped to succeed in business	**Direct benefits** o SMEs increasingly using available information resources o SMEs willing to provide information on business o SMEs knowledgeable of their business and their competitive position o SMEs aware of the need for good management information as competitive advantage o SMEs aware of assistance, support and financing possibilities o SMEs aware of issues and regulations affecting them in relation to Poland's entry to the EU	**Direct benefits** o Increased number of start-ups and higher rate of start-up survival o Enhanced capabilities of SMEs to expand and grow o SME investment in new and advanced technology increased o SME investment in capacity skills and quality increased o Working capital base for SMEs enlarged o Asset base of SMEs enlarged and improved	**Direct benefits** o Business expansion capabilities of SMEs improved o Improved product and process development in SMEs o SME personnel skills and capabilities improved o Production capacity of manufacturing SMEs increased o Quality of SME products improved o Enhanced service capability by service SMEs o Environmental impact of SMEs improved o Efficiency of SMEs improved

Table 1 continued

Products

o SME awareness training for government institutions
o SME policy development programme
o Fiscal regulations monitoring project
o Public procurement project
o Sub-contracting—issues and opportunities
o Cross-ministry regulation monitoring and SME impact project
o SME representation awareness programme
o SME membership enhancement programme for business organizations
o Business education for elementary schools
o Business as a career for – secondary school and – university graduates
o Public SME awareness campaign and contemporary issues of business and free market economy
o Business community input to the government budget project
o SME lobbying programme
o Networking for SMEs project
o SME organizations institution building

Products

o Start your own business counselling and training
o Education programme for entrepreneurs
o Advisory services for SMEs network
o Company Development Programme
o Technology development services
o Business development, counselling and training (strategic and change management)
o Sector-specific services
o Business-to-business training and counselling programme
o Mentoring services
o Consultancy initiative
o Product and service design services
o Marketing for small enterprises
o Quality development and assurance services
o Training programme in public procurement issues
o Business clustering programme
o Local market development programme

Products

o SME Information Centre
o Aid programmes on local, regional, national and international scenes
o National and regional business information
o Regional information points for SMEs
o Training for SMEs in accessing and using information for competitive advantage
o Training for information professionals in information provision for SMEs
o Information bulletins for SMEs
o Technological and sectoral information programme
o Information channels for European Union issues
o SMEs and the environment information programme
o Information on sub-contracting programme

Products

o Regional mutual guarantee schemes
o Revolving regional loan funds
o Equity funding for selected SME segments
o Interest subsidy programme
o 'Kick-start' grant programme
o Re-equipment and development grant programme
o New financial instruments development and utilization programme
o SME awareness and lending training programme for bank management and staff
o Banking efficiency and new technology programme
o Re-guarantee scheme
o Banker/business workshops
o Retained income training and counselling programme for SMEs
o Treasury management programme for MEs
o International investment for SMEs
o Financial linkage programme

Products

o Specialist SME sector incubators
o Sectoral product and process upgrade programme for SMEs (value engineering)
o Technical skills development programme
o Regional business parks programme
o R&D facilities programme
o Databank and unwanted assets adaptation programme
o Interactive skill and technology development programme
o SME adoption programme
o Technology transfer for SMEs
o Technological park programme

154

Key factors in the foundation's operations

The foundation's strategy was developed in response to the needs of Polish small and medium enterprises, with the aim of expanding the creation of quality services and support, and facilitating access to them. The strategy is based on the concept of partnership, that is the foundation will seek to fulfil its functions through equivalent and long-term alliances with existing organizations active in the field of SME support.

The foundation is an apolitical and quasi-governmental organization, whose role in relation to the Ministry of Industry and Trade and other ministries and government institutions lies in implementation, information and consultation. The foundation will endeavour to play the role of linking SME and entrepreneurs' organizations with government and international institutions. An important element in the implementation of the foundation's strategy will be based on integrating the activities of other organizations and institutions in SME development with the aims of government policy and the priorities of business self-government. This approach will allow for greater co-ordination and the concentration of effort, while at the same time existing programmes and activities will be involved. By definition, the field covered by the Foundation will be narrower than the fields of interest of other organizations working for SMEs within broader remits (chambers of commerce, associations of entrepreneurs and employers, Regional Development Agencies), but at the same time it will be more in depth (as eventually it will include all areas of relevance to the activities and well-being of SMEs).

In its work the foundation will build on the experiences and achievements of other organizations and programmes, especially in the areas of project management and the use of 'market' mechanisms and incentives to ensure effective public activities. At the same time the foundation—which is responsible for public funds—will guarantee fully professional and transparent management of funds and support projects.

The composition of the foundation

The foundation is composed of a council, board of management and staff of experienced young Polish professionals. The council is representative of the key actors in the public and private sectors. The foundation management and staff have experience in developing, implementing and evaluating programmes and projects supporting the development of SMEs in Poland. These executives have been responsible for implementing two PHARE programmes in Poland involved in SME and private sector development. The implementation of these programmes has resulted in the establishment of some 32 Business Support and Information Centres, support to the Polish Chamber of Commerce and 12 regional chambers of commerce and the co-financing of training programmes for the SME sector.

With the experience of the management and staff and the support of a representative council, the foundation will form the key agency for the support and development of the Polish SME sector and play an important role in implementing the government's policy for the sector. The foundation's operations and programmes are funded by government, national organizations and international donors.

The foundation—linking the SME sector and government

As stated, working both with the government and the SME sector, mainly through its organizations, and serving as a channel of communication between these actors, is seen by the foundation as one of the essential requirements for its success. The foundation will undertake this task in three principal ways.

The council of the foundation. The council of the foundation is the controlling body of the organization. Under its statute, it is chaired by a representative of the Minister of Industry and Trade, with members representing three other ministries, and seven non-government organizations: the National Chamber of Commerce, the Chamber of Crafts and Small Business, the National Association of Regional Development Agencies, the Polish Agency for Regional Development, the Business Centre Club (an organization of leading businessmen), the Association of Polish Banks, one of the big Polish banks (Powszechny Bank Kredytowy). Therefore, it covers a wide representation of both public and private institutions active in the field of SME development. The council is a supervisory and policymaking body for the foundation, empowered to take the most important decisions: setting the direction of its activities and rules for their implementation, approving annual plans and budgets, as well as annual reports, and so on.

Apart from these functions, directly related to the activities of the foundation, the council—as agreed by the Ministry of Industry and Trade and the council members—will serve as a forum for the exchange of information, views and discussion between the representatives of the government and the SME sector on wider issues important for the development of the sector, and particularly on government policy towards the sector. In this way the Foundation Council will play the role of a working channel of communication between these actors. It will greatly assist not only the successful operation of the foundation, but also the development of a better understanding of SME needs and concerns by relevant government agencies and ministries.

Partner Organizations. The council, although the most important, is not the only instrument enabling the Foundation to fulfil its function as a link between the government and the SME sector. The foundation will also achieve this by working in co-operation with local, regional and national organizations representing the SME sector and providing services to it.

156

One of the essential elements of the foundation's operations will be assistance aimed at enhancing the skills and capabilities of these organizations and institutions to enable them to serve the needs of the SME sector better. The Foundation's programme will be developed in consultation with and implemented through these organizations. In this way, the foundation will 'translate' SME policy into practical measures and programmes aimed directly at the development of the sector and the institutions which support it. Conversely, feedback from the sector, the institutions and the implementation programmes will be channelled back for input into the creation, adaptation and development of future policy and programmes.

Undertaking SME sector studies. The foundation will undertake studies on a regular basis of the SME sector and its support institutions in order to keep informed of their changing needs. These will form an essential element of the foundation's market intelligence programme, aimed at developing an appropriate response in its activities to the changing needs of the sector. These studies will also be used to provide input to the government and to the formulation of institutional policy and programmes in relation to the sector. Particular areas of study will be: commercial and industrial law; fiscal law and regulations; banking law and regulations; disclosure of information; business registration; technology development and innovation; and sectoral and segmental studies.

These studies will greatly benefit the council of the foundation in considering the development of the foundation's strategy. The results of the studies will be shared with partner organizations to enable concerted efforts to be made to influence government policy and to create a cooperative aproach to addressing issues affecting the development of the SME sector.

Conclusion

The above gives a brief picture of the Polish Foundation for SME Promotion and Development, the reason for its establishment and its strategy and objectives. The foundation has before it a formidable task to achieve its objectives; however, in undertaking this task it has been provided with the appropriate structure and staff, has the full backing of the Polish Government, and has as its council members representatives of those organizations and institutions, public and private, which are the key to the implementation of a coherent and relevant SME policy.

The foundation therefore represents the key component for the implementation of government policy for small business, established as it has been not only to implement policy but to act as the conduit for SME input to that policy and through its council to provide a forum representative of all the interests of the SME sector through which the voice of the small business entrepreneur can be heard.

The Polish–British Enterprise Project (PBEP)

MIKE HARDY

POLAND IS EMERGING rapidly as a competitive and decentralized market economy, though it is acknowledged that some regions, including eastern Poland, are lagging behind. The growth of small, medium and microenterprises will have an important impact on regional transition and growth, but difficulties with access to finance and effective business support services are acting as major constraints on the formation and growth of SMEs.

The Polish–British Enterprise Project (the PBEP), financed by the UK Know-How Fund, was started in the autumn of 1994 to provide an integrated programme of support to address these constraints. The PBEP is a large and innovative project, targeted on two selected provinces (*voivodships*) in eastern Poland, Lublin and Bialystok. These areas were selected by the Government of the Republic of Poland as suitable beneficiaries on the basis of their relatively depressed economies and emerging SME populations.

The five-year project combines technical assistance with funding for financial and enterprise support instruments. The project is being delivered through, and will strengthen the capacity of, networks of regional and local business support organizations in each province.

The PBEP objectives

The stated aim is 'to accelerate the economic development of Bialystok and Lublin by facilitating the development of SMEs within the context of the transformation of Poland to a competitive and decentralized market economy'. The primary objective, then, is to promote the development of SMEs in both provinces. This objective is achieved through three independent but complementary strategic aims:

○ to consolidate and develop the performance of existing SME support services;
○ to provide new instruments to tackle the constraints on SMEs' formation and growth;
○ to foster the efficient operation of markets, where high-quality suppliers of information and services are able to meet the needs of knowledgeable

Mike Hardy is the Director, Private Sector Development, at The British Council, and has been working on the Polish–British Enterprise Project, financed by the UK Know-How Fund.

buyers in SMEs who are willing to pay a commercial price for a quality of service they value.

The methods employed and the policies developed within the programme to achieve these strategic aims have implications for the underlying theme of the PBEP to foster market relations and market forces. These action strategies are being realized through a co-ordinated package of financial and technical assistance with four interlinked programmes. The business development programme (BDP), promotes and supports networks of business services organizations and provides incubator facilities and workspace in each region. A market development programme (MDP) helps to train and equip SMEs to secure new markets, both at home and overseas, thereby creating new demand for the region's products. An equity investment fund (EIF), is planned to address the undercapitalization of SMEs in the targets areas by providing medium-term finance in the form of equity participation. Finally, a loan guarantee fund (LGF), is designed to tackle the problems that SMEs often encounter in providing collateral for loans sought from the commercial banks.

Delivery of the project in each target area is being overseen by an Apex Co-ordinating Agency (ACA), formed within existing local development foundations in Lublin and Bialystok, working largely in partnership with existing or new business support agencies and intermediaries to execute the programmes.

The expected duration of the PBEP is five years, by the end of which time the executive agencies supported by the project would expect to be self-sustaining, drawing on a combination of revenues and other grants. The donor's operational association with the programme will then terminate.

Coverage of the programme

The programmes are open to all off-farm sectors (except, for example, tobacco) and operate at two distinct levels. Firstly, individual enterprises and clusters of business enterprises are actively targeted in each area's predominant industrial sectors (food/agro/timber processing and construction), together with those engaged in exporting and tourism. Secondly, the programmes respond reactively to businesses in other sectors.

Although the programmes are open to established, private enterprises (with 51 per cent or more of their equity in Polish hands), employing between 1 and 100 full-time equivalents, firms employing between 5 and 50 full-time equivalents are the primary target group. Enterprises of similar size owned by the provinces or local authorities and undergoing privatization are also eligible. The Business Development Programme is additionally available to business start-ups.

Constraints affecting SMEs

The programme design reflects the experience of economic restructuring and transition showing that three primary constraints operate to slow the development of SMEs in market economies. These are: a weak enabling environment for SME development; difficulties in gaining access to competent business support and advice; and difficulties in securing finance, either because of exacting collateral requirements, the high cost of borrowing, or risk-averse, short-term lending horizons. Measures which stimulate and sustain a rapid growth of SMEs invariably address all three constraints. It has been found that approaches designed to deal with one factor in isolation from the others are consistently ineffective, undermined by the mutual interdependence of the constraints.

The fieldwork undertaken prior to project inception confirmed the impact of these constraints within the local areas. In particular: the business support provision in both areas was highly limited; the difficulties encountered by SMEs in accessing finance closely mirrored those experienced elsewhere in Poland and other developing market economies; and many SMEs in the target areas were failing to exploit fully market opportunities both at home and abroad. The PBEP, then, provides a co-ordinated and focused approach by means of four complementary SME-support programmes.

The Business Development Programme

This programme aims to:

○ improve the coherence of existing business development services;
○ consolidate the competence of current business development organizations, helping them to take on new activities or complementing them with new agencies where this is necessary; and
○ provide a high visibility for the delivery of business development activities through a network of business incubators in each area.

The Equity Investment Fund (EIF) and Loan Guarantee Fund (LGF)

The main objectives of these funds is to stimulate the growth and long-term viability of SMEs by improving their access to finance.

The EIF provides access to medium-term finance in the form of equity participations. The funds will be used flexibly and creatively to finance a range of SME development stages, although the primary target is to facilitate increases in the productive or operational capacities of existing firms. The EIF provides no direct up-front grant to individual enterprises. It is expected that the fund will make a return from successful enterprises by selling the equity at market-based rates after the firm has achieved profitability. Sales will be in the first instance to the enterprise or if not feasible to other investors. The target scenario for the fund is to achieve an increasing survival rate over time from 40 to 60 per cent of assisted enterprises and to earn a real rate of return of 20 per cent over 4 years from the surviving enterprises.

The LGF, on the other hand, will improve the ability of SMEs to access loans by stimulating bank lending to SMEs. A primary objective is to encourage better training and awareness of small business in banks, and to tie in the role of business advice and support to the process of financing SMEs. The LGF will operate on a commercial basis and under acceptable assumptions of failure rates and lending multiples, will be sustainable.

The Market Development Programme

This programme aims to:

o stimulate SME growth by equipping firms with the information and skills to secure new, and develop existing, markets at home and abroad;
o provide low-cost expert marketing consultancies;
o research and evaluate domestic and export markets;
o write and implement marketing strategies;
o encourage the development of markets for private sector marketing consultancy in each of the areas; and
o develop international business-to-business links.

It should be noted that strong emphasis is being placed on creating or enhancing the capacity of existing local business support organizations to deliver these programmes. Also, in analysing the impact of the programmes, an assessment was made of the extra value-added which the project overall would need to generate from year 5 for the following 10 years to justify the initial investment ($19m). With a discount rate of 12 per cent, the project would need to generate additional value-added each year of about $4.4 million. Assuming a target of surviving SMEs supported of 150, with an average employment of 10, this translates to a value-added per employee of about $3000, and is considered to be an achievable target.

Strategic issues and early lessons

In practice there are many more issues that need to be addressed than are covered in the broad strategy and implementation schemas outlined in the project memorandum. Factors such as the institutional structures being created, their form, role and function within their regions, the process by which the 'ownership' of the project and its impact will be transferred to local Polish management and, importantly, the way in which a five-year programme to assist regional economic development through the promotion of SMEs interrelates with the broader issues of transformation to a market economy in Poland, which may take a much longer period.

161

The 'vision' for the longer term (both for the PBEP and its impact) revolves around the nature of the institutions that are eventually established. A key question concerns the long-term role and status of the ACAs and their sponsoring development foundations, including the relationships between the ACAs, their parent foundations and other organizations or structures created or supported under the auspices of the PBEP.

The project design takes full account of the existing business support organizations and their activities in each area. In line with this, the project's operational emphasis is to complement and strengthen the performance of existing SME-support services, and only provide new instruments to tackle constraints where these are not already being addressed. These partnerships will have a significant impact on the project's performance.

Early experience within the project has confirmed the importance of the inception period, which has allowed considerable attention to be paid to a thorough analysis and articulation of SME needs, and of the capacities and attitudes of key partners and intermediaries. Increased attention has also been placed on the institution-building element, particularly of the two crucial Apex Co-ordinating Agencies.

Finally, the strength of the project design lies in its co-ordinated and integrated approach to addressing the full range of local constraints to SME development and growth in the two areas. Strong project management has been essential to ensure that the different project components do not develop separately, creating eight projects rather than one.

The employment service's assistance to small and medium business in Russia

V. PONOMAREV AND NATALIA GRIBANKOVA

THE ECONOMIC SITUATION in the Moscow district and the state of the labour market makes the development of various forms of enterprise and self-employment into a task of the utmost importance. The high scientific potential and the educational level of the population creates propitious conditions for the development of small and medium business. Regional employment programmes and similar programmes throughout the district also provide for the resolution of social objectives, in particular helping the population to adapt themselves to work in the new economic conditions.

Moscow district (oblast), as is well known, has a high level of machine building, and a developed defence industry, the conversion of which is proving difficult; there are also many textile enterprises in the district. The most extreme employment situation arises in the scientific cities, of which there are more than 20 in the district. Agriculture is also going through a difficult time. However, regardless of the risk inherent in business formation and the unpredictability of the results, many inhabitants of the Moscow district are currently striving to set up their own business so as to solve the problems of unemployment.

Problems facing small business development

In co-operation with executive agencies and also with organizations involved in the creation and support of small and medium business, the employment services have taken the first steps to assist business. There are a whole set of problems on the path to the development of small and medium business in the district. The chief among the existing problems is the need to re-establish the tradition of private business, lost for 70 years, and to foster a psychological reorientation of people's thinking.

A lack of background in private business demands special training and the acquisition of practical experience, for which time and appropriate conditions are needed. In addition, there are serious supply problems for new small businesses in obtaining the materials and labour they need.

V.A. Ponomarev is the Director of the Moscow district centre of the employment service of the Russian Federation, and N. Gribankova is a senior official of the service in Zhukovsky, near Moscow.

163

Also, the current system of taxation does not encourage the development of private business at any level. A large number of promising business projects are also being hampered by the lack of investment by domestic and foreign investors. Such a situation is being exacerbated by the lack of start-up capital to buy the necessary equipment, raw materials and the rent of premises.

The system of property ownership and of health and life insurance for members of a private business organization have not been fully worked out and the inadequate legal framework also seriously restrains the pace and scale of organization of small and medium business.

Overcoming all these problems is only possible by the combined efforts of state and non-state business partners. Some of them need decisions on the federal level, others on the regional level, and it is also possible to resolve many of them successfully at the municipal level.

How the employment service is helping small business formation

In the work of the employment service, assistance for business activity and the self-employment of citizens is one of the basic focuses of employment policies, and is provided in the following ways:

- o financial support on a competitive basis for business people who create jobs;
- o assistance and financial help to the unemployed to develop their own business, or to become self-employed;
- o training and retraining of the unemployed in activities connected with business;
- o creation of the infrastructure for the adaption of people to the market economy and the support of business activity;
- o developing connections with foreign firms who are prepared to co-operate and invest in the development of small and medium business in Russia; and
- o participation in the district programmes of support for enterprise development and the integration of the efforts of various district-level organizations in the work of promoting small and medium businesses in the Moscow district.

Transition to a competitive basis of financial support for employers who provide additional jobs for the unemployed furthers the growth in the number who wish to enter commerce and found their own business. A lot of attention has been paid to those who have been paid off, and the unemployed who wish to start up their own business. Various ways of providing help have been used: the provision of advice on legal questions concerning the founding of one's own business, help in the preparation of registration documents, payment from the resources of the employment fund for

164

expenditure on the registration of an enterprise or of an individual trade, allocation of subsidies, and so on.

In 1994, with the help of the employment service, 94 people opened their own business, which was nearly twice as many as in the previous year; 556 people became self-employed, the majority of whom received financial assistance from the employment service. The employment service carries out its training and retraining of the unemployed by instructing in the basics of business, accountancy, management, marketing, and other forms of individual trade as part of professional training for people engaged in business. Every fifth person sent for training learns a profession connected with the development of small business. In 1994 around 2000 unemployed underwent training in the basics of business, and more than 1500 of them are now self-employed or have opened their own business.

Professional understanding of and psychological support for the unemployed is very important at this stage. This part of the work of the district employment service provides help in the choice of profession, based on the inclinations and potentials of the unemployed. The psychologist helps to assess personal qualities and advise which sort of work is suited to the client. Attention has been paid to giving professional advice to the unemployed, with the aim of persuading them to work in small and medium business or to start a business. These sessions differ from the usual advisory work of the employment services.

Founding the Social and Business Centres

A basic focus in the work of the employment service is helping to develop organizations which support business, and which aim to help the population adjust to the new reality of the changed labour market.

In order to seek out and attract partners to joint activity in the towns of the district for solving the unemployment problem, the Moscow district employment service became the founder (co-founder) of new bodies— business centres for the adaption of the population to the changed needs of the labour market.

The business centres are aimed at helping local agencies reduce unemployment, carry out socially significant projects, implement co-operative programmes for the creation and preservation of jobs, and, above all, support new private business.

The original idea was for the establishment of business incubators; however, Russian conditions and the traditions of social protection led to a significant broadening of functions, aimed at the social support of unemployed citizens and their adaptation to the labour market. The first business centre was created in 1993 in Orekhovo-Zuevski and currently eight more centres have been created. Out of the nine social and business centres (SBCs), two have been operating for more than a year, and the rest from two to six months. More than 2.5 thousand people made use of the services of the SBCs in 1994, and more than half of them dealt with issues of business activity.

There has been some success in the Moscow district in establishing new businesses. There are already barbers, shoemakers, shops, sewing and knitting units, and bakers, begun with the assistance of the district employment service and supported by the social and business centres. Several dozen miccroenterprises have been established with the assistance of the employment service and the SBCs, which is encouraging working from home.

Using foreign expertise

Particular attention has been given to the arrangement of mutually profitable links with foreign partners to attract resources and experience to support the economic reforms and the acceleration of the development of business and self-employment in the Moscow district. Centres for business partnership and business support services, established jointly with Canadian advisers in fostering and the development of social and economic links, are operating through the initiative of the Moscow district employment centre. The project 'The future of urban association', recognized in Canada, USA and Britain as a project aimed at the resolution of the problem of increasing unemployment and the enhancement of business activity, is a basic part of the work of the centres. Centres have been established in the city of Zhukovski, and in the municipalities of Orekhovo-Zuevski, Voskresenski, Pushkinski and Mytishchinski.

The assistance of Canadian specialists and their help have enabled the business development work to be raised to a high quality. A series of documents have been issued in the centres on:

○ the technology of the centre's work;
○ official instructions for managing staff;
○ way of receiving credits; and
○ materials and recommendations for how to repay the credits.

Out of five centres for the development of business, four were created immediately as structural sub-divisions of the employment centres and one in Orekhovo-Zuevski as a constituent element of a social and business centre.

The first service for enterprise support was established with the assistance of Canadian advisers in the city of Zhukovski in March 1994. The basis of the project is the need for a sub-division in the structure of the employment centre for the development of business and the support of enterprise. Various bodies have been attracted to work on this project including the urban administration, and various social organizations such as the city council of trade unions, the society of disabled people, and Afghan veterans.

166

Financial support

The enterprise support service also provides consultative and investment help for small business. The basic sources of finance are: the resources of the employment fund and of the fund established by the Canadians. Investment support in the form of loans has been received by 9 small business enterprises, through which 102 jobs have been created. Investment for the support of five particular projects has been received from Canadian resources. Financial help has been given only for the creation of jobs on socially significant projects.

The enterprise support service also provides advice on business issues, helps draw up the set of founding documents, and explains issues of financial management, market analysis, and personnel questions (on this they work closely with the psychological service working in the employment centre).

Since the start of the business support service, three people have set up their own business with the help of the service, for the establishment of which subsidies to the amount of a year's unemployment benefit were given to them.

In practice the business support service tackles three basic tasks:

○ it provides information services for any inhabitant of the city;
○ it provides advisory and other services to those wishing to work for themselves, i.e. for individuals working without forming a legal entity; and
○ it supports already existing small and medium businesses.

Four other business support centres were opened at the beginning of 1995 and are in the trial period of setting up and working out a mechanism for carrying out the basic ideas of the project. It is still too early to talk about any achievements. Extensive and protracted preparatory work preceded the opening of the centres, in which the Canadian specialists, local administration, representatives of business circles and employees of the employment agency and other bodies took part. On the basis of an analysis of the economic situation and a public opinion survey, concrete conclusions were reached for each of the municipalities on the expediency of opening centres for business partners and the development of the project in the future. At present the credit resources for newly established centres have not been provided by the Canadian partners.

The municipal administration, the employment centre, the social and business centre and business bodies took part in the implementation of the Russian-Canadian project carried out in Orekhovo-Zuevski. It is proposed that the basic sources of finance for the project will be the federal employment fund and the investment of the Canadian partners. The project is aimed at organizations which support business, which encourage small enterprises and the creation of infrastructure for helping in the development of business.

A public opinion survey of all strata and groups of the population was carried out, the outcome of which clarified their attitude to business, the need for more business organizations, and other factors which are hindering the development of business.

Voskresenski business development centre

The business development centre of Voskresenski provides economic and legal help in the form of advice to businessmen and the unemployed. Help in planning commercial activities and in drawing up business plans is given. The business development centre has also begun to carry out market research for investigating the volumes and patterns of demand in Voskresenski City.

Issues concerning the financing of employers and of businessmen are to be found in the advisory board's introduction. This is the highest decision-making body of the centre and consists of representatives of the employment service, administration, social organizations, businessmen and others.

Financial help was given to the co-operative agricultural firm 'Luch' for expanding the production of chicken meat; the resources came from the employment centres, jointly with the administration of the city of Voskresenski.

The development of the centre has the following objectives: the broadening of the range and quality of advisory services; the incubation of businesses that are starting up; more active search for investors (attracting bank capital and insurance companies to the financing of future projects); the establishment of regional investment companies; and the setting up leasing companies.

The Pushkinski centre

The concrete goals and aims of the Pushkinski centre for assisting business development are connected with the support of the traditional branches of industry; with the study of the basics of business and accounting for those citizens who are interested in the establishment of their own enterprise; with the drawing up of business plans and with financial help for the provision of new jobs on a concrete basis.

Active work on developing documents to guide the business centre in its activity is being carried out at the moment, and computers and suitable software for working out and estimating business plans are being acquired.

Six entrepreneurs have come to the Pushkinski centre with projects. Three were refused because of the insolvency of the projects, two were recommended to do some more work on the projects and one project was allowed to compete for funding. This bakery enterprise envisages the creation of 39 additional jobs and is socially beneficial for the town.

Lessons learned

On the whole the project could support more promotional action to develop small and medium business. At the same time, more serious market research and much deeper study of the focus of business is essential at the preparatory stage, to allow the strategy and tactics of the business partner centres to be drawn up taking into account the special features of each municipality.

There is a need to finish working out a strategy for centre staff conduct. The establishment of a Russian-Canadian school for the training of the centres' staff, the establishment of close contacts between the Canadian and Russian partners and the organization of internships for the managers of the business partner centres in Canadian business centres would increase the efficiency of the work of the staff.

There have been a number of cases where the provision of credit from the resources of Canadian partners for particular entrepreneurial projects is essential. It is important to set the conditions and mechanism for the provision of credit provided by the Canadians in more detail.

Taking into account the complicated system of taxation in Russia, it would also be important to consider the proposal to conclude an inter-governmental agreement on taxes on the Canadian funds provided for the implementation of entrepreneurial projects, or an increase in the funds provided, to take into account the taxes that have been paid.

The first business partner centre is not yet two years old, and practical results are already visible. It can be said with confidence that these new bodies working in co-operation with the employment service will find their place in the region's socio-economic framework and with favourable conditions should become influential centres in their own cities or municipalities for all social groups.

Higher education institutions' involvement with business development projects in Romania and Krasnoyarsk, Russian Federation

ROBERT R. TOLAR

THE WASHINGTON STATE UNIVERSITY Small Business Development Center Office of International Programs operates two projects in the emerging democracies of Europe and Asia. The programmes are quite similar in nature and design; however, they have been in operation for differing lengths of time: the Romanian project is in its fourth year of operation, and the programme has finished year one in Krasnoyarsk.

The underlying theme of these projects is 'Economic development can best occur in a setting in which the private sector, the public sector, and higher education work together'. Both our strengths and our weaknesses come from the emphasis placed on higher education. Colleges and universities of Central and Eastern Europe, Russia, and the Newly Independent States have been around much longer than most of the businesses in those nations, and certainly longer than the governments now in power. For that matter, many institutions have seen entire systems of government come and go, yet they remain remarkably the same as they have always been.

Changes made within higher education may last much longer than if change were attempted within a particular government agency or a chamber of commerce alone. It is not easy to change a university curriculum, however, or the attitude and mind-set of a faculty, and this is as true of the United States as it is of Romania and Russia.

Working with universities may bring about long-term change by altering the curriculum, but that in itself does little in the short term. In an attempt to have immediate impact, the Washington State University Small Business Development Center provides management training seminars to start-up and existing businesses, and to government agency officials. The Center is in the process of training university administrators and faculty in the merits of land grant, or extension education.

Washington State University first became involved in Romania in 1991 as part of the USAID-funded Management Training and Economics Education initiative. During the first two years the Washington State University Small Business Development Center worked jointly with the University of Washington: the Small Business Development Center providing the management training and the University of Washington

Robert Tolar works at the Washington State University, Small Business Development Centre, and has also been involved with the setting up of the SBDC in Romania.

of Washington concentrating on the economics education component. Our Romanian partners were the Polytechnic University of Bucharest and the Academy of Economics, also in Bucharest.

Project description

In 1993 Washington State University strengthened its co-operation with the Polytechnic University of Bucharest. The Center received one of the four 'Center of Excellence' grants awarded by USAID. Basically, the CBE (Center for Business Excellence) project consisted of four components: (1) counsellor training; (2) management training for privatization, and continuing education through an extension or 'land-grant' model; (3) human resource management development; and (4) information resource development.

The counsellor training programme is conducted at four sites: two in Bucharest; one in Timisoara; and one in Craiova. Business faculty members complete a series of training modules on management, marketing and sales, including advertising, finance, planning, and personnel. They then co-counsel clients with American counsellors, teach in a team with members of the Washington State team, and eventually counsel and train on their own. They may be certified as professional business counsellors, capable of counselling start-ups and existing businesses; and master business counsellors, qualified to train other counsellors. To date, there are 27 professional business counsellors and 8 master business counsellors in the programme.

Management Training for Privatization (MTP)

The second round of the Management Training for Privatization (MTP) programme has recently finished. The first round consisted of a series of seminars presented at three sites in the country to top managers of 14 firms on the list for privatization. The objective of the programme was to enhance the management skills of each company so as to make the firms more attractive to potential investors, customers, and suppliers. An outcome was a collection of presentation materials—transparencies, spreadsheets, and company histories—suitable for immediate use.

An independent evaluation was conducted on the MTP programme in the summer of 1994, and adjustments were made as a result. The new programme spends less time on the preparation of materials, and concentrates more on team building, personnel management, and attempting to address problems within the companies themselves. The aim is to try to convince firm managers that funds for expansion, upgrading, and new product development will be more likely to come from savings they make in-house than from investments from abroad.

Human Resource Management (HRM) Development

A third component of the Romanian project is the establishment of a centre where personnel managers or general managers are trained in some of the basics of human resource management, i.e., how to do job assessments, how to write job descriptions, how to interview and select the right personnel, how to develop benefit packages, and so on.

Another purpose of the HRM centre is to serve as a placement centre for university graduates. While personnel managers are learning how to interview and select the right personnel, university students are learning how to prepare for the job search, how to write resumés, and how to present themselves in the best possible light during an interview.

Information Resource Development

One of the most critical areas of need is the dearth of up-to-date information on technology, markets, and suppliers. There is a need to train business men and women in how to access information which is available; institutions of higher education on how to begin developing information resources in-country; and government agencies on how to support such activities.

Lessons learned

The first rule that has been tested and proven is: 'The map is not the territory'. No matter how much is read, how many predeparture training sessions the staff go through, or how many briefings are provided by former residents of Russia and Romania, upon arrival nothing is as expected. And while things really are different in Romania from the USA, the host country nationals may not fully understand how different. There is a Chinese proverb to the effect: 'If you want to know what water is, don't ask a fish'. Those who work in Central and Eastern Europe, Russia, and the Newly Independent States might do well to heed that advice.

From time to time expatriate advisers are criticized for 'not understanding the situation here', or failing to realize that 'that's not the way we do things here'. The immediate reaction to such criticism is often to accept it as true and try to make adjustments. In some cases, however, the critic may be like a fish trying to describe water! A view from the outside is often helpful in projects in the emerging democracies.

It is obvious that there may be an unrealistic view of how businesses operate in the West—examples are plentiful of such views. A commonly held view is that businesses are started in the West by going to the bank and telling them how much money is needed; or that a business idea is sent to the government, and the funds come by return mail.

Businesses are started the same way the world over: with money from savings, from family, and from friends. Bank loans generally come after those investments, despite what entrepreneurs in the emerging nations believe. It is essential therefore that SME loan funds require a minimum equity prior to any loan, and whenever possible, this requirement should be made known to all. To do anything less is to place start-up businesses in a false world.

Some businesses which find financing too quickly or too easily may lose focus, and may become overly diversified too soon. This phenomenon has been observed many times and has led to the conclusion that loans should be tied to required counselling activities, i.e., monthly or bi-monthly counselling sessions should be made a part of the loan repayment programme.

Counsellors are not the answer to all business problems, however, regular meetings with a business counsellor make business owners better planners, and help them identify potential problems earlier than they might otherwise. Counsellors, without the vested interest of owners, may be better able to offer objective suggestions.

It still seems astonishing the nonchalant manner in which governments, donor agencies, and enterprise funds deal with information. If they provided accurate, timely, and meaningful information regarding loan availability, a far more positive relationship with SMEs could be established. Rumours cannot be totally controlled, but nevertheless, accurate and straightforward announcements could be made regarding financial assistance to SMEs. If nothing else, brief announcements stating the earliest date loans will be available, specifically what types of businesses will be eligible, and other to-the-point information should be made.

Many people knew, but others did not want to hear, that: 'change will take much longer than was originally thought'. Certainly we at the Small Business Development Center were naive to believe that our objectives would be met within the first three years. We understood that universities would be difficult to change, but we were certainly wrong in believing that the mind-set of the population would be so difficult to change.

Another lesson learned is that bureaucracy may spring up where you least expect it. The problems encountered have not come from USAID or other donor agencies, nor to any great extent from the host countries; rather, difficulties have come from institutions with which we work and from our own institution, the Small Business Development Center. Patience is needed for projects both in Romania and in Russia. Things take longer to accomplish in those countries than they do in the United States. This is not always because of red tape. Too often it seems the reason for the delay is simply because someone did not want to do what was necessary, and hoped that the problem would just go away.

Sometimes in the projects it seems to be like the blind leading the blind: nobody has helped anyone convert to a market economy before. There is a lack of knowledge about how to get through the transition to a full market economy. Advisers may know where they would like to see companies once the transition is over, but it is very difficult for them to understand the subtleties of operating in the present economy. There is much to be learned about how companies are operating in the present situation, and how the programme should be adapted accordingly.

Up to 1995, the project councillors have advised over 7000 business owners and managers at the four SME development offices in Romania and the one in Krasnoyarsk. Attendance at seminars at several sites has been approximately 10 000.

Challenges to face and future plans

Future plans are to fully institutionalize the programme at the Polytechnic University of Bucharest so that business counselling will continue; seminars will be offered at numerous sites in the country; new counsellors will be trained; a human resource management centre will be fully operational, serving also as a placement centre for university students; and a research and information centre will be fully operational, providing technological information in support of business counselling.

One of the biggest challenges we face is in gaining more municipal and regional support for the centres so as to ensure sustainability. It is important that officials in Bucharest, Timisoara, and Craiova gain a sense of ownership of the centres—and are convinced of the role the various centres can play in economic development.

A problem faced early in the projects was the desire for business owners and managers to be counselled only by American counsellors. With the certification process fully implemented, and professional and master business counsellors providing services, that problem has been successfully addressed. As a result of this experience, minimum standards for SME counsellors and assistance providers should be established so that entrepreneurs and business owners throughout the country can be assured of receiving relatively accurate information. This does not mean that all business counsellors should be trained by the same body, or that all business counsellors possess the same expertise in all things. There should be a minimum standard of counselling service, however, just as there are minimum standards of care in medicine and dentistry.

The two most common complaints from SMEs both in Romania and in Krasnoyarsk are: first, that meaningful technical information is unavailable; and that secondly, planning is difficult without knowing what the government is going to do with taxes. Donor agencies are doing much to address the first issue. Considerable additions to libraries have been made; internet connections are available at countless sites; and opportunities to travel to the West have been extended to many.

174

Just how well the second issue is being addressed is questionable. Countries which have developed strong SME economies generally have one thing in common: tax codes which are consistent over long periods of time. Those codes may change with newly elected governments, but the changes are minimal. Taxes on SMEs in one country may be much higher than in another country, but the rates—within a few points—can be anticipated within countries for relatively long periods of time, and companies may plan production, procurement, and pricing with those rates in mind.

Promoting women in business in Uzbekistan

T.D. SAIDIKRAMOVA

THE UZBEKISTAN BUSINESS WOMEN'S ASSOCIATION was formed four years ago on 21 June 1991 as a public organization, and is registered with the Ministry of Justice of the Republic of Uzbekistan. The Association aims to strengthen the efforts of women to set up businesses, and to create a public awareness of the importance of women being active in business. The Association has 3000 individual and corporate members, and is financed from membership subscriptions, as well as by small contributions from economic organizations. Membership of the Association is open to women working in all organizations, whether private, state or public sector.

In setting up a small business, most new entrepreneurs come up against a number of problems. Observation and analysis of entrepreneurs' activity indicate above all problems of a lack of business education; of information on partners, and on equipment and products; and, difficulties in finding premises and finance, in processing documents, and in the registration of businesses. There is a lack of a proper infrastructure to develop and support small and medium-sized business. The first steps to remedy this are now being taken. Hence the need for this type of organization, since many problems for new entrepreneurs need resolution.

The Uzbekistan Business Women's Association is a partner in a number of support projects: the Business Communication Centre (BCC), the Market Skills Development Centre, the UN network of Business-Incubators Project, and on the GTZ network of the Business Promotion Centre. This latter project is of special significance.

The Business Communication Centre

A Business Communication Centre has begun to operate successfully in the Republic. This programme is being implemented with the involvement of the Danish Institute of Technology, although there have been, and still are, problems in setting up the project. The project is most important as one of the critical elements of the infrastructure needed to promote the development of small and medium-sized business.

Many new entrepreneurs are currently receiving real help from the centre in the form of help with their economic calculations for their

T.D. Saidikramova is the President of the Uzbekistan Women's Association.

business activity (compiling business plans), finding partners in the European market, and help with participation in the 'Europartneriat' (Gdańsk and Dortmund) and the 'Medpartneriat' (Istanbul). Business women members of our Association work in close contact with the Business Communication Centre as partners in many activities organized by the Centre.

The Business Promotion Centre

One element of the infrastructure to support small and medium-sized business in training entrepreneurs, improving their knowledge and also providing consultation services is the Business Promotion Centre, which was established in the Republic with the assistance of the German Organization for Technical Co-operation (GTZ), in which the partners are the Business Women's Association and the Republic's Union of Entrepreneurs. The project was proposed by the GTZ and carried out by Luso Consulting (a German Consulting firm based in Hamburg), and is estimated to last six years. The centre was first registered in November 1994.

In planning and developing this project there have been problems common to all such projects, such as finding premises, getting registered, and so on. Usually the partners in international projects are independent organizations (in this case the Business Women's Association and the Union of Entrepreneurs), which are unable to provide premises for the project or to make a sizeable contribution to financing the operations. However, such organizations can be effective in resolving problems, and have a great interest in such projects, appreciating the significance of their eventual impact.

The people implementing this project have to be given the credit for well thought-out organization in implementing each stage. The first stage was a joint seminar held in June, 1993 between the GTZ, the Business Women's Association and the Union of Entrepreneurs on the theme 'Ways to develop small and medium-sized business in Uzbekistan within a framework of technical co-operation with Germany'.

The participants in the seminar were representatives from the Cabinet of Ministers, the Business Women's Association and the Union of Entrepreneurs. The seminar concluded that there is a widespread lack of business education. A declaration was adopted, stating that the Business Women's Association and the Union of Entrepreneurs had approved the fund document and were approaching the Federal Government of Germany to request organizational and financial support for the project. The project was approved in 1994.

In February 1995 active work on the Business Promotion Centre began: drafting the foundation documents; and experimental courses with entrepreneurs, business college students and business institute students and representatives of the Peace Corps. In order to evaluate the economic situation in the Republic the programme council and the trainers from

Luso Consulting together with the project partners visited the regions of Fergana, Syr-Dar'ya, Samarkand and Tashkent. Meetings were arranged which provided the opportunity to understand the problems of developing and strengthening small and medium-sized business in the republic.

Among these were the process of developing effective market relations. Many organizations are still at the formative stage, amendments are being made to laws, the currency is not convertible, production within the country is limited, many raw materials have to be imported from other countries, and so the list continues. However, positive aspects of the development of small and medium-sized business were also discovered, despite the difficulty of the economic situation. Small and medium-sized businesses have already made a notable contribution to resolving current problems in Uzbekistan. There is a striking diversity in the types of business, of the equipment, business strategies and ways of resolving external problems, and the enterprise spirit is already evident. It is their serious .approach to studying the economic situation in the Republic and their familiarity with the psychology and culture that has enabled the Luso Consulting representatives to work out what kind of material to use for training, how best to bring it to our business women, and what steps to take. Many examples and cases would subsequently in training sessions be taken from the real-life situation of private business development in the Republic.

Training local trainers

The project is based on the CEFE programme (Competency-based Formation of Entrepreneurs). This is a programme developed by GTZ to develop and train entrepreneurs in various developing countries. The CEFE programme in Uzbekistan has had to be adapted to fit the special conditions of the country. CEFE in Uzbekistan will be used somewhat differently than in other countries. Our German colleagues have taken a sensible approach to training local 'trainers', since they have a better idea of the situation, the socio-economic conditions, as well as the psychology and, not least, the language in which training is to be conducted.

An announcement was made in the local press for a competition to train trainers. A lot of questions came from those wishing to be trained and to answer them an information evening was held for the candidates. There were 37 applications. The first course for 'trainers' was successfully completed by 25 people. The best trainers were selected to work on the staff of the Business Promotion Centre.

The next stage was working with the staff: refinement of the content of all courses, and of the methodology; one had to remember that it was difficult for local trainers to enter an auditorium, overcome the psychological barrier and speak confidently. Their experiences as trainers had only just begun.

All stages of the project were covered periodically by the local press, and television programmes were organized and transmitted. Each piece of information generated great interest among readers and viewers, and today the centre is progressing.

The Business Promotion Centre is known not only in the Republic but our trainers have also visited the Ukraine, and there have been expressions of interest from Kyrgyzstan and Novosibirsk in Russia. A month-long training session was held in 1995 at Kokand in the Fergana region, which is inhabited by half the population of the republic (10 million people). After a successful training in Tashkent, further training is to be organized in the Fergana Region.

At the instigation of those who attended the training sessions we are preparing to set up a CEFE club. The Business Promotion Centre also works with other projects, such as the Market Skills Development Centre, the Regional Bank Training Centre and the Business Communication Centre.

Those listening to presentations of business plans are representatives not only of local banks, but also of German banks accredited in the Republic. By the end of 1995 the Business Promotion Centre had trained 150 potential entrepreneurs.

Looking to the future

Today in Uzbekistan the CEFE method has proved successful: many questions have been discussed, solutions found, and a lot of material has been amassed.

What further problems have we to face tomorrow? Is it still worthwhile to continue to finance the project? All outstanding questions were discussed during a seminar in November 1994 on 'Objective definition and planning'.

The main stages of the seminar were:

○ the definition of objectives;
○ the analysis of results;
○ the development of measures for the further progress of the project.

During the seminar the current economic situation in the Republic was discussed, as well as recent Republican legislation. Conditions are currently being created in the Republic to support and develop private business: the decrees and resolutions of 1994 and 1995 on 'Initiating and Stimulating Private Business' are evidence of this. For without an economic and legislative climate that is favourable towards small and medium enterprises, the task of creating businesses, employment and economic security by men or women will be a difficult one.

A note on the Donor Committee for Small Enterprise Development

The Committee of Donor Agencies for Small Enteprrise Development (referred to here as 'the Committee') which sponsored the International Conference for Economies in Transition in Central and Eastern Europe and in the former Soviet Union (CEE/FSU) in Budapest in June 1995 was established at a meeting in Berlin in October 1979, convened at the invitation of the World Bank. Present were representatives of bi-lateral and multi-lateral donor organizations engaged in programmes of assistance for small enterprises in developing countries. The participants in Berlin welcomed the opportunity to exchange information on the programmes undertaken by agencies in this field and on the experience gained in the implementation of these projects. The donor agencies' representatives agreed that supporting small-scale enterprise development was a rapidly growing area of interest to all development assistance organizations, and that increased exchanges in relation to programmes would help harmonize thinking and prevent conflicting approaches.

Accordingly, an informal steering committee was set up to plan the form that future contacts and activities of the Committee should take. It was also agreed that contacts should be made with the representatives of developing countries to broaden the dialogue on the projects supported by the donors. The aim was to hear their views in assessing the success that had been achieved, and how approaches and the content of projects might take greater account of past experience.

By 1995, the Committee, whose secretariat is located in the World Bank, represented 17 bilateral agencies, 15 multi-lateral institutions and 2 other international development organizations. Despite its increased size, it has still retained its informal character with no established legal status, but it has effectively served its function of exchanging information on programmes of participating donor agencies, sharing what has been learned in the course of the implementation of projects, and seeking to co-ordinate the efforts and the approaches in support of small enterprise development.

There have been regular meetings, virtually annually, in Paris, Washington, Geneva, Bonn and Vienna, as well as meetings at the end of a number of regional and other conferences. These gatherings started with a Conference of Asian countries in Colombo in December 1981, which focused on issues and features of special interest or concern, and on situations prevailing in the region which were important for donor agencies to recognize and take into account. These included cultural, social, economic and political factors impacting on the successful development of SME support programmes. Further regional gatherings were held by the Committee in Abidjan, Ivory Coast for African countries in June 1983, and in Quito, Ecuador for Latin America in April 1985.

The regional meetings highlighted a number of themes and these became the subjects of global meetings. Conferences of this nature included: the role of commercial banks (London, 1986), and assistance programme for women entrepreneurs (Ottawa, 1987). In view of the increasing involvement of donors in supporting NGOs and microenterprises, the Committee sponsored a large International Conference on Microenterprise Development in Washington in June 1988.

Subsequently, as concerns increased on the importance of policy changes and the effect of structural adjustment programmes on the African countries, special meetings were convened on this subject. The Norwegian aid agency NORAD sponsored a meeting in Oslo in 1989 on policy changes and their relation to SME development. The Committee organized a further conference hosted by the Netherlands in the Hague in 1991, which explored the way the policy environment impacted on the development of programmes for small business assistance in Africa. Papers at that gathering reviewed the effects of structural adjustment programmes on SME sectors in various countries of the region. Following the active exchange at the Hague conference the committee decided to convene a further conference in Africa in Abidjan at the end of 1993 to discuss the subject in greater detail. The Abidjan meeting, organized by the Canadian aid agency CIDA, changed the focus of the previous Hague meeting away from the definition of appropriate policies and towards the details of designing and implementing such policy changes. The conference explored ways in which countries could overcome the obstacles or policies that impeded small enterprise development in Africa. The Committee also sponsors a journal, *Small Enterprise Development*, which has been published since 1990 by IT Publications, London.

Until the end of 1989 the focus of activities of the donor agencies was providing support for small enterprise development in the developing world of Asia, Africa and Latin America. But political events of monumental proportions took place during 1989–90 which, among other more far-reaching effects, also provided a new focus for part, at least, of the donor agencies' activities. In November 1989 the Berlin wall came down and this was followed in the subsequent two years by the collapse of the communist central planning regimes throughout Eastern and Central Europe and then throughout the vast area of the Soviet Union as well. These countries clearly expressed their intention of turning their backs on the past decades and taking steps to establish a market economy and build up a significant private sector to act as the engine of growth of their economies. Accordingly, the donor agencies quickly developed aid programmes to help in the creation of a strong private sector and more specifically to help in the development of SME. Naturally, since the aid experience of donor agencies at that point had been virtually only in the Third World, background and expertise were drawn from developing countries and from the donor countries themselves. This was what was applied in many situations in the countries of CEE/FSU that sought donor help.

Donors, aware that there was a compelling need to respond rapidly to these new challenges, hastened to develop projects to deal with a situation which had come upon them with little previous warning. They offered advice and assistance on the policies and measures to be introduced, the economic environment to be created and the support services needed to stimulate the emergence and growth of a private SME sector. Advice and training were given by the consultants and specialists sent by the donors, but finance, because of uncertainty in the donor camp and of absence or inadequacy of appropriate counterpart organizations, was significantly slower in coming. Not only was finance to start businesses in short supply, but even funds to cover operating costs for the proposed services at promotional or SME centres were lacking.

Over the five years 1990–95 a variety of initiatives and a wide range of activities were promoted in the CEE/FSU countries with the support—and in most cases on the advice and recommendation—of the donor agencies themselves.

www.ingramcontent.com/pod-product-compliance
Lightning Source LLC
Chambersburg PA
CBHW072128020426
42334CB00018B/1714